Harvesting Minds

HARVESTING

MINDS

How TV Commercials
Control Kids

Roy F. Fox

Foreword by George Gerbner

PRAEGER

Westport, Connecticut
London

Library of Congress Cataloging-in-Publication Data

Fox, Roy F.
    Harvesting minds : how TV commercials control kids / Roy F. Fox ;
foreword by George Gerbner.
        p.   cm.
    Includes bibliographical references and index.
    ISBN 0–275–95203–7 (alk. paper)—ISBN 0–275–97101–5 (pbk: alk. paper)
    1. Commercialism in schools—United States.   2. Television
advertising and children—United States.   3. Television in
education—United States   I. Title.
LB1044.8.F69   1996
305.23′083—dc20   96–10438

British Library Cataloguing in Publication Data is available.

Library of Congress Catalog Card Number: 96–10438
ISBN: 0–275–97101–5 (pbk.)

First published in 1996

Praeger Publishers, 88 Post Road West, Westport, CT 06881
An imprint of Greenwood Publishing Group, Inc.
www.praeger.com

Printed in the United States of America

The paper used in this book complies with the
Permanent Paper Standard issued by the National
Information Standards Organization (Z39.48–1984).

10 9 8 7 6 5 4 3 2 1

For
Joel Frederick Fox
Emma Caitlin Fox
and all kids

Contents

Foreword: Invasion of the Story Sellers

Harvesting young minds for private profit in a field set aside for that purpose and visited voluntarily has its problems. That is why commercials on children's programs are subject to special codes, loose as they are. However, harvesting young minds for private profit in the schools—a public preserve specifically set aside for resisting such blandishments—is more than problematic. It legitimizes an historic departure, with far-reaching implications. I would like to sketch those implications and thus place this ground-breaking book in the broadest human perspective. Our brief journey will look at the distinctive feature of human socialization and its principal transformations, leading us to the predicament we confront today.

Most of what we know, or think we know, we have never personally experienced. We live in a world erected by the stories we hear and see and tell. Unlocking incredible riches through imagery and words, conjuring up the unseen through art, creating towering works of imagination and fact through poetry, song, tales, reports, and laws—that is the *true* magic of human life.

Through that magic we live in a world much wider than the threats and gratifications of the immediate physical environment, which is the world of other species. In our world, stories socialize us into roles of gender, age, class, vocation, and lifestyle, offering us models of conformity or targets for rebellion. Stories weave the seamless web of our cultural environment, cultivating most of what we think, what we do, and how we conduct our affairs.

This story-telling process used to be handcrafted, homemade, and community inspired. Now it is mostly mass-produced and policy-driven. It is the end result of a complex manufacturing and marketing process. This situation demands a new diagnosis.

The stories that animate our cultural environment have three distinct but related functions: 1) *they reveal how things work*; 2) *they describe what things are*, and 3) *they tell us what to do about them*.

Stories of the first kind, which reveal how things work, illuminate the all-important but invisible relationships of life. They help us perceive the invisible and hidden dynamics of daily reality. Fairy tales, novels, plays, comics, cartoons, and other forms of narrative imagination and imagery are the basic building blocks of human understanding. They show complex causality by presenting imaginary action in total situations, coming to some conclusion that has a moral purpose and a social function. You don't have to believe the "facts" of Little Red Riding Hood to grasp the notion that big bad "wolves" victimize old women and trick little girls—a lesson in gender roles, fear, and power. Stories of this kind build, from infancy on, the fantasy we call reality. I do not suggest that the revelations are false, which they may or may not be, but that they are synthetic, selective, often mythical, and always socially constructed.

Stories of the second kind depict what things are. These are descriptions, expositions, and reports abstracted from total situations, which fill in with "facts" the gaps in the fantasies conjured up by stories of the first kind. They are the presumably factual accounts—the chronicles of the past and the news and science of today. Stories of what things are usually confirm some idea of how things work. Their high "facticity" (i.e., correspondence to actual events presumed to exist independently of the story) gives them special status in politics and law. They emphasize and lend credibility to selected parts of each society's fantasies of reality, alerting us to certain interests, threats, opportunities, and challenges.

Stories of the third kind—those which tell us what to do—clinch the lessons of the first two and turn them into action. They typically present us with a valued objective or suggest a need or desire—and then offer a product, service, candidate, institution, or action to help us attain it. For example, the lessons of the fictional Little Red Riding Hoods prominent in everyday media stories not only teach lessons of vulnerability, mistrust, and dependence, but also help sell insurance policies, burglar alarms, and guns.

Hence, stories of the third kind sell ways for us to adjust to our society's structure of power.

Ideally, these three kinds of stories check and balance each other. But in a commercially-driven culture, stories of the third kind pay for most of the first two. This creates a cultural environment which is climate-controlled to breed only stories that sell. In the electronic age, this cultural environment is monopolized, homogenized, and globalized. We must look at the historic course of our journey to see what this new age means for our children.

For the longest time in human history, stories were told only face to face. A community was defined by the rituals, mythologies, and imagery held in common. All useful knowledge was encapsulated in aphorisms and legends, proverbs and tales, incantations and ceremonies. Writing was rare and holy, forbidden for slaves. Laboriously inscribed manuscripts conferred sacred power to their interpreters, the priests and ministers.

State and church ruled the Middle Ages in a symbiotic relationship of mutual dependence and tension. State, composed of feudal nobles, was the economic and political order; church its cultural arm. The industrial revolution changed all of that. One of the first machines stamping out standardized artifacts was the printing press. Its product, the book, was a prerequisite for all the other upheavals to come. The book could be given to all who could read, requiring education and creating a new literate class of people. Readers could now interpret the book (at first the Bible) for themselves, breaking the monopoly of priestly interpreters and ushering in the Reformation.

When the printing press was hooked up to the steam engine, the industrialization of story-telling shifted into high gear. Rapid publication and mass transport created a new form of consciousness: modern mass publics. Publics are loose aggregations of people who share some common consciousness of how things work, what things are, and what ought to be done—but never meet face-to-face. That was never before possible.

Now, stories could be sent—often smuggled—across hitherto impenetrable or closely guarded boundaries of time, space, and status. The book lifted people from their traditional moorings, as the industrial revolution uprooted them from their local communities and cultures. They could now get off the land and go to work in faraway ports, factories, and continents, and have with them a packet of common consciousness—the book, the journal, and later the motion picture—wherever they went. Publics, created by such publication, were necessary for the formation of individual and group identities in the new urban environment, as the different classes and regional, religious, and ethnic groups tried to live together with some degree of cooperation and harmony. Publics were now the basic units of self-government, electing or selecting representatives to an assembly trying to reconcile diverse interests. The maintenance and integrity of multiple publics made self-government feasible for large, complex, and diverse national communities. People engaged in long and costly struggles—now at a critical stage—to be free to create and share stories that fit the reality of competing and often conflicting values and interests. Most of our assumptions about human development and political plurality and choice are rooted in the print era.

One of the most vital provisions of the print era was the creation of the only large-scale folk institution of the industrial society—public education—the community institution where face-to-face learning and interpreting could, ideally, liberate the individual from both tribal and medieval dependencies and cultural monopolies.

The second great transformation, the electronic revolution, has ushered in the telecommunications era. Its mainstream, television, is superimposed upon and reorganizes print-based culture. Unlike the industrial revolution, the new upheaval does not uproot people from their homes, but transports them in their homes. It re-tribalizes modern society and changes the role of education.

For the first time in human history, children are born into homes where mass-mediated storytellers reach them on the average of more than seven hours a day. Most waking hours, and often dreams, are filled with their stories. These stories do not come from families, schools, churches, neighborhoods, and often not even from the native countries. They come from a small group of distant conglomerates with something to sell.

Giant industries discharge their messages into the mainstream of common consciousness. Channels proliferate and new technologies pervade home and office while mergers and bottom-line pressures shrink creative alternatives and reduce diversity of content. The historic nexus of church and state is replaced by television and state. These changes may appear to broaden and enrich our horizons, but they also homogenize our viewpoints and limit our alternatives. For media professionals, the changes mean fewer opportunities and greater compulsions to present life in saleable packages. Creative artists, scientists, and humanists can still explore, enlighten, and sometimes even challenge, but increasingly, their stories must fit marketing strategies and priorities.

Despite being surrounded with sales messages, or perhaps because of it, a Consumer Federation of America survey concluded in 1990 that "Americans are not smart shoppers and their ignorance costs them billions, threatens their health and safety and undermines the economy. . . ." Viewing commercials is "work" performed by audiences in exchange for "free" news and entertainment. But in fact we pay dearly to subsidize commercial media through a surcharge added to the price of every advertised product. We also pay dearly by allowing advertising expenditures to be tax-deductible business expenses. These give-aways of public moneys for private purposes erode the diversity of our cultural mainstream.

Broadcasting is the most concentrated, homogenized, and globalized medium. The top 100 advertisers pay for two-thirds of all network television. Four networks, allied to giant transnational corporations—our private "Ministry of Culture"—control the bulk of production and distribution, and shape our cultural mainstream. Other interests, minority news, and the potential of any challenge to dominant perspectives, lose ground with every merger.

All of this leaves education as the only large-scale institutional corrective capable of reordering priorities and cultivating within students some sense of detached, analytical skill. We have to depend upon public education—as we have since it was founded—to play a liberating role. Education must restore a balance of stories of all three kinds, to stimulate a skeptical and critical view. Education must illuminate—rather than promote—the dominant role of the stories that sell.

But what happens when the historically protected and increasingly valuable sphere of the public classroom is invaded by the very images and messages that it should help students to evaluate? The remarkable and timely study that follows addresses that question. So let the story begin.

George Gerbner
Dean Emeritus
The Annenberg School for Communication
University of Pennsylvania

Acknowledgments

Many good people helped with this book. My current and former colleagues at the University of Missouri have encouraged this work, mainly by demonstrating their own belief in the power of *all* kinds of literacies. I especially thank Peter Hasselriis, Richard Robinson, Carol Gilles, Wayne Dumas, Dorothy Watson, and Ben Nelms. I thank Rebecca Cramer and Laura Beattie for their kind assistance. I am especially indebted to Leslie Gant and Harry Carrell, teachers and Missouri Writing Project colleagues, who helped ensure that this research focused on individual kids.

My research assistant for one year of this study, Lucy Stanovick, proved invaluable—as a conscientious, skilled colleague; as a gentle, perceptive questioner of kids; and as a natural at analyzing media and responses to it. I thank former Greenwood editor Lynn Flint for believing in this project, and Liz Murphy for shepherding it through. I am also indebted to editors Marcia Goldstein and Kim Mrazek Hastings for their excellent work. Finally, once more, Beverly Fox provided skilled editing, advice, and abundant patience.

Introduction

"What products are advertised on TV, here at school?" I asked a group of ninth-graders sitting around the table with me.

"Cinnaburst," replied Eric. "You know—it's that gum that has these little red things and—"

"No," interjected Lisa, "those are *flavor crystals*."

Lisa's interruption was spoken softly, politely. Eric, seated across the table from his classmate, Lisa, hesitated for a second and then muttered, "Oh yeah, flavor crystals," and quickly nodded in agreement, before recalling other television commercials that he'd seen in school this quarter.

When Lisa voluntarily corrected her classmate, two students sitting near her also silently nodded their heads in agreement: Lisa was right; Eric *was* talking about "flavor crystals." It was the exact phrase used in the gum commercial.

None of the other five students sitting around the table questioned the accuracy of this label. None of them found anything unusual in the fact that Lisa expressed this information with these words and retrieved them so easily. There were no raised eyebrows, no shades of doubt. Everything was normal.

Nobody in the group saw any differences between the real thing they were talking about—the gum—and the label they had so quickly and naturally affixed to it—"flavor crystals." This hollow phrase simply enhances the product, making it seem better than it is. The students were unaware that they'd given this gum a positive evaluation by using the advertiser's exact words.

Lisa, Eric, and the others sitting around the table on this October morning are scrubbed, decent, bright kids. They attend a consolidated school in rural Missouri, where most students are signed up for the hot lunch program. Every day, when Channel One broadcasts into their classroom, Lisa and her friends absorb commercials not only for bubble gum but for Snickers, Levi's 501 jeans, Milky Ways, Sega video games, Gatorade, Doritos chips, Sure deodorant, Little Caesar's pizza, and a gaggle of other products.

Every day at school Lisa and her classmates are systematically exposed to high-impact TV commercials. So are eight million other American kids who attend schools that have contracted to receive the Channel One broadcast: ten minutes of news and two minutes of commercials.

These commercials now constitute our national curriculum. More than any other experience or text, commercials are "read" by more students, more often, than *Romeo and Juliet* or *A Tale of Two Cities* or *Huck Finn* or *The Catcher in the Rye*. This book addresses one main question: What happens to kids when they are held captive to TV commercials?

I have mentioned only a few facts about this complex, social phenomenon. But there are many more stories to tell—especially those told by students themselves, whose voices are seldom heard in the debates about television advertising. This is one reason why I wrote the book.

Chapter 1, "Kids and Commercials," looks at the closed world of public school students and TV commercials. It also answers some essential questions: (1) Does watching Channel One help students become more culturally literate? (2) What do we know about the effects of commercials on kids? and (3) How does Channel One function like a propaganda machine? The final section of the chapter describes the methods and procedures used in this study.

I chose to study TV commercials within Channel One schools because they represent a largely "controlled" or "pure" environment in which to explore the effects of persuasive messages. (These same qualities attracted advertisers to schools in the first place.) The qualitative research described in Chapters 2–6 was carried out between 1993 and 1995. My purpose was to describe students' responses to Channel One's commercials: how kids interacted with the viewing experiences, what and how they thought about them. The results of this exploratory study (which employed small focus groups of students at rural schools) are presented in the following chapters: "How Well Do Kids Know Commercials?" "How Do Kids Respond to Commercials?" "How Do Kids Evaluate Commercials?" "How Do Commercials Affect Kids' Behavior?" and "How Do Commercials Affect Kids' Consumer Behavior?" After summarizing conclusions and recommendations in Chapter 7, the final chapter, "What Can We Do Right Now?" describes approaches for helping kids (and adults) better understand a world hot-wired with commercials and other media.

I wrote this book for several reasons. Although it is critical of TV commercials beamed at captive audiences of school kids, it is not critical of media itself. On the contrary, I have always been awestruck by images—wherever and however I encountered them—in media, in language, in art, in music, in nature, in mind. I have long regarded images (and imaging) in the same way that scientists view DNA—as the most fundamental element of human life, representing the most basic unit of thought and communication. So my first reason is an unshakable optimism and faith in the roles that images play in our thinking, communicating, and culture-making.

Although I am not a media-basher, I am a concerned parent and teacher, which leads me to the second reason for writing this book: something as elemental and valuable as media should never be abused—especially if kids are the "targets." So, to answer the question, "Why did you write this book?" I point to each page, to each story told. I point to Eric, Lisa, and all the other kids I talked with—the normally naive, good-hearted, open-faced kids who, on trust, absorb the world around them. "Flavor crystals" should never have been allowed to invade Lisa's and Eric's growing psyche. They have more important things to do—like being allowed the freedom to grow up nurturing their own images, not images that sell products.

The fragile selfhood of children—especially children in school—belongs to them and to their parents and families and teachers and friends and pets and communities—not to advertisers, marketers, and manufacturers. Yet Lisa and millions of American schoolchildren are being bombarded, day in and day out, with high-voltage commercials that have proven infinitely more interesting to them than anything that could happen at school.

Most people, though, don't think twice about school-sponsored television commercials. Why should they? After all, TV is a close, common presence in our lives. We think of it in the same ways that we think of loading the dishwasher and brushing our teeth—as a normal part of daily life. We regard television sets as furniture. However, for these reasons and more, we forget that the TV commercial is a commodity, sold in units of viewers-per-thousand. But our children are not commodities to be obtained, defined, labeled, and sold. Children should enter their school each day without being "targeted" by advertisers and corporate investors.

Most important, we must accept "flavor crystals" for what it really is—a hollow, euphemistic, silly ad phrase. That Lisa and Eric so easily absorbed this phony representation of reality into their consciousness serves as a visible reminder of something more serious that's hidden from view, an internal hemorrhaging of the spirit that seems to afflict children who are held hostage to an endless stream of ads. America has not held so many people captive for purposes of selling for profit since lines of ragged slaves clambered up the auction block. This parasitic practice, systematically inflicted upon American youth, must stop. That is the message in this book.

1

Kids and Commercials

HUCK AND JIM ON THE PLANET OF THE ADS

I think it's stupid. I don't know why athletes do that—pay all that money for all
them ignorant commercials for themselves. Guess it makes everyone like 'em more
and like their team more. Doesn't Emmitt Smith have a bunch of commercials that's
makin' everybody like his team better?

Debbie, the ninth-grader quoted above, was telling me why she thinks
professional athletes make the television commercials that she watches at
school on Channel One. After Debbie's response sunk in, I decided to ask
each group that day the same question: "Why do professional athletes make
commercials?" The next group brainstormed the following reasons:

- It motivates athletes to play better.
- It's a reward for athletes.
- It helps the team.
- It enhances the athletes' status among peers.

After talking with Debbie and other students, I realized that they usually
did not consider commercials to be messages aimed at selling something.
Instead, they viewed Nike commercials solely as advertisements *for* the
athletes—perks that *athletes* pay for themselves to bolster their own egos

and their team's reputation. Few kids mentioned that a product was being sold or that the athletes wanted to earn money for themselves.

Instead of seeing the athletes as endorsing the products, many kids saw the products as endorsing the athletes—the opposite of testimonial advertising, whereby famous people recommend products. Greg, a senior, said, "If you're good at what you do, you need to be recognized for it." Most students I talked with found many ways to embrace commercials, to trust them, to view advertisers' motives in a positive, trusting way.

Over a two-year period I talked with roughly 200 kids in rural Missouri schools about how they interpret the television commercials that are part of Channel One's twelve-minute broadcast into 40 percent of America's classrooms. Established by Whittle Communications in 1989 and later sold to K-III Communications, Channel One now broadcasts over 700 commercials each year and reaps over $100 million annually (Kozol 1992). The ads promote such products as Sega video games, Bubblelicious bubble gum, and Snickers to eight million kids every day. (In the schools I visited, many of the advertised products were sold in vending machines at school.)

Students' responses to the commercials continued to surprise me. Heather, a senior, became frustrated when she couldn't articulate why she and her friends so firmly believe that the Pepsi commercial we had just watched was true. "Well . . . I don't know," she finally concluded, "it just *feels* real!" Heather and her classmates had offered other reasons for their judgment: "they [the kids in the ad] dress like us" and "they goof around like us." But this didn't entirely satisfy her. In this commercial, larger forces shaped her judgment; she just could not put it into words. Heather and the other kids' insistence on the commercial's authenticity demonstrates its success. Pepsi's "It's Like This" commercials *do indeed* look real. They are constructed to look very much like public service announcements (PSAs). Because Channel One also airs PSAs, this blurring seems more than coincidental. Pretending to be documentaries in which "kids talk about their problems," the Pepsi ads incorporate close-up shots of red, white, and blue Pepsi cans between black-and-white and muted color shots of kids talking directly into the camera.

In discussing the same ad with 29 students from a different school, I discovered that only 12 thought it was a real commercial; 6 thought it was both a news item and a commercial; 4 thought it was purely news; and 7 didn't know how to define it. Indeed, when my student teacher saw this ad, she herself didn't know if it was a commercial or a news item—and she is a very bright, fifty-year-old former editor. One ninth-grader, though, tried to sort it all out for us when he pronounced, "It's not really a commercial—it's just a commercial *sponsored* by Pepsi."

To Heather and millions of other kids, the ad's rapid-fire editing and its swinging, seemingly random camera angles convey an image of kids spending a knock-about day at the beach cavorting with pals. Most students told me they could easily be friends with the kids in this commercial. Why? Because they look and dress and act the same as the students. When I asked, "From whose point of view is this commercial told—who is telling this story?" Brad replied that "it's not a story." Brad and others did not define the commercial as a yarn made up by someone else. They mentioned no director constructing its message, no creator "standing outside" and calling the shots.

Of the 150 students who discussed this commercial with me, only five said it had been fashioned by an external force such as the Pepsi Corporation, its marketer, or its commercial producers and directors. The students never acknowledged any *external* people involved in making or telling the ad's story. They seldom viewed commercials for what they are: highly contrived constructions that have been filtered through countless other people and processes, each with its own purposes. Like Brad, most students stated that the Pepsi commercial's point of view is expressed only by the kids who appear in it. After all, if nobody "outside" the message created it, then the point of view must come only from the "inside"—the actors who appear in the ad. The majority of students I talked with felt that no matter *how* the commercial is defined, Pepsi is really more concerned with "doing good" than it is with selling soft drinks:

RF: Do any of you see this commercial as trying to sell Pepsi, the soft drink?

Ellen: Since that commercial reaches people, it kind of makes them think that Pepsi is a good cause. . . .

Chad: [Interrupting] And they care.

Ellen: And they care about people, so they want people to support Pepsi so that they can support the commercials.

Ellen's choice of the word "support" indicates the trust and warmth with which many of these kids regarded the advertisers.

Documentary-style commercials aren't the only ones that infiltrate kids' language and thinking and blur the message. Gina and Blake discussed an acne medicine they had just seen on a Channel One commercial. Both referred to the product, Clearasil, by its name. But near the end of their conversation Gina unknowingly substituted the phrase "washing your face" for the brand name. Neither student noticed that they were equating the advertised ointment with the concept of cleanliness. The students did not realize that the advertisers had defined reality *for* them—in ways that simultaneously enhanced the product but devalued the students, in ways that added to sales but took from kids.

Channel One bombards students with commercials, repeating the same ones over and over, an experience that those of us not attending Channel One schools have never had. But it's routine for kids in Channel One schools. A few years ago the "Be Like Mike" (Michael Jordan) ad played repeatedly for months. Moreover, the ads informally "rerun" every time students randomly sing the catchy jingle or mimic parts of the commercial—whether in the hallways and locker rooms, in the cafeteria, on the bus, or outside of school. Students commonly report talking about commercials *outside* of school. Beth, a ninth-grader, regularly phones her friends and tells them which channel to tune in to whenever a funny commercial comes on. Every time students informally talk to each other about or re-enact commercials, they elicit (in varying degrees) the original ad's images, language, and music—for themselves and everyone around them.

Many students told me about a recent football game between their school and a neighboring small town. During the game the bleachers full of home-team students chanted in unison, "Got-to-be, got-to-be—Dom-in-os!" The exact same scenario occurs on a Domino's Pizza commercial that airs on Channel One: a football crowd chants the same line to an old rock song ("We will, we will—*rock* you"). The replay itself became a kind of sporting event, with people chanting, clapping, and stomping to the beat, fully acting out the commercial. Here, the many participants internalized this ad the most, because they were so viscerally and intensely engaged. But the ad message was also replayed to everyone within earshot.

Commercials are also replayed in other, more subtle ways. For example, ads starring Shaquille O'Neal replay every time a kid like Jason Smith signs his name in a yearbook as "Shaq Smith." And when I asked a student named Alex to evaluate a shampoo commercial that contained the line "Gimme a break," he replied by singing these same words, but to a tune that advertises *another* product, Kit Kat candy bars.

In this environment nothing should surprise me, but it does. Susie, a ninth-grader, described her dream about a McDonald's commercial, carefully noting the discrepancies between her dream and the reality of the ad. In both stories, the Big Mac starred. In art class Jason and his classmates were given empty Pringles potato chip cans to make into sculptures. They were asked to create a self-portrait that would reflect who they were. Jason's final product looked exactly like the little man on the can of Pringles chips.

Commercials effectively penetrate students' language and thinking. In one ad, for two nanoseconds, viewers glimpse a man and woman on an airplane; students later recalled the plane's seats as "red with little blue squares that have arrows sticking out of them." If such commercials strike deep, they can also strike fast. One day on Channel One I watched a David Robinson commercial with the students. They told me it was brand new—that they'd never seen it before. During the rest of that day, most students reported that the thirty-second commercial had "three parts," which they remembered in the correct sequence: first, Robinson goes to college and earns his master's degree; second, Robinson becomes a naval officer; third, he goes to the Olympics twice before becoming a professional ball player. Even though the students and I began that morning on the same level "viewing" field, I could remember none of these things—not even immediately after watching the commercial.

Of course, Channel One's commercials infiltrate kids' language and thinking for one reason: to get them to *act*, to buy specific items. That's why Channel One ads cost twice as much as those on prime-time network news. Monica, a high school senior who lives by herself, delights even at the memory of the special-effects commercial that prompted her to buy a pair of shoes:

I bought some Fila tennis shoes 'cause I seen 'em on a commercial. I mean, they had this basketball player, but I don't know who he was . . . he was jumping. Anyway, the shoes have like, little flaps on the sides of 'em, like little wings. They're velcro . . . anyway, they come off, and they started flying [giggles]. They flew off of the building, so I had to have them shoes!

Like Monica and many others, Evan, a diminutive ninth-grader, also buys items he sees for the first time on commercials at school. He enlisted the help of his grandmother to save up $114 to buy Michael Jordan Nike basketball shoes. When I ask why, Evan drawls matter-of-factly, "Saw 'em on a c'mersh'l." Never mind that Evan's family can't afford them. Never mind that Evan doesn't play basketball. Never mind that some kids are beaten and murdered for such shoes.

At the end of small-group sessions, I asked students, "Is there anything else about commercials that we haven't talked about?" "Yes!" they enthused, "We need *new* commercials!" Their answer is not surprising if you place it within its rightful context: operant conditioning. Anybody who watches so many commercials, every day for nine months, with some ads repeated endlessly, develops a craving for *new* commercials, a desire for *more*. Especially young people.

Channel One's commercials employ classic propaganda techniques such as repetition, testimonials, bandwagon appeals, transfers of one quality or element to another, and highly synthesized music and imagery. We've long known that such propaganda is most effective in closed environments, where outside stimuli can't interfere with the intended messages. And classrooms of captive students make up the perfect controlled environment: no external noise or outside distractions interfere with the flood of commercials, which star—the students tell me—"kids just like us." But advertisers don't call this propaganda. Instead they camouflage it in techno-market-speak, such as "brand and product loyalties through classroom-centered, peer-powered lifestyle patterning."

Why do we accept this corporate feeding on our young? Mainly because our own notions of propaganda—what it is and where it occurs—are based, ironically, upon obsolete media images: gray prisoner-of-war camps with grimacing North Korean guards; Winston Smith's *1984* torture by rats, and Angela Lansbury's dark, darting eyes in *The Manchurian Candidate*. These images never surface when we enter the bright hallways of public schools and are jostled by the scrubbed kids from small towns. Nor do mass publications such as *Newsweek* (1994b) serve the truth: one article praising Channel One assures us—in boldface and all-caps—that "NEWS + ADS = LEARNING." Learning what? How to wait in a holding cell for your next shot of Kit Kat candy bar serum? Gimme a break.

One thing remains certain: kids have not changed. They're as open-faced and open-hearted as Twain's Huck Finn was a hundred years ago. When he and Jim escaped on the raft, they fled a kind of slavery that they could see, hear, and feel. Today, of course, we no longer physically auction off slaves. We do, though, merchandise large units of children to those who bid highest for advertising time. Huck and Jim could jump on a raft, but how can today's kids purge themselves of "flavor crystals"? How can they erase the emotional imprints of laser-laced images, each frame meticulously crafted to sell expensive running shoes? My guess is that Huck and Jim handled the fraudulence of the King and the Duke more adroitly than today's kids can control TV commercials.

A person's mental images and language create his or her sense of selfhood. And this selfhood—especially during our formative years—is the most valuable, fragile quality we'll ever embrace. Private, vulnerable, and sacred, a human being's psyche is not a commodity to be sold. But it happens, every day, for millions of American kids.

This book tries to describe how kids interact with commercials and how they influence kids' thinking, attitudes, values, and behavior. The remainder of this chapter provides background information for the study. The first section examines the broader social context of Channel One. The second section explores the effects of advertising on kids; the final section describes how the study was conducted.

PUNDITS, PROPAGANDISTS, AND PROFITEERS

What is Channel One? How did it establish itself in the classroom, allowing TV ads to become America's common text—in effect, America's national curriculum? And finally, does Channel One develop students' cultural literacy?

What Is Channel One?

Christopher Whittle, former owner of *Esquire* magazine, initially achieved his wealth and fame designing ad messages tailored for highly specific audiences, such as patients waiting in doctors' offices—what is known in the ad trade as "captive-audience marketing." In January 1989, Whittle Communications, based in Knoxville, Tennessee, announced plans to test its Channel One broadcast in six school systems. In exchange for Channel One, 90 percent of a school's students must watch Channel One for 92 percent of the on-air time (schools must supply Channel One with attendance records); each program must be watched in its entirety; shows cannot be interrupted; and teachers do not have the right to turn the program off. In return, schools receive approximately $50,000 worth of installed electronic hardware, such as a color television set for each classroom, VCRs, and a satellite dish (capable of picking up only Channel One's signal). Schools can use the hardware for projects in addition to Channel One but must return the equipment if they stop requiring that kids watch it. Created for a young audience, the Channel One program and commercials feature news anchors and correspondents who appear to be under twenty-five years old.

My own observations are consistent with many other reports (e.g., Carmody 1989; Rudinow 1990; Toch 1992) in concluding that Channel One's production techniques closely resemble those of MTV or music television: very brief segments, slow-motion and soft-focus video images, bursts of images, rapid camera cuts, and background rock music. Also, these sources and others cite Channel One's reliance on feature and human-interest stories over hard news. For example, in October 1991 Channel One broadcast a five-part series on teen fashion that focused on the histories of sneakers and jeans, as well as a profile of "trendsetters" such as the hip-hop group "Fly Girls." Also, the series featured tours of four teenagers' wardrobes (Toch 1992).

Channel One has since revised its news programs to be more professional, but there are no guarantees it will remain so; media formats change as quickly as new directors are hired. Regardless of the newscast, two minutes of high-impact commercials will always remain—for Levi's jeans, Bubblelicious bubble gum, and other items aimed at kids. Because students (grades 6–12) buy $80 billion worth of products each year, the thirty-second commercials aired on Channel One cost advertisers $157,000 each—twice the cost of a commercial on prime-time network news (Kozol 1992, 274). The bottom line is that Channel One is "ringing up over $100 million a year in advertising income" (Toch 1992, 89). These dollars come from America's poorest schools. In fact, a University of Massachusetts study found "Channel One in 67% of the schools that spend less than $10 a year per student for textbooks, and it's in only 19% of the schools spending $75 or more. Ten percent of the schools that spend more than $6,000 a year per student take Channel One, and 60% of those that spend less than $2,600 are aboard" (McCarthy 1993, 4A).

Channel One has spread dramatically since 1989. It is now being received by over twelve thousand schools in forty-eight states, and many more are waiting to have equipment installed (Cramer 1993). Approximately eight million students—over one-third of America's teens—are now watching Channel One (Solomon 1993) more than any other television program except the Super Bowl (Goodman 1989).

America's New National Curriculum . . . Brought to You by Pepsi

Since the publication of E. D. Hirsch's *Cultural Literacy* (1987), professional debates have raged in journals, in teachers' lounges, in classrooms, and on convention floors over what constitutes our literary and cultural heritage: Which texts should all students be required to read? Should we even *have* a set of common literary experiences, regardless of classroom setting, instructional needs, and students' gender, social, racial, and cultural makeup? Ironically, when nobody seemed to be watching, all these concerns were preempted by television commercials. It's no longer a debate about whether students should focus on *King Lear* or *One Flew over the Cuckoo's Nest*. It's not even a disagreement between *The Color Purple* and *The Band*

Played On. No longer can anyone question which texts should make up our culture's canon or national curriculum.

Why? Because one private corporation sold a core curriculum to thousands of schools—wrapped in a glitzy commercial television package. Many people who haven't actually watched Channel One think of it as educational TV, because that's how it has been marketed. The notion conjures up images of college profs in horn-rimmed glasses holding pointers at blackboards. But that's not the case. Actually, Channel One is more commercial than network TV: it's hipper, faster-moving, full of loud rock music—and, directly and indirectly, it's always selling something.

In short, the most standardized text—experienced the most frequently, by the most students—is the TV ad. Kids who are captive to Channel One's ads and buy the products (sometimes sold within their schools) are in fact the only people who are paying for this enterprise—not just in terms of time and money but also in terms of learning, language, thinking, attitudes, actions, and values.

Is Chernobyl *Really* Cher's Full Name?— Channel One as Bogus Cultural Literacy

Channel One was sold to schools with promises of improving students' "cultural literacy." Americans in 1989 were perfectly conditioned to accept the simple, concrete solutions that allowed Whittle's commercial TV into the classroom. In addition to Reaganomics, several popular books laid the foundation for Channel One: Hirsch's *Cultural Literacy* (1987), Bloom's *The Closing of the American Mind* (1987), and Bennett's *What Works: Research about Teaching and Learning* (1986). These books created a crisis climate for education by arguing that Americans were culturally illiterate and should "get back to basics." According to Hirsch's definition, Americans wouldn't be "culturally literate" (another way of saying "cultured") unless they read and memorized the list of texts in the back of his book. Fortunately, critical consciousness has never been achieved by reading someone else's list. Hirsch's book exploited one of America's oldest and deepest feelings—our inferiority complex. Deeply embedded within our cultural myth and identity, we Americans fear ignorance. In literature this theme is embodied in the country bumpkin image, the rough-hewn, unsophisticated American. The theme recurs throughout the history of American culture—from Twain's *Huck Finn* to *The Beverly Hillbillies*, to *Dumb and Dumber*. Hirsch's book offered a quick, simple salve to heal this feeling of being "less than," in the same way that images of Einstein are used to sell computers. Hirsch's book succeeded because it simplified academic success and reduced cultural knowledge to a list of items to memorize. But it's never been that simple.

First, a notion so broad as cultural literacy cannot and should not be defined solely in terms of any *single* topic, be it current events, American literature, post–World War II history, the plays of Tennessee Williams, or the films of Alfred Hitchcock. Similarly, cultural literacy is a *process*, not a product. Cultural literacy implies active critical thinking, building interactive networks of concepts, and personal construction of in-depth knowledge. Any type of literacy includes thinking, knowing, and doing—forming connections across disciplines, in the arts, sciences, and humanities. Whittle successfully packaged the term "cultural literacy" to mean watching an eight-minute TV program. This is absurd. Poet Howard Nemerov (1977) best summarizes the foolishness of such simple answers to complex questions:

> A sandwich and a beer might cure these ills
> If only Boys and Girls were Bars and Grills.

The flames of educational crisis were fanned by Whittle's friends and insiders, some of whom cashed in on Channel One. They include Chester Finn Jr. and Lamar Alexander (former secretary of education), who led the National Commission on Excellence in Education when it released *A Nation at Risk: The Imperative for Educational Reform* (Kozol 1992). Like the books by Hirsch (1987), Bloom (1987), and Bennett (1986), this document was another high-profile chunk of firewood for the cultural literacy bonfire. And Whittle and Alexander had close connections: "Alexander, a friend of Whittle's for some twenty years, initially served on Whittle's board and also worked as a consultant to, and held stock in, his corporation—a relationship from which he profited financially. (Having bought four Whittle Communications shares in 1988 for $19,000, Alexander and his wife then sold them back to Whittle for $330,000 five months later)" (Kozol 1992, 274).

In 1989, two years after Hirsch and his colleagues began softening up Americans by convincing them that they were illiterate and uncivilized, Whittle moved in for the kill. He took Bloom's snake-oil approach one step further. If Hirsch promised that Americans could become culturally literate by reading a list of books, then Whittle guaranteed the same thing for students by watching a ten-minute news show with ads: "Whittle pledged to produce a 'news and current events' broadcast that would bolster the cultural literacy of the nation's students. Many kids think 'Chernobyl is Cher's full name,' he quipped" (Toch 1992, 86).

In sum, a false need was created within the collective mind of the American public—a need for "cultural literacy" and "basics" in education. In addition to saying that schools needed more electronic equipment, this was Whittle's primary reason for developing Channel One. Moreover, he somehow convinced everyone that the *same* twelve-minute TV program and commercials would work equally well for millions of different kids, enrolled in thousands of different schools, spread across forty-eight different states. This cycle of create-a-need-and-then-fill-it has long been the golden rule of marketing. Whittle's comment about Chernobyl should be remembered for what it is: a sound bite manufactured to stimulate sales. The real priority was profit.

Do Kids at Least Learn Current Events?

Even if TV news shows don't constitute cultural literacy, another question remains: Do these news programs at least help students become more aware of current events? The bulk of the evidence says no. Research indicates that there is little reason to believe that viewing Channel One effectively teaches students about current world and national events. Whittle Communications' pilot study found that students who watched Channel One had significantly more correct answers on a current events test. However, the raw data and test instruments used in this research (reported only in press releases) could not be obtained by outsiders (Rudinow 1990).

Although Greenberg and Brand (1993, 147) concluded that "Student viewers of Channel One knew more about news events broadcast on the program than nonviewers," they also found no differences between students with and without Channel One on a measure of "general news knowledge." However, when they were retested two months later, Channel One students knew more about general current events. Greenberg and Brand, as well as Johnston and Brzezinski (1992), found that watching Channel One made no differences in students' interest in news topics and that students who watched Channel One did not report increased use of other media, such as daily newspapers and monthly news magazines.

Although nearly 75 percent of the students in Carlin's study (1992) reported that Channel One gave them new ideas to think about, most did not search for more information about topics covered on Channel One. Johnston and Brzezinski (1992, 3) also determined that although students *believed* they were learning significant information, average viewers scored only 3.3 percent higher than nonviewers on a current events test. Cramer's subjects (1993, 63) likewise reported increased knowledge of current events merely by watching Channel One; however, Cramer concluded that "test data did not support that belief."

In a study evaluating both Channel One and *CNN's Newsroom*, a similar program produced by Turner Educational Services, students in two states did not know any more current events than those who did not watch these shows (Educational Technology 1991). Tate (1989) found that students who had viewed Channel One made the same score on a current events test as those who had not watched the program. Knupfer and Hayes (1994, 51) studied 2,267 students and found "no significant differences in current-events test scores between students who received Channel One and those who did not receive the broadcast." Tiene (1994) reported a similar finding. More important, "Students remembered the advertisements"—not just because they are aimed at a young audience, but also because students "saw them repeated so many times" (Knupfer and Hayes 1994, 53).

WHAT DO WE KNOW ABOUT KIDS AND ADVERTISING?

In the past thirty years considerable research, theory, and direct experience have led to a generally accepted definition of media literacy: the ability to "decode, evaluate, analyze, and produce both print and electronic media" (Aufderheide 1992). Although most of the research has focused on young children, consensus remains on several issues: (1) that media have ideological and political implications; (2) that each medium has its own aesthetics, codes, and conventions; (3) that people usually negotiate and construct meaning from media; and (4) that media not only can reflect reality but also can help create it.

Although television ads in the schools began with Channel One's broadcasts in 1989, other kinds of direct and indirect advertising in American schools are nothing new. Two studies, *Report to the Legislature on Commercialism in Schools* (Washington Office of the State Superintendent of Public Instruction 1991) and *Captive Kids: A Report on Commercial Pressures on Kids at School* (Consumer's Union 1995), identify numerous commercial ventures ranging from formal business-education partnerships to free teacher-workshops that introduce new textbooks. Indeed, corporate-produced instructional materials are common in classrooms. Most are thinly veiled sales pitches that can badly distort the truth. The following examples from Karpatkin and Holmes (1995, 74) masquerade as legitimate and objective curriculum:

Campbell's "Prego Thickness Experiment" [is] designed "to help your students become aware of the many situations in which scientific thinking plays a part." The experiment quickly degenerates into a way for kids to prove its ad claim—that Prego spaghetti sauce is thicker than Ragu spaghetti sauce.

National Live Stock and Meat Board teaching kits plug pro-meat viewpoints into almost every curriculum area. "Digging for Data," which ostensibly teaches methods of scientific inquiry, provides data and actually leads students to deduce that early American settlers were short because they didn't eat enough meat.

Although these ventures have the same goal as Channel One—to make money from students—they differ in significant ways. For example, they do not seize students' attention on a systematic, daily basis, as Channel One does. Also, they do not blend the many finely integrated electronic techniques available for imagery, language, graphics, voice, sound effects, and music. Channel One has greater marketing resources for crafting more powerful messages "targeted" at specific, captive audiences. Makers of television commercials routinely field-test and hone their messages with computerized equipment, including the eye-scanner, T-Scope, and analog machine (Consodine and Haley 1992, 104).

Another concern is that Channel One can affect students' perceptions of social reality. In her review of research on the effects of television on *noncaptive* audiences, Greenfield (1984) concludes that "The evidence overwhelmingly indicates that television does influence children's views of social reality" (37). In other words, the media influence what kids think about other types of people—how they imagine what others are like, how they respect differences in others, how they communicate with others, how they treat others. The main concerns about TV commercials' effects on students' perceptions of life are summarized in the following sections.

Gender-Role Stereotyping

Television—with and without commercials—encourages viewers to form unrealistic and clichéd opinions about both genders. Even three-year-old children who are heavy television viewers have demonstrated more rigid attitudes about what jobs men and women should have, as opposed to their peers who view less television (Greenberg 1982). Consider female stereotypes in advertisements and TV commercials. Over twenty years ago, the United Nations Commission on the Status of Women reported three ways in which women in advertisements suffered from stereotyping:

a. Women are usually portrayed as unable to think for themselves; they defer to men to make decisions.

b. Loss of masculine approval is viewed as a threat; the advertised products are used to gain approval from men.

c. According to advertisements, women seem to be obsessed with cleanliness; they express a "gamut of emotions" in embracing whiteness, brightness, and freshness. (Washington Office of the State Superintendent of Public Instruction 1991, 91)

This report also describes research on the following areas of TV commercials for gender stereotyping: voice-overs or off-screen narrators, roles, activities, settings, and the ages of men and women. Following are a few of the findings:

- Almost all commercials with voice-overs are spoken and sung by men.
- Commercials show men in more roles than women, and they more often show women in family roles.
- Commercials show women doing activities in the home and show men as the beneficiaries of those activities.
- The settings of commercials show women inside the home and men outside the home.
- In commercials during children's programming, women and girls are seen less than men and boys.

Despite the evidence presented by such studies, people often argue that the media does not create stereotypes. One argument is that the media merely *reflects* contemporary society—that it doesn't create stereotypes at all. If more women enter the work force, the reasoning goes, then the television industry will produce more programs focusing on women in the work place. This argument is only partly accurate. Instead, market researchers comb their data for trends within sample populations—for what relatively small numbers of certain people are doing, so that producers can offer cutting-edge programming. When these new shows catch on with viewers, imitators are spawned. Soon, viewers begin to feel as if *everyone else* lives and breathes in sync with the current line-up. This situation often makes viewers feel alienated because they know that *they* are not like Seinfeld or the doctors on *ER*. The popular media characters create the illusion that everyone else is like them, when in fact this cannot be true.

Another common argument is that one TV show or film cannot create stereotypes because, after all, only a handful of characters are portrayed.

How can a single Archie Bunker represent millions? This argument does not account for the prevalence of media outlets, or the frequency of media images, or the way in which people perceive media images. Nor does it account for the power of symbols or icons.

First, there's not just one Archie Bunker—there are as many Bunkers as there are television sets tuned into him. And there are probably more television sets than people per household! Hence not only can the image and persona be realistic to most viewers, but that image is everywhere as well. Also, if even a single character or other symbol gains enough popularity, that symbol soon represents not only all other instances of that type but also the "best" qualities of that type. Babe Ruth symbolizes all baseball players and the game of baseball. He embodies the best qualities of the game: sportsmanship, humor, and skill. When single characters or single symbols represent so much, they can hardly escape becoming a stereotype.

Gender stereotyping has changed minimally over time. The independent Murphy Browns are relatively rare on TV. Although women are now more often *identified* as having a career outside the home, they still are usually shown performing domestic tasks at home. We know that Jill, the wife on the television program *Home Improvement*, has a career outside the home; but we usually only see her in the kitchen, placing canned goods into cupboards. If regular programs reinforce stereotypical views of gender roles, then as Greenfield (1984) concludes, commercials are "outstanding culprits" in doing the same thing:

One group of high school girls was shown fifteen commercials emphasizing the importance of physical beauty, while another group was not shown the commercials. The girls who watched the commercials were more likely than the others to agree with the statements "beauty is personally desirable for me" and "beauty is important to be popular with me." However . . . television, even without commercials (for example, in Britain twenty-five years ago and in Sweden today), influences children to attach more importance to appearance in general and clothes in particular. (38)

These same high school girls have watched TV commercials since they were young children—the age at which ads begin conditioning them to accept conventional gender roles. Ross and Campbell, et al. (n.d.) examined characteristics of television commercials for toys that were associated with girls and those that were associated with boys. The characteristics of ads for boys' toys were loud music, rapid camera cuts, and sound effects. Conversely, ads for girls' toys had more background music and gentler camera shots, such as fades and dissolves. Most of the children who viewed mock commercials (which showed shapes instead of real toys for boys and girls) correctly identified them according to the gender for which they were tailored.

Research results on gender-role stereotyping within Channel One commercials echo these findings. Mueller and Wulfemeyer (1991) obtained videotapes of Channel One pilot programs used in six secondary schools. The researchers analyzed the content of every commercial aired during this period and coded each segment for a variety of qualities including gender. They concluded that for most of the time the commercial's single, dominant character was a male. Although most Channel One commercials were aimed at both genders, 27 percent targeted males, whereas only 7 percent targeted females.

Similarly, Belland (1994, 96) shows how gender bias functioned in a Channel One news broadcast. For example, he presents a drawing representing one frame of the news story and observes that "the male anchor is shown in a superior position in the upper left of the picture." Belland notes that this positioning was typical for the week of programming he analyzed. He concludes that the Channel One news program "overwhelmingly showed males in key roles," for example, as spearheading advancements in technology.

Social and Racial Stereotyping

Media, including commercials, often present the following scenarios as reality: Men make the big decisions. Women do child care and clean house. White males possess technological expertise. The disabled population are "Amazingly Accomplished Surmounters; Pitiable Victims of Fate; Courageous Copers" (Moog 1990, 190). Nonwhite people are poor, ignorant, law-breaking, untidy, athletic, and violent.

The way in which the media portrays or "re-presents" certain groups of people (often categorized by gender, race, age, and social class) can affect viewers' attitudes toward that group. Evidence of the effects of media stereotyping has accumulated since 1933, when Peterson and Thurstone found that a single viewing of D. W. Griffith's *The Birth of a Nation* correlated with a negative shift in adolescents' attitudes toward African Americans.

But the effect can work both ways. Positive portrayals of groups can improve viewers' perceptions of these groups. Research on the influence of television revealed that minority kids watching *Sesame Street* rated higher than nonviewers of this program on measures of self-confidence and cultural pride, and that white children watching *Sesame Street* viewed cultural and racial differences more positively than nonviewers (Christensen and Roberts 1982). One study surveyed over 1,200 students' attitudes toward race and ethnicity, as well as their perceptions of television's influence on them (Lichter and Lichter, 1988). Forty percent said they learned "a lot" from TV; 25 percent agreed that "television shows what life is really like" and that "people on television are like real life." About one-third of those who expressed opinions stated that the ethnic characters they watch on TV influence their attitudes toward these same groups in real life. Rossiter (1980) found that *all types of characters* in TV commercials—human, nonhuman, and cartoon—prompted kids (even young ones) to form stereotypes of people's race, gender, occupation, and social behavior. Mueller and Wulfemeyer (1991) found that Channel One commercials were dominated by white teens and that the dominant characters were Caucasian 87 percent of the time and were male 57 percent of the time. De Vaney (1994) agrees, concluding that Channel One ads are "peopled with white teens" (150).

Throughout the present study I often observed stereotypes in Channel One commercials; I also observed students who generalized from commercials to form real-life judgments. For example, the Little Caesar's commercial that was highly popular with students during the time of my visits featured an elderly couple. Students often referred to the woman as "the old lady" and partly attributed her failure to apply lipstick evenly to her age.

Appeals to Sexuality and Physical Appearance

Advertising has traditionally emphasized sexuality and physical appearance to sell products, from soft drinks and deodorant to cars (e.g., see Hayakawa's "Sexual Fantasy and the 1957 Car," 1962). Moog (1994) shows how print advertising communicates immature attitudes about sexuality to young people; consequently, their definitions and perceptions of sexuality and gender identity become "stunted." This prevents both men and women, Moog maintains, from developing humane and mature gender identities and relationships.

Mueller and Wulfemeyer (1991) identify the personal values that Channel One advertisers use to target the youth market. About half the values are related to kids' sense of their own sexuality and appearance. These include appearance/sexuality, youthfulness/cleanliness, leisure/pleasure, status/self-esteem, love/affection, belonging, and community (140). De Vaney (1994, 150) would agree. She uses the term "Bacchanalian" to describe the world of

Channel One commercials. Indeed, her description of a potato chips commercial shown on Channel One illustrates how blatantly some ads use erotic metaphors to appeal to sexuality.

Cavorting on the Farm

SCENARIO. In this thirty-second spot for Pringles corn chips, six teens (four girls and two boys) dance and play in a corn field. As the scene opens, one boy, standing in the middle of the corn field, is slowly detassling an ear of very yellow corn. The other is standing on a ladder propped against a silo. He has a paint roller in his hand, but is facing away from the silo and into the camera. Four girls, waving yellow cans of Pringles at the boys, arrive in a speeding yellow jeep. Girls and boys come together. They dance and feed one another corn chips. Magically, the silo turns into a yellow can of Pringles. A large banner appears across the screen in block letters, "FEVER RELIEVER."

AUDIO. A musical jingle runs throughout this ad. The jingle compares corn chips to fresh corn and tells the students, "You have the fever of a fresh corn flavor." The rhythm and volume of the jingle gradually increase until they reach a "fever pitch." After the jingle ends, a rich deep male voice-over says slowly, "The fresh corn fever-reliever."

VIDEO. The video track is in the form of a music video. Although a story is told, dramatic narrative codes are abandoned in favor of MTV codes. Approximately seventy shots occupy the thirty-second slot. Very fast-paced cuts articulate the shots, half of which are not matched, but are jump cuts. The boys are dressed in jeans and T-shirts, but the four girls are dressed in tight, bright clothes that call attention to their bodies. The two girls whose images occupy most of the music video are blond. Each wears an off-the-shoulder top. Their shoulders are bare. The pacing of the cuts increases as the rhythm of the music increases, until it reaches a fast-cut culminating scene. This scene is a very tight shot of a boy's lap. He is supposed to be seated in the corn field. His face is not shown. With one hand he holds a detassled ear of yellow corn erect in his lap. A female hand (no face) reaches for the corn. Magically, the corn turns into a stack of corn chips about the size of an ear of corn. The female hand plucks a corn chip, and the stack turns back into an erect ear of corn. By repeatedly intercutting the ear of corn held by the boy's hand and the female hand reaching for the corn/chip stack, the producer shows the stack of chips gradually diminishing. The scene closes with a close-up of the girl's ecstatic face. The scene switches to the closing series of shots next to the silo where the "fever reliever" banner is rolled. (De Vaney 1994, 146–147)

Appeals to sexuality and physical appearance are more commonly used to sell products such as cigarettes and alcoholic beverages. Younger kids are now associating sexuality with such products. Even fifth- and sixth-graders remember TV commercials for beer—and kids may watch more than 2,000 beer and wine ads each year (Schwed 1995). What's more, young kids link the drinking of beer to "romance, sociability and relaxation" (Columbia Daily Tribune 1994).

Materialism

According to Carol Herman, Senior Vice President of Grey Advertising, "it isn't enough to advertise on television . . . you've got to reach kids throughout the day—in school, as they're shopping in the mall . . . or at the movies. You've got to become part of the fabric of their lives" (Washington Office of the State Superintendent of Public Instruction 1991, 16). Indeed, advertising *is* "part of the fabric" of kids' lives. When they are not in school, kids watch TV more than they engage in any other activity—an average of three hours each day on school days and an average of six to eight hours each day on weekends (Medrich et al. 1982). After age two, the majority of children watch TV every day and are exposed to over 20,000 commercial messages per year (Adler and Faber 1980), whereas the average adult American sees 32,000 commercials per year (Consodine and Haley 1992, 98).

Many researchers have linked advertising to consumers' materialistic attitudes. Hite and Eck (1987), for example, conclude that ads not only (1) make kids materialistic but also (2) generate friction between parents and children, and (3) limit the formation of "moral and ethical values." In another study, viewers of Channel One commercials evaluated the products advertised more favorably than nonviewers did. The same study found that Channel One viewers had a greater desire to buy the products shown, concluding that "we found Channel One viewers to hold more materialistic attitudes" (Greenberg and Brand 1993, 150).

Advertising—indeed, all visual media—consists of nothing but visible, tangible objects. And when we see something that we don't have, we naturally want to obtain it for ourselves, to consume products that we believe will define us and our reasons for living. Greenfield (1984) notes that British children who watched television in the 1950s—the BBC, which contained no commercials—developed more materialistic attitudes than those who did not watch television. Greenfield observes that

Adolescent boys who watched television . . . were more focused on what they would *have* in the future; adolescent boys without television were more focused on what they would be *doing*. The longer the child's experience with television, the more this materialistic outlook increased. (51)

Materialistic attitudes can become stronger when the tangible products that kids buy cannot live up to the *intangible* values that the ads promised. That is, when kids are saturated in advertising, their appetites for products are stimulated. At the same time, kids desire the values that have been associated with those products—intangible values that, like sex appeal, are impossible to buy. Even when a product fails to deliver something it never could, kids will buy it again, trying to fill the void. Throughout this book, behind all the thinking, language, attitudes, and behaviors, readers may sense in kids an overall materialistic world view—a global conception or internal map that defines and describes the world as a place where goals are achieved and problems are solved through buying and selling, a world that crowds out the life of the body, the mind, and the spirit.

HOW WAS THIS STUDY CONDUCTED?

This book describes how two hundred students attending Channel One schools respond to TV commercials: their language, attitudes, values, and behavior. The study describes not only what the kids say but also how, when, and why they say it. The following general questions guided the investigation: How well do kids know commercials? How do kids think about commercials? How do kids evaluate commercials? How do commercials affect kids' behavior? How do commercials affect kids' consumer behavior? How can the total context of commercial television in the schools best be described? I analyzed kids' language for their semantic reactions to commercials—for how their internal maps of reality, constructed by both language and images, did and did not match up with reality. Sometimes kids were aware of their responses; sometimes they were not.

In the pages ahead I have tried to let the kids speak for themselves. I present their thinking as completely as possible. I did not attempt to verify or "correct" any of their statements for accuracy (although I believe most students were quite accurate in their recall of brand names and other information). Also, all the information obtained from kids came from nonthreatening and naturalistic inquiry, in as normal an environment as I could create. Throughout the taped interviews, my most common response to what kids said was, "Why?" I wanted to know the pathways of their thinking; I wanted to know if they could provide examples and illustrations to support their responses to commercials. They often could. This made it easier to "show and not merely tell" what they were thinking and feeling, to make the contours of their reasoning more visible. I have tried equally hard to be concrete and detailed when reporting language and behavior that the kids did *not* seem aware of at the time.

Removed from their teachers, guaranteed anonymity, and comfortably situated within small groups of their peers, sitting in a circle, these kids spoke honestly and directly. During small-group sessions I did not ask for or use their names (however, I have supplied fictitious names here). Also, I have edited their words as little as possible, because their *own* language rings truest. Kids' own language best reveals the human beings lined up in front of the TV sets. Finally, kids have a right to their own language, especially when the issue at stake is the appropriation of their voices.

Sources of Data

Most of the interviews occurred during the school day at two rural, public high schools in central Missouri, about 60 miles apart. Data was gathered from October 1993 to March 1995. Each school was located in a town of approximately 8,000 people. Each school was located about 100 miles from an urban center (St. Louis or Kansas City). The educational and economic profiles that follow show the areas to be roughly equal. This information was provided by school district personnel and census data.

School District A

From 1980 to 1990, census data showed a 43 percent loss of farming families from this district's rural areas, whereas the small towns gained in population. Seven percent of the district's residents over age twenty-five have a college degree; 20 percent have less than a ninth-grade education. Forty percent of the county's adults are high school graduates. The main types of employment are agriculture and agribusiness industries. According to the 1990 census, the county's individual median income is $21,726—considerably lower than the median state income of $26,362. With 14 percent of the population below the national poverty level, about 270 children received Aid for Families with Dependent Children (AFDC) benefits every month in 1992. Nearly one-third of the live births in 1990 were to unwed mothers.

School District B

Overall, this district's demographic and economic situations are similar to those of School District A. From 1980 to 1990 the county lost approximately 6 percent of its population. About 11 percent of the residents over age twenty-five have a college degree; nearly 16 percent have less than a ninth-grade education. Thirty-four percent of the county's adults are high school graduates. As in School District A, agribusiness industries represent the main type of employment. In 1989 the county's individual median income was $21,685—considerably lower than the median state income of $26,362. Also, 12.5 percent of the population was below the national poverty level. Nearly 40 percent of the live births in 1993 were to unwed mothers.

The Students

The main source of data for this study consisted of small focus groups of five to eight students each, totaling approximately two hundred students. About 90 percent of the students were ninth-graders. Students came from required courses, primarily from English/Language Arts classes; thus I could talk with a representative sample of kids who were not tracked by ability level or test scores. There were roughly the same number of males and females. The large majority of students at both schools were Caucasian. Overall, the students in this study were as average and as typical as central Missouri could offer.

Secondary Sources of Data

Other data sources included the following: (1) written notes of observations of students watching Channel One broadcasts; (2) interviews with teachers, administrators, and parents; (3) Channel One published materials (e.g., viewing guides, contracts with schools); (4) journal and newspaper articles; (5) materials published by Whittle and K-III Communications; and (6) the results of anonymous written surveys completed by approximately 140 students attending the same schools where the interviews occurred. The surveys were completed several weeks before the in-school interviews.

Methods and Procedures for Focus Groups

My assistant and I met with each focus group for 45–60 minutes without their teacher present. Occasionally I conducted one-to-one interviews with key informants—kids selected because they had shown (during small-group conversations) some special reason, ability, or knowledge that I wanted them to explain in more detail. All sessions were audiotaped. Early in the study I began using a mixer board that could handle five separate microphones, because kids usually became excited and spoke at once.

Because of the nature of the television medium, the genre of commercials, and the fluid quality of human responses to television, an emergent design was the logical choice for this study. Students' experiences with television are much like the medium itself—fast, emotional, imagistic, fluid, and fleeting. Commercials as a genre possess an abundance of these qualities. For instance, a televised documentary on sea life would be slower and less emotional than a fifteen-second ad for Levi's jeans. Therefore, I began with a specific agenda but pursued other directions as they arose. Following are the primary questions used throughout the study:

- Can you retell, in as much detail as you can, exactly what happens in a commercial of your choice?
- What is your favorite Channel One commercial and why? Tell us as many details about it as you can remember.
- From whose point of view is the story or information in this commercial told? Who is telling this story?
- Have you ever seen a commercial that somehow motivated you to buy something? If so, what can you tell me about it?
- What are the differences between a commercial and something you watch that *isn't* a commercial? How do you know?
- What makes an effective or "good" commercial?
- What makes an ineffective or "bad" commercial?
- Can you analyze or evaluate the strengths and weaknesses of this commercial? If so, please explain.
- What is this commercial selling?

I always tried to establish an atmosphere that helped students relax. I did not want them to think the questions had a single, right or wrong answer. Nor did I want students to fear that they were "sounding dumb" or "going off on tangents." An atmosphere of trust and honest exploration were crucial for enabling students to share their thoughts. Therefore we met in random, small groups, removed from teachers. I guaranteed students anonymity and did not refer to them by name. Each group began with the following announcement:

I have specific questions to ask you, but I'm really more interested in whatever it is that *you* want to say—so don't let these questions stop you if you've got other things to say. Also, please remember that there are no right or wrong answers here.

As students responded to my predetermined questions, I followed up on their responses, searching for the emotional heart or center of gravity of their comments. In this way I could approach what the kids were most intensely feeling or thinking about commercials, and why. Blindly following predetermined questions would not allow us to explore this uncharted territory, so some questions evolved during our discussions. The open-ended "Why?" made the students think more about their reactions and feelings, and better explain them.

Other Procedures

Although most of the time was devoted to asking the main questions and then following up on them, I sometimes used additional methods to elicit responses: (1) we watched commercials together, stopping the tape and reviewing as either of us deemed necessary; (2) the small group would reach consensus about a question or issue (e.g., recall as many details as possible about a specific commercial); (3) the kids explored a written transcript of a commercial without seeing the video; (4) they ranked commercials we had just viewed from best to worst and then explained their choices; and (5) the kids watched commercials in small groups, with the instruction that they were free to "think out loud" about what they were viewing.

Analysis of Data

Research assistant Lucy Stanovick and I discussed our impressions following each meeting with the focus groups, as well as on the following day. These observations and issues were then described in written notes. Working from approximately five hundred pages of notes and typed transcripts—from over forty hours of taped conversations—I analyzed and labeled each phenomenon observed, placing them into groups or categories. The categories often shifted as data was analyzed again and again. Sometimes categories combined; sometimes they separated into two groups. My research assistant and I agreed upon the final groupings, definitions, and placement of examples within them.

Data was analyzed through the following (often overlapping), disciplinary principles: media literacy (e.g., cultural codes, conventions); general semantics and propaganda analysis (e.g., two-valued orientation, levels of abstraction); semiotics (e.g., association, transfer); gestalt psychology (e.g., perception of whole structures vs. parts and "law" of proximity); reader-response literary theory (e.g., focus on transaction between reader and text); rhetorical persuasion; critical thinking; and audience-based film criticism.

The primary, specific criteria for determining students' effective and ineffective analysis of commercials included their ability to apply rhetorical persuasion and propaganda techniques derived from general semantics, semiotics, and rhetorical persuasion, which include bandwagon, testimonial, association, and others. To gauge these, I employed Rank's (1976) "Intensify/Downplay" schema. Students' language was analyzed for both its stated and implied uses of these analytical tools; however, I did not expect students to employ the exact terminology of any of the critical frameworks used to examine their responses.

Limitations

The project has definite limitations. First, the study simply describes ways that individual kids responded to and interacted with commercials. My aim is merely to identify basic categories of reactions. I do not mean to state or imply that all kids think, say, or do everything described here.

Second, the study focuses on kids' personal responses to television—which may have been the first time they verbalized such feelings. The best approach for this type of exploration is through the kids' own thinking and informal language. Hence, numbers are largely irrelevant. Where I have observed clear trends or patterns in responses, I indicate a crude approximation in simple words such as "most students" or "some students" or "a few kids." In those few instances when I kept track of frequency counts, and when I think it's especially important, I quote them (e.g., "twenty-two out of thirty-three kids I talked to about violence, said that . . . ").

Third, keep in mind that Channel One schools represent a unique type of environment that affects the way in which kids respond to commercials, even those they watch at home. Why? Because Channel One schools are "closed" environments, where certain factors are controlled or eliminated. For example, students lack freedom to change the channels, to mute the audio, to leave the room, and to avoid excessive repetition of commercials over a period of weeks and months. These factors alone affect how they respond to commercials.

Fourth, how we interpret or understand any text (print, audio, or visual) depends on our prior knowledge, previous experiences, background, culture, gender, age, and other "filters." This is the prevailing paradigm for response to literature and media research. I firmly believe in this paradigm, but mainly for free or open environments. Although the students discussed here definitely interacted with media and processed it through such screens, they generated much less personal meaning than expected. Rather than interacting on a deeper level with texts, they often merely mirrored them or replayed them in ways that did not lead to further understanding or analysis.

Fifth, the study focuses on the commercials the kids watched in their classrooms; it does not try to gauge the influence of ads viewed at home or elsewhere. In all interviews I tried to make this as clear as possible. I have tried to clearly identify those few times when students *do* refer to commercials that aired outside of school.

Finally, because many of these kids were reflecting on commercials out loud for the first time, their thinking often evolved *as they interacted during our small groups*. It's natural for all symbols—words, pictures, music, and the like—to generate thinking, which in turn often generates *more* thinking and symbols. This new thinking in turn modifies the kid's concept of the original symbols. Mixing one symbol system with another creates mental combustion. Mixing kids with other kids to explore commercials creates even more combustion. Meaning-making, especially as it occurred during these focus groups, was a social, evolving process subject to renegotiation and redefinition.

2

How Well Do Kids Know Commercials?

Sara: My favorite was the Little Caesar's commercial about the kid who brings pizza onto a plane and then the woman puts lipstick on all over her face.

Joyce: That was a good one. We all laughed all the time whenever we saw it. When it would come on, everybody would get quiet and just watch it.

Lynn: Yeah, that was the best one.

RF: You liked it that much, all year?

All: Yeah!

RF: About how many times did you watch that commercial?

Sara: From the beginning of the year, in late August, until Christmas break, every day or every other day.

Lynn: It was like the "Be Like Mike" commercial. Sometimes they showed that one twice in one day.

How well do kids know commercials? Extraordinarily well. Even when the novelty fades, they still enjoy watching their favorites. They tolerate commercials more than the average adult, as this boy makes clear: "Everybody liked Shaq [Shaquille O'Neal, basketball player] last year because he was new and he was hot and everybody paid attention. The Emmitt Smith commercial is still interesting because it's not *every day* of the week—it's just once or twice a week. You don't get to see it very often, and it's still fresh when you do see it."

Just how well kids retain and know the basics of commercials was a question that I pursued throughout this study. Without a doubt, kids consistently demonstrated a very high recall of commercials' content and structure, including an intimate knowledge of details, even down to how certain products are packaged.

Connections between commercials' symbols (e.g., characters, jingles) and brand names were firmly established. In small groups, if one student said "Gatorade" then most of the others would voluntarily chime in with "Chuckie V.!"—the name of the character who stars in Gatorade commercials. Conversely, if a student described a commercial as being about "cinnamon gum and people kissing," others would jump in with "Big Red"—the product's name. Product names quickly and easily elicited commercials' key features or symbols, and the ads' symbols (e.g., the Nike swoosh) did likewise for the product names. Many students also demonstrated a sophisticated knowledge of the relationships among commercials, products, and members of product "families."

KIDS KNOW THE DETAILS OF COMMERCIALS

Kristy: There was an M&M commercial on this morning that I saw for the first time.

RF: What do you remember about it?

Clark: It's about "Don't ask—you *always* ask questions."

Kristy: Yeah. The guy who plays Eldon on *Murphy Brown* plays the guy who has two little M&M's. He has a green M&M in his hand and one M&M asked Eldon what green meant, and Eldon said it meant "go," like "go ahead and eat it." And then Eldon got to the red M&M, who asked him, "What does red mean? Doesn't that mean stop?" And then Eldon said, "Yeah, stop asking me questions." And then he ate that one. And then one started walking out and said, "Why do you ask so many questions?"

Clark immediately retells the commercial in nearly the exact words of the ad (as opposed to a summary or overview). This type of response was typical throughout the study. Even though Kristy had only seen the commercial once, she also describes it in considerable detail.

One simple but major finding of this study—and one that should come as no surprise—is that most students could easily recall microscopic levels of details about commercials. Students knew the direction in which a model swung her hair or how many rings another model wore. They even recalled tiny details about ads they had not seen for over a year. Also, many students made precise distinctions within and between commercials and products, including packaging. When I replayed a commercial to check on the accuracy of students' observations, the kids were generally correct (about 80 percent of the time). However, more important than their accuracy in recalling details was their *level* of specificity. By far the most important issue is the degree of focus and complexity of the pictures that students carry in their mind's eye.

Details about People and Places

The Little Caesar's pizza commercial was extremely popular in one school the year before my first visit. When I asked students to retell the commercial, nearly everyone recalled its sequence of main actions. At an airport, a boy grabs a slice of pizza and boards the plane. The cheese on the boy's slice forms a long strand, connecting it to the airport, even as the plane tries to fly away. This unknown tether causes the plane to fly in circles. Meanwhile, an elderly woman passenger leaves her husband to go to the plane's restroom and apply some lipstick. Because the plane keeps flying in circles, she teeters and smears lipstick all over her face. So goes the basic commercial. However, during and after retellings, I asked students to recall as many details as possible, to determine just how specific these images remained in their mind's eye. Every small group typically reported the following:

Inside the airport, a group of old people, the boy's relatives, are seeing him off. The boy reaches for a slice of cheese pizza from a Little Caesar's pizza box that bears a likeness of the Little Caesar's character, a little spikey-haired man holding a spear and two pizzas. This is the character who always utters, "pizza-pizza!" As the boy reaches for the pizza, the airport announcer says, in a sing-song voice, "Flight 409 is now arriving . . ."

The day is sunny. The plane is a white jumbo jet with red and blue stripes on the side. The nose of the plane is red. The elderly couple inside the plane is seated in the coach fare section, because they are in a row consisting of three red seats that have a pattern consisting of little blue squares with arrows sticking out of them.

The boy, about ten years old, has pudgy red cheeks, freckles, and sandy brown hair. He wears a red and navy blue striped tee-shirt and shorts and a black backpack. The elderly woman, about sixty-five years old, has gray, curly short hair that's a little frizzy. Her hair is partly dyed a reddish color. She wears brown, plastic glasses that have arms that curve down. She wears a white, short-sleeved Granny dress with blue and pink flowers. She wears clip-on, gaudy earrings and a bead necklace, which has a large centerpiece. She carries a purse, which has arched handles, in the crook of her arm. She applies fire-engine red lipstick. The woman's husband, seated next to the window, is old, gray, and bald. He wears glasses and a gray-brown suit, with a striped tie.

Again, the level of specificity reigns as most important. The commercials succeed in selling their product when viewers recall, with confidence, such minute details. Perfect accuracy is a secondary issue.

Details about Brand Names and Products

Students demonstrated a keen memory for the language, dialogue, and vocal intonations used in commercials. Because students' overall uses of language are best classified as "replay phenomena"—that is, their language often merely replayed or mirrored the language used in commercials—it is explored in detail in Chapter 5. Here, I will review only how students used specific details to talk about commercials and products. Consider the following conversation:

Shawna: I like that new commercial. . . .

Mary: The one with the little kid in it?

Shawna: Yes!

Mary: Isn't he cute?!

Shawna: It's about this man and woman sitting at a table and she says, "Have you ever tasted anything better than *Little Caesar's* pizza?" and—

Mary: [Interrupting] No—she says, "Have you ever seen anything more amazing than this?"

Students would often interrupt each other to make sure that their class-mates were using the *exact words* of the commercial—usually the names of products, characters, phone numbers, or ingredients of products. For example, students consistently knew what "flavor crystals" were—the ad phrase for the tiny bits of candy in Cinnaburst chewing gum—and would correct their peers when this term was not used.

One year after Pizza Hut advertised a phone number for obtaining direc-tions to its nearest restaurant, students still knew it. Although the number *appeared* as "513–839–3939," students *said* it as "513–83–93–93–9"—the way the commercial's narrator said it, repeating "threes," which lead up to the long vowel sound in "nine." In short, students recalled the exact numbers *and* the exact phrasing. Shawna uses the brand name in her retelling, which was not part of the original ad. After she was interrupted, she continued:

Shawna: It was the pizza—and she looked up and the kid had a cat on his head and he was balancing all this stuff. And the guy looked up and he looked down and said, "No."

Mary: And the little kid was singing "Give My Regards to Broadway." It's soo cuute!

Shawna: And then he just looks down and says, "Nope!"

Mary: And that's the end—but it's really cute!

RF: And this commercial is for . . .?

Shawna: Little Caesar's—

Just after Shawna said, "Little Caesar's," one of my microphones picked up a third girl whispering, "pizza-pizza!"—the Little Caesar's slogan uttered at the end of its commercials by the little man who also appears on Little Caesar's boxes. The point here is that commercials often elicited brand names, slogans, jingles, and other memorable "tag lines" associated with them. The reverse was also true: students often launched into descriptions of commercials when someone else mentioned a brand name or slogan. In one conversation, in the space of about three minutes, one girl kept referring to a commercial as the "I love Jukie" commercial— and a boy in the group corrected her three times, saying, "You mean the *Sprite* commercial." One begets the other: the brand name evokes an image, creating an echo-chamber environment where ads and products can hardly be forgotten.

Sometimes students used the exact language from a commercial to describe it. One student describes a Pepsi ad: "It's mostly about inner-city kids, not gang stuff. Ya know, it's like this, and the kids on the commercial just said what they were feeling." The commercial that this student describes is titled, "It's Like This!"—which also functions as a slogan, because it is orally and visually repeated during the ad. However, this student did not seem aware that she was using the Pepsi slogan to describe the ad.

Details about Packaging

Randy: The Nike symbol is a "swoosh" and the Fila symbol is an upside-down Nike swoosh—and Reebok has their own version of the Nike swoosh.

RF: Someone this morning called it a "swish"—so which is it?

All: A swoosh!

RF: Does Nike ever use this word in a commercial or magazine ad?

Randy: They have it on the boxes—in real little letters on the side of the box.

In addition to knowing the details about commercials, kids knew about packaging. I gradually learned that many students do not view packaging in the way that most adults do—as mere containers or wrappings of products. Instead, many kids regard packaging as integral parts of the products themselves.

Mike: I bought a big, remote-control truck, which I saw on commercials like "The Bandit."

RF: Was it expensive?

Mike: A hundred dollars.

Jessica: Jeez! For a remote-control truck? How big is it?

Mike: Big.

Jessica: How big? The size of a Nike shoe box?

Mike: Bigger than that.

Jessica's final comment caught me off guard. We had never discussed Nike shoes up to that point, and her metaphor—what she chose to measure her world by—contained a brand name. The old comparison line, "bigger than a shoe box," had taken on a new twist. This comparison was evidently a common frame of reference for these kids. Intrigued, I asked other kids to describe Nike shoe boxes:

Debbie: They're really big if you get high-tops. They're orange, gray, and white. They have a bright orange top and it goes down on the bottom and there's about that much you can see on the bottom [holds fingers apart], and it's dull gray and white striped.

Zack: That's not *always* it, though. Michael Jordan's shoe boxes are different than all the other kinds. [Two other kids agree.] The others have a pull-off top and his just flaps back and it's like the whole box, and the way it comes down is, like, it starts really small at the top and works its way down, to be really big. It's black and gray and stuff—kind of like a person with a basketball. It's on all his shoes and stuff.

Zack refers to "Michael Jordan's shoe boxes," and *not* Nike's shoe boxes. Nike has so thoroughly imprinted Jordan on its product that, to Zack, Jordan now owns the company. When I learned that this same group of kids drank Gatorade, also advertised on Channel One, I asked them to tell me about the bottle it comes in:

Jessica: I bought Gatorade one time because the label had a picture of Michael Jordan drinking it. I thought that was cool.

Zack: Sometimes I buy it 'cause it says you can win something.

Jessica: Yeah! That's why I buy Dr. Pepper.

RF: Can you describe the bottle?

Jessica: The color of it depends on the flavor. They have the Michael Jordan citrus flavoring and that's why I buy that one, because it has Michael Jordan on it. And that label is an orange-yellowish.

RF: Do you remember what the label says?

Jessica: It just has Michael Jordan drinking it and behind him are X's and O's, for plays, like when you play basketball.

Zack: There's a yellow lightning bolt on it, too, right beside the word "Gatorade," and it says "Thirst Quencher" right under it.

In these few minutes, Jessica mentions Jordan four times, consistently using his first and last name. Jordan's presence clearly motivated these kids to know and use the products. Another group of boys recalled the Gatorade bottles even more precisely:

Larry: It depends on what flavor you get. They're in glass bottles. If it's punch, it's red; grape is purple. The lids are all the same color. The word "Gatorade" is in white print, and the lightning bolt behind it is usually the color of the flavor.

Paul: They've also got two-gallon jugs and those are different from the bottles. Because on the two-gallon jugs, some of the print is a different color. On the bottles, it can be a fruit punch flavor, but the label will be red and the print white. But on the two-gallon jug, sometimes the letters might correspond to the flavor, and the background will be a different color.

Such recall of small details and fine distinctions tell me that, for these kids, appearance is extremely important. They pay keen attention to it. During the conversations about packaging, students were animatedly talking all at once, often trying to be heard above each other. Also, throughout these conversations the students never questioned *why* I would ask them about something so irrelevant. Clearly, they viewed packaging as integral to the product.

KIDS KNOW THE STRUCTURE OF COMMERCIALS

One day, we watched a commercial that aired for the first time on Channel One. This thirty-second ad featured the athlete David Robinson. Throughout that day, most of the kids told me that this commercial's structure consisted of "three parts," which they recalled in the correct sequence:

(1) Robinson goes to college and earns his master's degree; (2) Robinson becomes a naval officer; and (3) he goes to the Olympics (twice) before becoming a professional ball player. (Right after watching it, I remembered none of these things!)

Students could also recall the three-part structure of a Sure deodorant commercial: (1) a marching band takes off in a different direction, away from the boy who has body odor, (2) a girl in a red shirt dances and raises her arms, revealing the visible traces of body odor, and (3) a boy in a movie theater puts his arm around a girl and withdraws it because he is "unsure" if he has body odor. Students' details of each vignette and how they were sequenced were often correct.

In "continuing" commercials, those that form a series (e.g., ads featuring the Energizer Bunny), a few students quickly identified their conventions, or key features.

A lot of commercials are really neat the first time you see them. Like the "Energizer Bunny" commercial. The newest one is about Darth Vader, from *Star Wars,* who's trying to get the bunny, and Vader's laser runs out of energy and he pulls out his batteries and they're a different brand. You really want to know what's going to happen in the next commercial. And then you wait and wait and wait and wait, and they finally show you.

Jerry was at least vaguely aware that series commercials are connected in some way: "I think there are three Chuckie V. commercials. When we first came to school, he was telling us about going to Hawaii. And then in the second one, he advertised that we'd get a shirt and win a trip to Hawaii; and in the third one, he poured Gatorade on his head." Jerry, bright and articulate, seems to be on the right track, but he could make little sense out of the third ad in the series. Despite (or because of) Jerry's confusion and mild surprise, he was curious about what the next one would be.

Students' ability to recall narrative sequence—not their skill in analyzing messages—helped them understand commercials' structure. Never once did students discuss the parts of a commercial *out* of the order in which they appeared; their retellings always followed a chronological order. Students' awareness of how parts fit into a whole message seemed never put to any use, other than as aids for remembering commercials. The extremely rare instances when students *did* use their knowledge of structure occurred when they identified inconsistencies within commercials.

KIDS KNOW RELATIONSHIPS AMONG COMMERCIALS AND PRODUCTS

Jake: I can tell from the commercials that Coke and Pepsi compete with each other. The same goes for McDonald's and Hardee's, Wendy's and Burger King, and Mr. Pibb and Mello Yello.

RF: Can you explain a little more?

Jake: Well, it seems like Coke has copied off of Pepsi quite a few times—like with Mello Yello coming out after Mr. Pibb. Mello Yello and Kick are copied from Mountain Dew. Dr. Pepper is a Pepsi product and Mr. Pibb is a Coke product. Dad's Rootbeer was copied from A&W.

RF: Any others?

Jake: Mello Yello is Coke and Mountain Dew is Pepsi. Coke came out with Sprite and Pepsi has Slice. Coke had High C and Minute Maid and Pepsi has Orange and Lemon Slice.

Chris: What about Seven-Up?

Jake: Seven-Up is a separate company, but maybe Royal Crown Cola owns Seven-Up and Kick; I'm not sure.

Chris: What about Fresca?

Jake: That's Coca-Cola.

RF: Is there a copy of Fresca from Pepsi?

Jake: Squirt.

RF: Is Gatorade a separate company?

Jake: Yeah, there are a lot of things copied off of Gatorade. Allsport is from Pepsi and Powerade is from Coke.

Jake's knowledge of parent companies, spin-off products, and competing brands was greater than that of most kids I talked to. I asked him to create some charts illustrating these connections (see Table 2.1).

Throughout the study, students revealed knowledge about other relationships. One boy sketched a brief history of athletic shoe sales:

It was Converse at first—way back when—and then Nike was real high, way up there on a pedestal. And then Reebok started muffing 'em out, because they started doing endorsements with tennis players, so, in the early eighties, Nike brought in Jordan. Then, Converse came back with the "Ponies"—they're old. That's when they brought in Spud Webb, when they won the slam-dunk contest, and Dominique Wilkins, that's when he came out and endorsed them. And that's when Nike brought in Jordan Air and broke all those records.

Table 2.1
Jake's Diagram of Procter and Gamble's Products

Procter and Gamble		
Food	*Personal Hygiene*	
Crisco	Noxzema	Crest
Jif	Old Spice	Clearasil
Pringles	Ivory	Pampers
Fisher Nuts	Dawn	Tide
Hawaiian Punch	Cascade	Pepto Bismol
Folgers Coffee	Era	Sure
	Zest	Head and Shoulders

This boy's animated tone and attitude revealed that he regards athletic shoe sales as a kind of sport, complete with strategies, moves, countermoves, star players, losers, and winners.

One group of ninth-grade girls seemed to know every job that "the Noxzema girl" ever had, almost as if they had memorized her resumé. They knew not only her real name but also how many Channel One Noxzema commercials she had starred in, which ones had also aired on network television, which ones she had made for other products, which print ads she had appeared in, and which noncommercial acting roles she had performed.

Another group of five students revealed a knowledge of simpler relationships, yet nonetheless important: they informed me that Michael Jordan made commercials for four products: Nike, Gatorade, Wheaties, and Hanes underwear. They readily agreed that any of Jordan's several Nike commercials were far superior to his ads for any other products. They ranked Jordan's Gatorade commercials as second in overall quality, then his ads for Wheaties, and, bringing up the rear, his commercial for Hanes underwear. The Hanes ad was ranked last because Jordan appears in it the least. The length of Jordan's appearance seemed to determine how much the ad was liked. (And, of course, we should not overlook the fact that four out of these five students were wearing Nike shoes.) What students understood and how they evaluated ads depended on what was important to them—an expected consequence of knowing about and valuing products and ads in the first place.

CONCLUSION

Clearly, these students intimately know and recall commercials and the products they sell. My discussions with individuals and small groups vividly and consistently revealed their familiarity. The thoroughness and detail of students' knowledge of commercials and products can only be tapped by sitting down and talking to them at length. What students demonstrated in these informal conversations—including their nonverbal and intense personal involvement with commercials—could never have been determined through questionnaires.

Indeed, the survey I administered to 140 students in two Channel One schools did not come close to communicating what the interviews did. For example, one question ("Describe the Channel One commercial that you best remember. Be as specific and detailed as you can.") elicited sketchy, general responses from students. During interviews, on the other hand, we could continually follow up with questions to learn about the extent and depth of their knowledge about commercials. Even the question, "Write the names of as many products advertised in Channel One's commercials as you can think of," gives an incomplete picture of how well kids know commercials (even though students reported an average of six specific brands each).

Students know commercials so well, of course, because they see them in a controlled environment, over and over, during an entire year's period. These commercials contrast not only with the news portion of the program but also with a school environment that cannot compete with the many "jolts per minute" delivered by high-voltage ads for Nike, Gatorade, and M&M's.

Students also know commercials well because kids themselves repeat the messages again and again, in many ways. This replay phenomena involves students re-enacting or rerunning the commercial message in some way—by reciting or singing jingles to friends, by adopting the name of a favorite commercial character, by replicating an ad's words or images in a project for art class, or even by dreaming about the commercial. Although replay phenomena will be explored in detail in Chapter 5, suffice it to say here that students talk about commercials with each other and their friends and family. During interviews and in the questionnaire, 40 percent of the kids reported that they talk about commercials inside *and* outside of school. Slightly more girls reported discussing commercials with friends. Kids reported talking with friends and family about commercials in the following situations:

- Before, during, between, and after classes in the hallways.
- While watching television at home (several would call up their friends whenever a new or favorite commercial aired so they could watch it together).
- In locker rooms.
- While watching and participating in after-school sporting events and practice sessions (e.g., one student reported quoting lines of a commercial's dialogue while he was running cross-country track: "One state down and two states to go . . .").
- During bus rides to and from school.
- During lunch in the school cafeteria.
- While shopping.
- While signing yearbooks.
- While playing backyard football games.
- While viewing satires of commercials done in feature films, such as *Wayne's World* and *Stay Tuned*.

Finally, students know commercials well because they have been enticed by the advertisers and conditioned to *accept them* in Channel One schools and hence to *anticipate them*. At the end of each small-group session, I asked the students, "Is there anything *else* about commercials that we haven't talked about, that I should know?" Their consistent and unmistakable response to this question surprised even me. Invariably, groups would nearly shout in unison: "Yes! We need *new* commercials!" This response is logical if it's viewed within the framework of simple operant conditioning. That is, people exposed to so many commercials, every day for nine months, with some ads repeated endlessly, develop a craving for *new* commercials, a desire for *more*. Especially young people.

If these kids had *not* recalled so much about commercials and products, I would never have been able to observe how they think about commercials, how they evaluate them, and how their behavior is affected by them—all of which are explored in the chapters ahead.

3

How Do Kids Respond to Commercials?

Just as the viewers of medieval and Renaissance periods were social-ized to endow religious meanings to images, so contemporary adoles-cents are socialized to respond according to consumeristic cultural values.

Richard Beach 1993, 138

This chapter describes the twelve main ways in which kids responded to television commercials—the dominant patterns that emerged from analyses of the tapes, transcripts, and field notes. The responses can be thought of as types of perceiving or thinking about commercials. They can even be thought of as "stances" or "habits of mind" toward commercials.

Most kids, most of the time, could not resist doing or saying something in response to TV commercials. Their responses ranged from vigorous physical actions to passive uses of an ad's language. However you consider them, I want to emphasize two points. First, these responses come from normal kids who indeed know how to think. Second, most of these responses function in ways that benefit advertisers.

DEMONSTRATING

RF: Can you recall a commercial that's somehow connected to a product you've bought?

Cara: Oh, yeah, there was a new Skittles commercial this morning!

Susan: [Excitedly] Oh! That was cool! [Three other girls excitedly express agreement.]

Cara: Skittles would fall down this map and then they'd show people in this town—they had a pineapple poodle and stuff! [All five girls giggle.]

RF: I don't understand . . .

Cara: From the top of the screen, Skittles fall onto this map—

Susan: [Interrupting] And then they go to that town and they had banana watermelon that grew on trees and that orange grape thing. And these girls won something at a fair with these orange grapes, and this lady was unfortunate in that she mixed her French poodle with Hawaiian pineapple or something like that, so this poodle has this pineapple thing on his head! [All laugh.]

Speaking quickly and loudly, trying to be heard over the others, interrupting each other, and often bursting out in laughter, these girls described the ad they had seen for the first time an hour earlier. (Cara never did answer my question.) Although I never understood what they were describing, they physically and verbally demonstrated an intense engagement with the commercial. Throughout my conversations with kids, they showed consistently high interest and involvement. They were seldom passive or bored by commercials. Individually or in small groups, students discussed commercials freely and energetically, usually with minimal prompting. In spirited, emphatic tones, they openly expressed what they liked and didn't like. Students' interest in commercials ran high. Some teachers and students told us that kids were talking about our visits between classes; and some students, through their own manipulation, visited us a second time (as part of another small group) even though we did not request to see them.

One common indication of students' engagement in commercials was the obvious pleasure they revealed in the act of recalling commercials. If John said something about a Mintaburst gum ad, then another student would jump in and say, "Oh, yeah! I remember *that* one!" Or a student might interrupt with, "That reminds me of the Big Red gum commercial!" Students derived great pleasure in identifying and discussing these connections. If watching commercials in a classroom is a social experience, then actively exploring them in small groups became even more social and pleasurable. Students were especially engaged in commercials when they repeated—word-for-word and without hesitation—lines of dialogue, jingles, and other features of the ads.

Kids' personal involvement in commercials surfaced in other ways as well. A senior girl who lived alone and seldom attended school described the characters in a Pepsi commercial: "I know where they're coming from and they know where I'm coming from." She also said that she could "relate to" and "communicate with" the characters in this commercial, indicating a two-way communication street with the ad, where of course none could exist. Whether kids embraced or shunned commercials (usually the former), the ads often made deep impressions on them.

ASSUMING IDENTITIES

Kids were also involved when they assumed or "took over" the identities of people they watched on TV commercials. Kids assumed identities in many ways. Judson Wells called himself "Shaq" Wells (for Shaquille O'Neal, who is featured in many Channel One ads). Judson even signed his name in yearbooks as "Shaq." More often, kids appropriated the identities of an ad's characters when answering questions. They automatically "switched person" or "switched viewpoints" with a character in a commercial. When I asked Bryan what the new Gatorade commercial was about, he immediately replied with the commercial's exact words, "And the best part is, you get to go there and watch me!" The "me" in Bryan's reply is "Chuckie V.," the star of this ad. Bryan does not impose any clear or logical distance by introducing his response with a phrase like, "This commercial is about a triathlete who says, 'And the best part is . . .' " Instead, he leaps instantly and completely into the persona of the commercial's character, with no explanation.

When I asked the same question of another boy, he instantly replied, "Not only do you get the trip to Hawaii, you get to party after the triathalon with me!" Again, these words are identical to those of the actual commercial. Again, the student uses "me" when he *really* means Chuckie V. There is very little distance between these kids and the ad. Role-playing a character's identity seemed to be an abbreviated or "shorthand" way of communicating about commercials, however illogical it might sound. This type of thinking also demonstrates students' rapid recall of the commercial's details. However, its main effect, I think, resides in its "replay" function in that it reruns parts of the original ad message, eliciting the entire commercial message for everyone within earshot.

ASSOCIATING

Students *associate*, almost instantly, one commercial with another. Corporations spend billions of dollars on commercials to ensure that they are memorable—that they hook viewers' interest with highly synthesized language, images, and music. Hence, over and over during my conversations with kids, a word or phrase or image from one commercial quickly set off chains of associations—quick links to other ads. One symbol ignited memories of other *types* of symbols, even when the products and symbol system differed. For instance, one group of students read a printed transcript of a Head and Shoulders Shampoo commercial, in which one boy told his sister, "Give me a break." Next, when I asked students what this printed version of the commercial was selling, one boy jokingly replied, "Kit Kat" candy bars. This boy instantly associated the printed "Give me a break" (even though its product was shampoo) with the other "Gimme a break," from a song from a candy ad. Similarly, a musical phrase might invoke a punch line or an image—or another musical phrase. A detailed description of one commercial could provoke in students an image from another ad, or it could remind them of a word or phrase from another commercial.

Conversely, images could elicit language or music or other images. So it goes with such highly "intertextual" messages. Commercials can flag not only other ads but other types of messages, including noncommercial ones, regardless of where or when students encountered them. Pepsi's commercial for Crystal Light cola reminded one boy of a satire that aired on *Saturday Night Live*. However, the most common type of association in this study occurred when one student's recall of an ad triggered memories of other commercials. And another and another, sometimes spreading like brush fires on hot, windy days.

Remnants from past advertising campaigns were sometimes used to respond to or evaluate new ads. When I asked several students what a new Pepsi commercial was about, they replied, "It's about the Pepsi generation" or "the new generation" or "they don't want the next generation to be so prejudiced." Even though the commercial we were talking about said nothing about generations, students nonetheless relied on these defunct slogans to evaluate the new ad. Another student voluntarily compared a current Gatorade commercial featuring Chuckie V., who was training for the triathlon, to a "Dave and Dan" Reebok commercial that had aired a year earlier (Dave and Dan were also athletes). This intertextuality of commercials mainly helps advertisers. Channel One sometimes airs slight variations of the same basic commercial, such as the three Gatorade ads featuring Chuckie V. For students, it becomes a game to figure out how one ad differs from the others. Such "games" translate into more active involvement with advertising messages, increasing students' attention to the commercials and, in turn, bolstering sales.

Finally, the "automatic" nature of associations can have the opposite effect. Responding to commercials via associations (whether language or images or both are evoked) sometimes restricts, controls, or "frames" whatever happens next in kids' thinking or talking. In short, associating can have a "chilling" effect on kids' thinking and talking. In answer to my question, one girl reported that her favorite commercial was the current Gatorade ad. Her answer immediately triggered an association in the boy beside her, who flatly repeated the ad's slogan, "Obey your thirst." The conversation died instantly. Why? Because this key line, packed with associations of language and images, represented the entire commercial for the other kids in the group. In effect, the compressed one-liner replayed the original commercial, leaving nothing more to say.

MIRRORING

"What's advertised on Channel One?"

"Cinnaburst," replied Eric, a ninth-grader. "You know—it's that gum that has these little red things and—"

"No," interrupted Lisa, "those are *flavor crystals*."

Eric paused, muttering, "Oh, yeah, flavor crystals . . ." and quickly continued describing the other commercials he'd seen. When Lisa corrected her classmate with the ad's exact wording, the others nodded in agreement. To them, nothing unusual had occurred. Lisa's mirroring of the exact phrase (and her insistence that others do so, too) seemed perfectly normal. At least a few students in every small group parroted the exact lines and intonations from ads, sang jingles from commercials, and physically imitated the actions of a commercial's character. Although mirroring indicates involvement with commercials, it requires little, if any, autonomous, personal thinking.

Many students physically imitated how the woman from the Little Caesar's commercial applied lipstick, or how the model in the Finesse Shampoo commercial shook her head. While seated, other kids shuffled their arms and legs to mimic the dances seen on commercials. These mirrorings usually occurred spontaneously and voluntarily and focused on ads we were currently discussing, as well as others that the students recalled. Most students were aware that they were mirroring the exact words and actions from commercials, but not always. When a ninth-grader told me about the flavors depicted on a Skittles candy commercial, she answered, "There's a million and some flavors: cherry-orange, lemon-lime, raspberry-melon-lime; there's too many to say—millions and millions." She was unaware that she mirrored the commercial's exact words: "millions and millions." Finally, because mirroring is integral to other types of students' responses to commercials, it is also explored later in detail in this chapter, as well as in Chapter 5.

CONFUSING

Trying to be informed consumers, some students became lost in the tangle of an ad's pseudo-scientific images and verbal claims:

Gail: I bought Pantene Pro-V Shampoo because I saw it advertised in a magazine. And using it made me watch their commercials more—the ones with girls who have really long and silky hair that's always fixed neat. It shows the vitamin coating the hair.

Katie: I bought Finesse Shampoo after I saw their commercial. Finesse is the one that says, "Sometimes you need a little, sometimes you need a lot" [exact words of commercial].

Jo-Ann: [Quoting exact words of commercial] Yeah—"Never over-conditions, never under-conditions."

RF: What does that mean?

Katie: On the bottle it has a little thing, like a color scale, and if you're having a bad hair day because of weather, you may need more. But if it's a good day, you'll need less.

RF: So, when you need less, you just don't put as much shampoo into your hand, right?

Katie: No—I think it's supposed to be in the chemicals in the shampoo, so if you need more, it will give you more.

RF: So, the shampoo somehow knows this automatically?

Katie: Yes, it will know.

Jo-Ann: No. There are different formulas, like for permed or dry hair.

RF: So you have to buy different bottles to get different formulas?

Jo-Ann: No.

RF: So, what does "Never over-conditions, never under-conditions" mean?

Katie: Well, I think that's what that scale means.

Jo-Ann: I guess the shampoo *does* know this.

Although these girls replayed the ad's exact verbal claim ("never over-conditions, never under-conditions") and images (e.g., a model's long and silky hair), some confusion remains about what it all means and how it all fits together. The first girl who used Pantene Pro-V had earlier told me that she knew that "Pro-V" stood for vitamins, but she didn't know which ones. Neither did they know which vitamins were shown "coating" the hair in the commercial. Despite this puzzlement, the girls faithfully used the product and believed in its commercials.

SUBSTITUTING

> Sometimes, if I'm sitting at home and I'm hungry and like, a Taco Bell commercial comes on, I'll go out and get some Taco Bell.
>
> Rod

While talking, kids sometimes replaced the expected name or topic with something different, something that most listeners would not normally anticipate, as when Rod substituted the brand name "Taco Bell" for food. In typical cases of substituting, the sales message enhances the ad and product. A popular Gatorade commercial advertised a contest in which winners would travel to Hawaii to see a triathlon. In this ad Chuckie V. tells viewers he will participate in this triathlon. Because the name of the *contest* was the "Chuckathon," students sometimes substituted "Chuckathon" for "triathlon."

A few times when students made a substitution, they realized it and then corrected themselves. After one discussion of a Little Caesar's pizza commercial became side-tracked, I asked, "Now, where were we?" A ninth-grade boy answered, "We were talking about the cheesy—uh, I mean, the Little Caesar's commercial." The word "cheesy" is used in the commercial we were talking about and is emphasized in this ad campaign, but it had not been uttered in our discussion.

Another time, because I had to talk with a teacher who had just entered the room, students talked among themselves about an acne cream commercial (which we had just watched). Initially, the students called the product by its name, Clearasil. Within minutes, however, one student substituted the phrase, "washing your face" for the product's brand name. None of the kids in the group noticed that the advertised ointment somehow had become synonymous with cleanliness.

Substituting often did not occur as clearly as in these examples. When Laura, a ninth-grader, talked about an ad for Noxzema skin lotion, she stated that she had "bought Noxzema twice," and the first time she purchased it, she didn't like it. The second time she bought Noxzema, she explained, occurred after she had seen a commercial about a girl who was worried about a date. Much later, when listening to the tape of our conversation, I realized that Laura substituted herself for the Noxzema girl, in that her discussion gradually slipped into her own experiences. She concluded by saying, "I hate it if you have a boyfriend with perfect skin."

Most kids who made such substitutions didn't seem aware of doing so. Substitutions help illustrate (with specific evidence) the extremely close relationship between products, commercials, and kids' personal experience—sometimes so close that they become nearly indistinguishable.

FLUCTUATING

Fluctuating occurred when some kids' thinking moved quickly back and forth, between opposite points of view. With great *speed and fluidity*, kids vacillated back and forth—first liking a commercial, then hating it; first understanding, then becoming confused; first believing, then doubting, then believing, then doubting again—all in the space of a few minutes. Consider the following conversation with Alan, a ninth-grader.

RF: Can you remember a commercial that helped you decide to buy the product?

Alan: I know of a lot of people who saw the Crystal Pepsi commercial and said "I'm gonna go out and buy that." But I've never had Crystal Pepsi in my whole life! Also, there's like, name-brand shoes—but those are just advertisements—like Nike or something. But if I see that shown on TV, I'm not gonna run out and buy it.

RF: You've never bought Nike shoes?

Alan: Yeah, I have. I have some on right now [group laughs]. I like them—they're one of the better quality shoes, *I* think. . . .

RF: Why did you buy them?

Alan: Well, uh, actually, I didn't buy them. My dad went to Columbia and he came home with a pair of these.

RF: So, why did he choose Nikes?

Alan: I guess he figured out that I like them.

About ten minutes later, I asked these same students to describe how their watching of commercials differed from their watching of regular programs. Alan spoke first: "If it's something I don't really care about, I won't pay attention. I'll just try to do something else until the show comes back on. I mean, I like the Nike commercials that have a man dressed up as a referee and he talks about people and the NFL, like Barry Sanders and uh, Sharkie, or something like that, who plays for Green Bay. . . ."

First, Alan denies being influenced by any commercials and uses Nike ads as an example. Then, we immediately learn he's currently wearing Nikes because his father figured out that he likes them. Ten minutes later, when the topic of conversation shifted, Alan described a commercial that he did indeed like—which happens to be for Nike!

In another group, Jonathan, the only boy at the table, explained how his grandmother helped him save up to pay the high price of a pair of "Air Jordan" basketball shoes. *All* the girls around him immediately proclaimed how they would *never* spend that much money on a pair of Nikes. I then asked Jonathan why he didn't buy one of the other brands of shoes, and he answered that Nikes were popular. Then, Mary, sitting next to Jonathan, agreed strongly with him that it's important to wear what the other kids are wearing; in fact, she whispered to her neighbor, "Reeboks don't have anything to them." Next, Selena added, "Yeah, a lot of people wear Nikes, so you just wanna wear Nikes." The others nodded in agreement. This fluctuation occurred within about three minutes.

A group of ninth-grade girls fluctuated when focusing on the commercial's character and plight. Before discussing the plot details of a Clearasil ad, the girls informed me, in detail, about the model who starred in it: they knew her name, which magazines she had appeared in, which commercials (and their sponsors) and regular programs she had appeared in, and more. They also voluntarily praised her beauty—especially her skin, hair, and teeth. Without doubt, these girls worshipped this model. We next discussed the plot of the ad: a girl hopes that her date will take her to a dark place, so he won't notice her acne. The girls agreed that the model had perfect skin, even though the character she plays is worried sick that her boyfriend might detect a blemish. When I asked the students why they liked this commercial, they agreed that it was because they could "relate" to this character who doesn't want her date to see her in bright light—that they "really understood" her nervousness.

I then tried to counter their opinion by asking, "But you just said this model has perfect skin?" and the girls quickly agreed. Next, the conversation again turned to how fearful they felt about boys seeing skin blemishes on a date. And again I reminded them about the model's perfect skin, and again they agreed. And so goes fluctuation, all within a few minutes.

I can't say exactly *why* these students fluctuated in their thinking about commercials. But I can say that the reasons for such vacillation are bound up in many variables, which shift in complex relationships: peer pressure, need for approval, lack of self-confidence and self-esteem, varied interpretations of images and language, the contradictory nature of "post-modern" media, and so on. However, unlike fluctuating, the phenomenon I call "blurring" is created by the advertising and programming of Channel One itself.

GENERALIZING

Kids sometimes distorted commercials, products, or their own previous responses when they made generalizations or unwarranted "leaps." They formed opinions or drew conclusions about one commercial and then, later, applied those same conclusions to *other* commercials, even when the latter situation did not warrant it. Such inferences were based on what the kids had heard, what they had read in language printed across the screen, and what images they had seen in commercials. As noted earlier, kids recalled slogans or jingles from earlier ad campaigns (e.g., "Be young, have fun" from a cola soft drink) and generalized them to other commercials, saying, for instance, that the kids in the newest ad were trying to "be young and have fun," even though the new ad never stated this.

Many students also generalized from earlier commercials that displayed language printed on the television screen. Pepsi was very effective at this. One year's Pepsi commercials showed kids talking to the camera, with their name and school affiliation printed across the bottom of the screen. Even though the current commercials neither carried this print nor mentioned school names, most students automatically *assumed* that the newer commercials also employed actual students and not actors.

Kids based other generalizations purely on the images viewed in previous commercials. Note how Reed and Darcy generalize Nike athletic shoes to Chuckie V., the character in the commercial—even claiming that he is wearing them, when in fact his feet are never shown!

RF: What commercial do you like the best?

Reed: I like those Gatorade commercials . . .

Darcy: [Interrupting] For Chuckie V.!

RF: Why do you like those?

Reed: I dunno. I just kind of like him. I like his haircut.

RF: How many spikes are in his hair?

Both: Five!

Darcy: And he was wearing an orange tank top and blues. And the shirt had like a silhouette of his face.

RF: What was on the back of his shirt?

Darcy: It never shows the back.

RF: What kind of shoes was Chuckie V. wearing?

Darcy: You mean like Nike or Reebok?

Reed: They're probably Nike.

Darcy: Nike.

RF: How can you tell?

Reed: Because they're a popular shoe.

RF: Okay—but how *else* can you tell?

Reed: Because they're a good shoe.

RF: Okay—but how else can you tell Chuckie is wearing these shoes—when you can't see them well enough to know *what* brand they are?

Reed: I dunno; I can just tell. He might be trying to promote Nike, because he's a star or like a sports figure and people might look up to him.

RF: Let me ask you another way: the next time I watch that commercial and try to identify the brand of shoe Chuckie is wearing, what should I look for?

Reed: They have that little swish that looks like a check mark.

Because Chuckie V. is shown riding a bike, running, and swimming in this commercial, Reed and Darcy assume he is a serious athlete; therefore he *has* to be wearing Nikes! The commercial states nothing about Nikes or athletic shoes. Because these kids are familiar with athletes wearing Nikes from the Nike commercials, they assume that other athletes in commercials would be wearing them, too—even if the commercial is for a different product. (Note that Darcy first responded, "Nike or Reebok"—that she saw only two possibilities.)

Such generalizing from one commercial to another makes it easier for kids to make the final leap—generalizing to themselves. After one senior girl detailed her loyalty to Nike shoes, I asked her why she was so devoted to Nike. She replied without hesitation, "Because I lift weights and run": she was a serious athlete; therefore she wore Nikes! Hence, a student's line of generalizing or transferring a quality might go something like this: "If serious athletes in Nike commercials wear Nikes, then so do athletes in *other* commercials. And if all these other athletes wear Nikes (and if I'm an athlete), then I should wear them, too." Getting kids to generalize from commercials to themselves is a supremely effective sales technique.

SHRINKING AND EMBEDDING

"Shrinking" means that students often regarded a mere few seconds as enough time to constitute a commercial—and 30 or 60 seconds as appropriate for a noncommercial or regular program. This speeded-up perception is much less common in adults who grew up watching less television or did not attend Channel One schools. Commercials themselves have shrunk in recent years from the standard 30-second ad to 10- and 20-second spots (Postman and Powers 1992). However, in this study it was not unusual for students to regard a mere 1-second flash of a Pepsi can as a commercial. Because these flashes occur within an actual Pepsi commercial, they are really ads-within-an-ad—one ad embedded within another.

However, roughly half the students in this study considered the few flashes of the Pepsi can as an ad embedded within a "regular program." Students used additional terms, such as "comedy," "reruns," and "segment," to describe these commercials—terms that are usually reserved for *noncommercial* programs. One boy described the entire Pepsi commercial as a "regular program." One girl called it a "special program," because she reported seeing it only about once a week. Another student even referred to this ad as "a miniature talk show."

Many students, then, did not view these commercials for what they are: double sales pitches. When briefer commercials are embedded within 30- and 60-second ads, viewers regard the frame surrounding the momentary ad as something *other than* a commercial—this student saw it as regular programming. When students regard commercials as programs—and split-second flashes of products as commercials—they shrink conventional time frames for both regular and commercial texts. Kids' rapid perception (or shrinking) seems an inevitable result of at least three factors: (1) the increasing speed of computers and other technology, (2) the trend toward shorter commercials, and (3) the high frequency of commercials to which students in Channel One schools are exposed.

SEEING NO AUTHORSHIP

During small-group sessions, about 150 students viewed one of Pepsi's "It's Like This" commercials. I asked each group the following questions: "Whose point of view is being communicated in this commercial—if anyone's?" and "Who is telling the story in this commercial?" Students invariably replied that the ad's point of view came from its characters—those people who were on camera the longest time and who were the most active. Only five students (out of a total 150) indicated that it was the viewpoint of the Pepsi Corporation or its marketer or its commercial producers, directors, and editors. Over and over again, students seemed oblivious to the likelihood that any *external* people were involved in making or telling this story. Kids saw no human being behind the message, no mediator calling the shots from the outside. Kids were very aware of the commercial's internal narrative, but they seemed oblivious about its *external* story—the who, what, where, when, why, and how of the ad's construction. To underscore this point, consider the following exchanges with a couple of the very rare students who *did indeed* observe that the commercial was constructed by someone else:

RF: Who is telling this story?

Chad: The third person, because he knows about everybody.

Becky: No, he doesn't!

Chad: Yes he does, because they're ALL giving their opinions.

Becky: They're all telling it, but there's no one person.

Amy: You can't really tell who's telling the story, because there's not one person telling it.

Although Chad identifies an external person controlling this commercial, the two girls dismiss his conclusion because they cannot *see* the narrator on screen. Even with a group of intelligent seniors, extensive probing and follow-up questions were needed before one girl eventually recognized that a person outside the commercial—not one of the on-screen actors—was behind the message.

RF: How can you tell that the people in this commercial are not actors?

Bryan: They're too laid-back.

Leigh: Because it's too unorganized and too natural. The kids are doing spontaneous things, I think. When they're asked a question, they just answer with whatever comes out.

RF: Did you ever see a movie or TV show that seemed very real?

Leigh: You can tell the difference. By the time you're sixteen years old, you know what's TV and what's real. You know this by the time you're seven!

RF: What do you pick up on in order to say, for example, *this* is documentary and unrehearsed—and *these* are actors following a script—how do you know?

Bryan: They're not as straightforward. They can't say whatever they feel.

Leigh: They use real words like "um" and "okay" and "like," and they pause and jump around.

Candace: I don't think they're actors because I don't recognize 'em. Besides, they're at a beach and laughing and they interrupt each other.

Norma: Also, in that commercial, this girl says, "It's nice to hear a guy call another guy a jerk," and then she jumps on his back.

RF: Can't actors be told to do these things?

Leigh: Well . . . directors *could* make actors do all this—but what makes the commercial effective is that it makes you feel like they're real.

Of course, most students are indeed capable of understanding the concept of authorship. My point is that many commercials—especially ads that are well aimed at a student audience—are extremely hard for students to "get outside of" and view from a distance. This was very much the case with the Pepsi ad, which presented itself in the guise of a documentary. Most students defined this commercial as a documentary, not an advertisement.

Also, when kids perceive people on commercials to be "playing themselves," then it's easier for kids to identify the ad's point of view as coming from *inside* the narrative. Therefore, kids do not believe they are watching commercials whose purpose is to sell products and services—a point of view external to the "story within" the commercial itself. For instance, a Mountain Dew commercial featured several goofy young men who enjoy daredevil activities. Most students insisted these young men were "playing themselves," doing their own acrobatic stunts—even though viewers cannot see the faces of the people in action. One student described a boy on an ad as one who "knows a lot" and who "has a good perspective on things." She said she was able to draw these conclusions because he was not acting but "playing himself." If characters are merely "playing themselves," students reason, then they're likely not selling anything at all.

Finally, I was surprised to find so many students who could not readily admit that commercials are authored texts. The large majority of students did not quickly and consciously apprehend and discuss the basic notion that someone "outside" *made* commercials; that commercials were constructions or representations of reality—messages crafted by people with definite purposes. In its simplest terms, to view commercials in such a vacuum means that students see ads as benign, free-floating entertainment "breaks" that are unconnected to purpose, profit, ethics, and responsibility.

CONTRADICTING

RF: Have you ever bought something that you can connect back to a commercial?

Gina: Maybe if I walked into the store and I remembered that commercial, maybe it would remind me that I wanted to get some of that, but I don't think that

I'd go out there just because I was thinking, "Oh, I saw this commercial on Channel One this morning, so I've got to buy this Gatorade."

RF: How many of you have bought Gatorade? [All five kids raise their hand.]

RF: Did you try it because of the commercial?

Four Kids: Yeah!

Gina: Well . . . maybe I remembered it subconsciously.

Seemingly contradictory positions are common to human behavior. Kids consistently claimed that they didn't watch commercials—and when they did, they insisted that the ads never influenced them. In one group, Stacy chided her friend who had just sung the entire Diet Coke jingle: "That's all she ever talks about!" Stacy's friend, of course, vigorously denied the charge. We then watched a videotape of a commercial containing a shot of a tee-shirt with the Pepsi slogan printed on it. Stacy, the accuser, suddenly yelled, "Oh! I *have* that tee-shirt!" While she criticized her friend's knowing the words to a Coke jingle, she wore a tee-shirt advertising Pepsi. Stacy is not alone. Many kids expressed some type of disavowal about commercials, which in turn *allowed* kids the confidence—or somehow granted them "permission"—to watch and discuss other commercials and products.

Lee, a bright, articulate senior, told me that Channel One's Cinnaburst commercials were so "obviously aimed at a young audience" that he found them condescending. "It makes me not want to buy their product," he complained. Later, when I heard him recite, verbatim, the Cinnaburst gum jingle, I asked him if he chewed Cinnaburst gum. He replied, "I've got some in my pocket."

Students made other kinds of contradictions as well. Kids who initially told me that they did *not* talk about commercials outside of school often countered their answer with statements such as, "Well, I do if the commercial is real stupid or real funny or something." Then, they would often report in detail which commercials they hated: "The guy who advertises Sunbeam Dodge is so cheesy! He wears an orange shirt and this bright yellow, plaid sports jacket and . . ."

During a discussion about a Nike shoe commercial, some ninth-graders were proud that they recognized the "swoosh" as the Nike symbol. They stated that there was no need for Nike to actually show the shoe, or to say the word "Nike," or to explain what they were advertising. Students said they were so familiar with the symbol and product that they didn't need to watch the entire commercial. And, of course, they were sure that the commercial was trying to sell Nikes. We viewed the Pepsi commercial immediately after this discussion, and these same students insisted that

Pepsi was *not* trying to sell its product because the ad only showed its symbol (on the can) but *said* nothing about its product.

Granted, the context of viewing commercials during school helps elicit contradictory stances toward commercials, products, and other topics. Even a single commercial is fraught with oppositions, tensions, and blatant contradictions. Likewise, products that compete with each other are likely to appear in commercials that oppose each other in content, tone, or style.

Students usually seemed unaware that they had contradicted themselves. Although I avoided pointing out these discrepancies, the contradictions sometimes became very obvious to everyone. On these occasions the kids never seemed bothered by the inconsistencies: they never indicated that something was amiss. Their tolerance or acceptance of contradictions is reminiscent of George Orwell's notion of "doublethink" in *1984*, in which *recognizing* incongruities does not clarify thinking. This notion of the "two-part mind" means that one part recognizes falsity: "Yes, I realize I'm being manipulated by the Cinnaburst ad." Simultaneously, the other part remains blind to it: "I know the Cinnaburst jingle by heart, and I have a package of Cinnaburst in my pocket."

BLURRING

"Blurring" occurs when kids mistake one type of television text for another. Students blurred one commercial with another; they mistook commercials for regular programs, such as the news; and they confused commercials with public service announcements (e.g., drug abuse warnings). Blurring was the most surprising yet most commonly observed finding of this study. However, blurring is largely not the fault of kids. Sales messages—especially Pepsi's "It's Like This" commercials—were often disguised as entertainment, information, or altruistic public service announcements. Kids usually received the intended sales message, but they were often unaware that they were being sold something by people seeking profits.

Students' frequent failure to distinguish the boundaries among Channel One's offerings is due mainly to the commercials themselves, as well as to how Channel One presents them. Indeed, most adults in this situation would get things mixed up, too. Elizabeth Simons, a veteran writer and editor who had returned to college to become a teacher, kept a journal of her observations of Channel One broadcasts while she was student teaching in rural Missouri. Following are two of her early entries (Simons 1993):

September 21, 1993:

At 8:25 a Pepsi can appears on screen for about two seconds, followed by teenagers talking about dealing with stress. Their first names, followed by their home states, are shown on the screen while they talk. There is booming rock music in the background. The viewer is left wondering whether this was a commercial or not.

September 22, 1993:

At 8:32 there is a message from Pepsi. A TV star tells the audience that "you asked for fewer commercials," so Pepsi is sponsoring a spot with "real kids talking about real issues." Next, a Pepsi can flashes on the screen with the catchy title, "It's Like This." I realize now that what I saw yesterday was indeed a disguised commercial.

If Ms. Simons, a seasoned and articulate writer, editor, and teacher, can be confused, then so can kids. And they were. A full year after Ms. Simons' experience, many of the students I talked with were *still* unclear about whether these Pepsi ads were regular programs, news-documentary programs, commercials, public service announcements (PSAs), or hybrids of everything. However, even the kids who thought the ads were documentaries knew that Pepsi "sponsored" them.

Such confusion is understandable. As noted in Chapter 1, Pepsi's "It's Like This" ads look very much like documentaries and PSAs because the ads insert several close-up shots of red, white, and blue Pepsi cans between black-and-white and muted color shots of kids talking directly into the camera about their problems. One day, I talked to 29 students about this ad, and about half of these kids thought it was a commercial. The other 17 kids defined it as purely news or a combination of news and advertising; 7 could not decide. This ratio generally continued throughout the two-year study, even though the series of ads began a year earlier. Following are brief discussions of the four main types of blurring that kids demonstrated in their thinking and talking about Channel One commercials.

Blurring Commercials with Programs

When I asked Andy what he thought the difference was between a program and a commercial, he replied, "Commercials don't have as much time to get their message across. Programs are really long." Andy's distinction, that simple length of time separated commercial from noncommercial television content, was shared by most of the kids I interviewed. Few students stated that the main difference between commercials and programs was one of intent or purpose—that commercials are made to sell products. Kids know that commercials sell products and services; but when asked how programs and commercials differ, they never mentioned selling products. This failure to link commercials with sales reflects other findings of the study, such as when students used the phrases "regular program" and "talk show" to describe commercials. I showed one of Pepsi's "It's Like This" commercials to a college freshman who had never seen Channel One. This student, an English major who is also highly skilled in analyzing media, defined the ad as a combination of a commercial and a "preview" for a regular television program, such as "Friends." This student even guessed that some footage of the commercial had been excerpted from the actual program being previewed. Overall, the kids in this study did not regard commercials as fundamentally different from other forms of television.

Blurring Commercials with News

Brian blurs commercials with the news, being oblivious to the essential differences between these two types of texts:

Brian: I don't like commercials because they get old so fast. We've seen 'em since the beginning of this year, and we had them last year.

RF: If commercials get boring and old because you've seen them too many times, how do you solve that problem?

Brian: What I do in class is—if they're the same commercials, the same ol' basic stuff about Haiti or Bosnia or O. J. Simpson—I don't even watch. I just kind of block it out.

This bright student knew, I believe, that commercials do not advertise events in Bosnia and Haiti. Nonetheless he lumps commercials and news together. Also, students often blurred Pepsi's "It's Like This" ads with commercials and news footage from the previous year. These ads were crafted to look like documentaries or news programs. During Channel One's news and feature segments—as well as during "Pop Quiz" segments, which focus on kids from Channel One schools across the country—students appear with their name, school, and location printed across the bottom of the screen. In 1993 the Pepsi advertisers imitated this technique, as well as the style of PSAs. This resulted in commercials that blurred with other types of content.

Blurring Commercials with Public Service Announcements

When I asked Mindy, a ninth-grader, to describe her favorite PSA, she replied, "It's mostly about inner-city kids, about how one got shot and stuff. Ya know, it's like this . . ." Mindy's exact words, "it's like this," is identical to Pepsi's slogan currently airing on Channel One. Conversely, Sarah, a ninth-grader, described her favorite Pepsi commercial, "This commercial has kids telling about different issues, like racism and getting shot." Sarah and Mindy have blurred the two messages: it was the PSA that focused on a shooting and included a message from President Bill Clinton—not the Pepsi ad. Mindy and Sarah are typical of other students who mistook Pepsi commercials for PSAs, and vice-versa. Both were being aired on Channel One throughout the period of this study. Kids most frequently blurred Pepsi's "It's Like This" commercials and PSAs focusing on "Stop the Hate" and drunken driving. Also, a few students blurred a Nike ad featuring Al Del Greco with another PSA.

Like some other students, Mindy and Sarah seemed unaware that they blurred a message that seeks a profit with one that does not. Although most kids kept commercials very straight (in terms of plot, sequence, characters, etc.), they *still* blurred these fundamentally different types of messages. Note the following conversation about a PSA focusing on drunken driving:

RF: Do you consider the segment about drunken driving to be a commercial?

Jill: No, it's not selling anything. It's more to make you aware.

RF: Are there other things on Channel One that are similar to this?

Samantha: There's one that shows what kids like to do after school, and it's not selling anything.

RF: Can you tell us about it?

Samantha: They're kids about eighteen—aren't they a bunch of different nationalities? It's something about racial discrimination.

Rita: It just shows normal kids.

Samantha: Yeah, they just have kids trying to relate to you.

RF: So, is this a commercial or a public service announcement, like the one on drunken driving?

Samantha: It's a commercial that Pepsi sponsors. Like Pepsi's doing something good, so they put their name in there.

Greg: Yeah, they just flash it; they don't even say it.

RF: So—do you see this as selling Pepsi?

Samantha: I see it as Pepsi sponsoring this because they're trying to do something good, trying to help our generation.

Here, even though students were not shown this Pepsi commercial during our interview, and even though I never mentioned Pepsi in any way, it still arises, almost naturally, from the kids' thinking and talking about the public service message. These kids believed that Pepsi sponsored a PSA, when it did not.

In the following conversation, Jennie, who was in a another group, also blurred the Pepsi commercials with PSAs. However, her blurring remained, even when she recalled a strong image of the product:

RF: Are these commercials? Or are they something else?

Jennie: They're commercials, because they're advertising a product—but they don't do it directly. It's just sponsored by Pepsi. Sometimes they show Pepsi in the corner.

RF: How often do they show a can of Pepsi?

Jennie: I know that in one of them, there's a tee-shirt that has Pepsi written on it and it's laying in the sand at the beach, and then you see water wash over the tee-shirt.

RF: What was the purpose of that one?

Jennie: It was about racism.

Public service messages were appearing on network television and Channel One long before Pepsi's series of documentary look-alike ads, with their use of black-and-white, grainy-looking film, rough-cut editing, and overlapping voices. In imitating PSAs, Pepsi capitalized on a positive, respected, ready-made framework through which students could interpret the new ads. For example, one student said, "The hidden message in the Pepsi commercial is 'Stop the Hate.' " And the exact phrase used in a popular PSA is "Stop the Hate."

Blurring is nothing new to Channel One. Others have documented Channel One's previous attempts to merge the "neutral" content of news and features with commercials. For example, Halleck (1992) describes a series on Channel One called *Now That's Art!* After featuring Chuck Close, this segment turned its attention to the nineteenth-century painter Georges Seurat and his technique of "Pointillism." Immediately following the program was a Sprint commercial, showing viewers how the network's "points of light" helped to end Soviet communism. Interestingly, the Channel One contract addresses this issue of blurring: "ADVERTISING/PROGRAMMING DISTINCTION.

Any creative technique that may confuse the viewer by blurring the distinction between programs and commercials is unacceptable" (Whittle n.d., 12).

As you can see from students' comments throughout this section, the blurring of commercials and noncommercials helps kids view Pepsico, Inc. as caring—as deeply committed to helping them cope with their emotional and psychological problems. Most kids felt quite strongly about Pepsi's altruistic intentions:

Beth: I think Pepsi is trying to appeal to what we're going through right now.

RF: Do you think that commercial was trying to sell something?

Ellen: The main message is kind of like *sponsored* by them—but they're trying to appeal to the things that we're going through right now.

Paige: Yeah—Pepsi understands what we're going through.

Beth: Yeah, and on the side, they might be trying to sell Pepsi.

All: [Simultaneously] Yeah.

Beth: They're *not* saying, "Drink Pepsi and you won't be racist."

RF: How does all of this make you feel about Pepsi?

Beth: It's good that they're trying to help us with our problems.

Pepsi has succeeded in what most advertisers try to do—establish positive and even warm feelings about the product. One student told me, "They're not trying to hit you over the head and make you do something." However, not surprisingly, Pepsi was the product mentioned most frequently in survey questions that asked students to identify specific products. Also, students can purchase Pepsi in most Channel One schools.

CONCLUSION

The types of responses examined in this chapter provide the foundation for how kids evaluate commercials. As we shall see, kids judge commercials in both critical and uncritical ways—though mostly uncritically. In turn, how students evaluate commercials helps determine how ads shape the kids' subsequent behaviors. These topics are explored in the chapters ahead.

4

How Do Kids Evaluate Commercials?

RF: What is this Pepsi commercial about?

Jill: They're talking about their real problems and their real feelings.

RF: Are they selling Pepsi?

Jill: No. If I didn't see the cans and the logos, I wouldn't have known it was a commercial.

RF: When did you see the cans and logos?

Jill: At the beginning, middle, and end.

Angie: Yeah, they talk about our real problems. They really care enough about us to do this.

If kids thoroughly know Channel One commercials—and if they think and talk about commercials, even in ways that largely benefit advertisers—then it's natural that kids would, at least sometimes, evaluate the ads. And they do. As Angie and Jill illustrate, kids in this study consistently judged commercials in positive, benign ways. On the other hand, students seldom criticized the ads. In this study, the main criteria for determining students' ability to evaluate commercials was their facility in applying propaganda and rhetorical persuasion techniques to verbal, visual, and aural media. Such analytical tools include testimonial, association, bandwagon, unfair comparisons, selection, and the like. Students' language was analyzed for both its stated and implied uses of these tools. (Of course, I never expected students to use the formal terminology of these techniques.)

The first section of this chapter, "Analyzing Commercials Effectively," shows the thinking of the handful of kids (six out of more than two hundred) who demonstrated a thoughtful, critical analysis of commercials in the following ways:

- Mentally distancing themselves from commercials.
- Selecting appropriate elements to critique and then closely inspecting and comparing those elements.
- Connecting observations, ideas, and concepts from commercials to other elements.
- Predicting why commercial creators made certain decisions (about setting, music, etc.).
- Identifying the ad's tone and pointing to specific textual evidence.

The responses of the majority of kids are explored in "Analyzing Commercials Ineffectively," which describes the following types of responses:

- Overvaluing the audio.
- Drawing boxed-in conclusions about ads and products.
- Overvaluing the visual (including the length and frequency of appearances).
- Restricting their choices to just two options (i.e., either/or thinking).
- Describing intended and obvious inconsistencies within commercials.
- Denying that they watched commercials or were susceptible to their messages.
- Restricting their comments to single commercials only.
- Overvaluing the newest commercials.

This chapter's final segment, "Embracing Commercials," also describes ineffective approaches to evaluating ads; it focuses on the positive, warm, almost blind love that some students hold for specific values communicated in commercials. Because I found so many instances of students embracing commercials, this analysis deserves a separate section. Here, I also examine students' notions of why people create (and appear in) commercials in the first place. Once again, students hold positive and warm regard for advertisers' motives. Finally, this section describes commercials that target even more specific audiences within Channel One schools. I call these "The Groovy Fruitopians," "The Shoe Jocks," "The Mountain Dew Macho Men," and "The Hair Worshippers."

ANALYZING COMMERCIALS EFFECTIVELY

Of the two hundred students who participated in this study, only about six analyzed commercials in substantive, specific, insightful ways. In spite of this low number, reviewing how students evaluated ads effectively will help us better understand the kids' reflective responses to ads. Following are brief discussions of the main approaches used by these students.

Distancing Themselves

Students who effectively analyzed commercials imposed a sense of "distance" or objectivity upon them, clearly separating themselves from the commercial and/or product. Although Lana does not offer any critical insights about the ad, she nonetheless imposes some distance between herself and the ad—a detachment that most students did not demonstrate:

Lana: Or like, if you see a commercial—and you see it enough that you can say it word-for-word or sing the song they sing. And then you get to the grocery store and you see that product and all of a sudden you say, "I know that commercial!" and you start hearing the words and humming the tune.

RF: Can you give me an example?

Lana: Cheerios. [laughing] It's about school—and I *love* school! It tells about how Cheerios give you energy through the day until lunch. It was about this kid who woke up in the morning and didn't have time for anything else, so he grabbed a bowl of Cheerios and his books and went to school and the bell rang for lunch and he ate lunch.

Here, Lana views and describes the effect of commercials in the second person ("you"), which shows her to be at least somewhat distanced from the topic. Also, she recognizes *why* she likes the commercial—because it's about school. In other words, distancing means knowing why you respond in a certain way, as well as seeing from afar—describing and evaluating commercials as if you were looking down upon them and could exercise control over them. In the following quote, Julie also demonstrates some critical distance between herself and Reebok athletic shoe commercials: "In that Reebok commercial, it's like they think *everything* is based on athletics. If you're not a runner, you don't even exist." Unlike Lana, Julie reveals why she has gained some distance from this ad. Julie, a smart senior who seldom attends school and lives by herself, is seriously overweight. Her words and tone of voice suggest that Reebok implies superiority for people who are athletic. Indicating some bitterness about being excluded from this elite group, Julie distances herself from the commercial more than most kids do. But to do so, she must pay the high price of lowered self-esteem.

Selecting, Inspecting, and Comparing Elements

Derek, a perceptive, articulate high school senior, plans to play college football and major in law enforcement. The following conversation focuses on a public service announcement about the dangers of drug addiction. Like Lana and Julie, Derek expresses a separation between himself and his subjects; but his comments also reveal much more.

Derek: They have crack babies on these public service commercials. They say, "Why do crack? Don't you want your baby to look healthy?" And then they show a white baby. And then the narrator says, "Or do you want your baby to look like *this*?" And this is where they show the black baby, with tubes and everything. It comes out racial—like only black people do crack.

RF: What did you do about this?

Derek: I complained to those people sitting around me. I don't know what you can do about it. They should show both babies as black and white. There's probably a large percentage of crack babies who are black, but not all of them. And that commercial makes it seem like *all* crack babies are black.

RF: Are there other things on Channel One that, because of the choices made, lead you to believe that something is all one certain way and not another?

Derek: A lot of the violence shown on TV is done by blacks.

RF: Let me ask you and the others if you see any racism in all the Channel One commercials starring Emmitt Smith, Michael Jordan, and Shaquille O'Neal.

Derek: My point of view is that they show a lot of positive things—those guys aren't selling drugs or doing violent stuff. But you *could* be offended by them because they don't show many white athletes, so whites could think it was prejudiced against them.

RF: Could these commercials be viewed as prejudicial against blacks, too?

Derek: In a way, they could, because those commercials don't show blacks in an office building or behind a desk or as a professor or a doctor—only as sports players. These commercials and most of the sitcoms playing now are not like the *Cosby Show*, which was good, because the dad was a doctor and the mom was a lawyer.

Even in this brief time, Derek effectively selects, inspects, and compares components of commercials. Derek was the only student who chose to analyze a public service announcement and not a "real" commercial intended to increase sales. Further, none of the other students selected, inspected, and compared the babies shown in this ad, noting that the crack babies in the PSA were black and, conversely, that the healthy babies were white. Also, Derek compared commercials with regular programs, supporting his judgments with specific references to each.

During a discussion about sports stars Emmitt Smith's and Michael Jordan's endorsements of Nike shoes, Derek explained how he focused on the athlete more than the shoe; how the names and images of the celebrities "make the product" and consequently inflate the prices. Derek explained that if Jordan, for instance, were not endorsing Nike shoes, he (Derek) still would have purchased them, but he would not have paid so much money for them. Derek reported that when he was younger, he indeed bought shoes according to which celebrity endorsed them; but no longer. Among other qualities, Derek's distancing and comparing are especially useful here: he speaks about himself, in a sense, as two people, one younger and one older, and how each was influenced by celebrity endorsements; he further compares the effects that Nike ads would have, with and without Jordan's presence.

A ninth-grade girl compared (and examined at a distance) how a boy featured in an acne cream commercial was dressed in two different scenes: "When he has zits all over his face, he's wearing big old black glasses and dorky clothes. But when his zits are gone, he's dressed all cool, his hair is fixed, and he finds a girlfriend right away."

Another student made multiple comparisons of the people who appeared within a single Pepsi commercial: "There is one white guy, one Hispanic guy, one black girl, and one Chinese girl—you know what I mean? It's kind of odd to have one person from each of those groups!" This student, by inspecting and comparing each person in the ad, concluded that such a mix was contrived.

Overall, although students' selecting, inspecting, and comparing were limited to single ads, they still demonstrated a degree of critical thinking about commercials.

Making Connections

Connecting means linking observations, ideas, and concepts from commercials to *other* things, such as regular programs, different texts (e.g., novels, articles), abstract values, and even students' own lives. Although this occurred only a few times during the study, it is an important, effective type of analysis because students construct concepts or networks of meaning that depend upon *multiple* sources. For example, when I asked a group of seniors what a commercial we had just watched was trying to sell, Carl remained quiet. However, during his second interview a few weeks later, he volunteered this analysis: "If you pay attention to that commercial, you can make the connection that Pepsi and friendship go together." Carl consequently connected a value to a product.

Making Predictions

Predicting means making one or more guesses or hypotheses about *why* makers of commercials made certain decisions. Hypothesizing, or venturing guesses, *enlarges the pool of possibilities* for students to explain *why* something is the way it is. If kids are aware that there are multiple reasons that explain phenomena (and that the world is full of multiple causes and multiple effects), then they will *move more quickly to weighing the most reasonable options*. If kids have few options to choose from (or none), then they are less likely to compare, contrast, and evaluate them. One group of ninth-grade girls quickly hypothesized reasons why the makers of a Channel One M&M's candy commercial selected an actor who was also appearing on the *Murphy Brown* network television show:

RF: Why do you think they chose *this* actor for *this* commercial?

Lana: Because he's actually a painter.

Maggie: Maybe because everyone can relate to him because he's a painter on the show and they use and talk about the M&M's colors in the commercial. . . .

Diedre: He's a recognizable person.

Lana: To symbolize paint.

Elise: He's not an artist, but a painter. But he thinks of himself as an artist.

Although this analysis is a group effort, wherein one person's thinking evolves from another's, it is effective analysis nonetheless. The girls built connections and advanced their thinking *as they talked*. In the few seconds in which this exchange occurred, the students enlarged their pool of possible answers to my question—which, in turn, will move them closer to comparing and weighing the most reasonable options. One girl hypothesized about how a particular Pepsi commercial could have been constructed:

It was like somebody had a camcorder and just recorded a lot of time with kids talking about different things, and then sliced out bits of it and put it together— someone professional who obviously knows what they're doing. You can put something together extremely carefully, but also in a kind of orderly, chaotic manner. It's kind of like artists who argue for hours about how to lay a pencil to make it look like it was just dropped.

The more this student hypothesizes, the more distance she gains from her subject.

Identifying Tone and Pointing to Evidence

A few students began to analyze commercials effectively by first identifying the overall tone or prevailing attitude that a commercial communicated to them. In responding to a Pepsi commercial, one girl labeled its overall tone: "Pepsi tries to make it sound like they're counseling." She then pointed out some examples or evidence to support her judgment (e.g., the characters sit in a circle and face each other; they hug each other). However, it was the ad's overall manner or style that seized the kids' attention first. Notice how Rob, a senior, begins with his general complaint, then quickly gets down to specific supporting evidence:

I don't like it when I see how obvious they are—when they direct the commercials to young people. It's condescending. It's over-exaggerated. The ad will show a school setting or a party or they'll show a bunch of young people hanging out together. When I see this, it makes me not want to buy the product. I really dislike the Gatorade commercial that shows Michael Jordan—especially when they sing, "Be Like Mike," as if drinking Gatorade is going to make you like Michael Jordan. The first time I saw it, I couldn't believe they were so blunt.

ANALYZING COMMERCIALS INEFFECTIVELY

Most of the kids I spoke with did not evaluate commercials effectively. They were thinking, of course, but in ways that quickly dead-ended. For example, if kids believed that their only choices for athletic shoes were Nike and Reebok, then they closed themselves off from even thinking about other options. Such thinking did not lead to further or deeper thinking.

The first part of this section describes specific ways in which kids engaged in unproductive analyses of commercials: (1) overvaluing the audio; (2) drawing boxed-in conclusions; (3) overvaluing the visual; (4) making either/or decisions; and (5) describing intended and obvious inconsistencies. Also, when kids analyzed commercials ineffectively, they were often unaware of *how* their thinking restricted further exploration. Therefore, the second part of this section describes generalized or oblivious ways in which kids evaluated ads: (1) denying that commercials influence thinking or consumer behavior; (2) evaluating only one commercial at a time; and (3) overvaluing the newest commercials.

Overvaluing the Audio

To interpret media texts, people must attend not only to the audio and visual elements but also to the interaction between them. Throughout this study, visual elements were stronger influences than audio or verbal elements. But some students placed disproportionate emphasis on audio elements—especially rock music soundtracks.

When a ninth-grade boy purchased a Sega video game he had recently seen on a Channel One commercial, he *also* bought two CDs of the music used in the background. Although this study did not focus on background music, it surfaced naturally in several conversations about commercials. Students identified songs and musicians. Overvaluing the audio portion of commercials occurred most frequently with ads for acne medications, such as Clearasil, Oxycute, and Noxzema.

Anna: There's a boy on this Clearasil commercial that said he had real bad acne and then he used Clearasil and his face is all clear and everything.

Greg: Yeah, it says that it's guaranteed to get rid of 54 percent of your zits in three days or your money back.

RF: Fifty-four percent in three days? Is that exactly what the commercial says? [All five students nod and say yes.]

RF: How would you measure this?

Greg: I don't know. But the good thing about Clearasil is that they don't say you're gonna have a *perfect* face. They just say that you won't have as many zits. I like them better because they're honest.

Greg's response to this claim (54 percent less acne in three days or money back) was typical of other students: they believed the claim mainly because it didn't declare 100 percent perfection. However, nobody I talked to had informally "tested" this claim or even considered how anyone might determine the accuracy of "54 percent less acne." After watching other acne cream commercials, my interest was piqued even more during the following conversation:

RF: Do the kids in this commercial [we had just viewed one together] have acne? [All five agree that they do not.] Do you think these kids *ever* had acne?

Sally: Yes.

RF: You can tell that these kids *once had* acne? [All five kids in the group nod agreement, saying, "Uh huh" and "Yeah, they've had it."] How do you know this?

Sally: Scars and things.

RF: Hmm . . . I thought they had perfect skin. Did the commercial show these scars? Maybe I missed them.

Sally: No, but you can tell.

Wayne: Sometimes you can just see.

Sally: When you're staring across the room, you can just see. And they say you can get scars and acne and things, so. . . .

RF: I didn't see this in the commercial we just watched, but can you tell if people with good skin in *other* skin medication commercials *used to have acne*—and if so, how can you tell?

Maia: I know in that one commercial, the boy has a perfect face; but I think he puts his face up to the camera sideways so you can see his profile.

Angie: And he's smiling and stuff.

RF: And when you see his profile, you can tell that he once had acne?

Sally and Maia: [Nodding in agreement] Uh huh.

Wayne: I can.

RF: How can you tell?

Maia: 'Cause they got these tiny little holes and you can kind of see them when he puts his face up close. . . . He hasn't had a major problem, but just a few, in little places.

After watching the commercials several times, I concluded that the kids featured in them had flawless skin—even the ones who bemoaned their acne directly into the camera. I cannot fathom how the students I talked with could possibly detect that the people shown in profile (and in other angles) had acne in the past. I can, though, observe that other commercial elements, especially the voice-overs and dialogue among characters, treated the actors in the commercial *as if they had acne*. In one acne medication commercial a group of kids in a pizza restaurant whisper about "Paul the Pimple King"—a kid who appeared to me and my research assistant to have very clear skin. Yet students in this study typically viewed Paul as either currently having acne or as *having had acne troubles in the past*. In short, students overvalued the verbal and audio elements beyond the visual.

What might happen when acne medication commercials tell kids how to treat a problem that, at least on screen, does not exist? Assume you're a typical, relatively insecure teen watching such commercials. Further assume that you do indeed have a few blemishes or imperfect skin, like most of us. If you watch commercials that show people bemoaning their "problem"—and they also happen to look very good—you might conclude that if *they* have a problem, then *you've* got a massive dilemma—simply because you look worse than those who are labeled as having problems.

Students' perceptions of acne commercials and products, as well as their own real need for the product, are bound up in illusions and insecurities. Student viewers did indeed perceive that kids in commercials currently had acne or had it in the past, whereas I reached neither conclusion. Further, none of the kids I talked to had acne—even though they watched Clearasil and Oxycute commercials intently and bought the products. As one result of overvaluing the audio, these kids drew boxed-in conclusions.

Drawing Boxed-In Conclusions

Advertisers have traditionally portrayed certain products as being necessary for consumers to use—all the time—even if they don't need them. Deodorant, mouthwash, toothpaste, shampoo, acne medication, and other products are often presented in ways that make them seem absolutely essential. Students in this study often drew such boxed-in conclusions about shampoo and acne medication.

RF: I'm surprised that you guys buy this acne medication because your skin is perfect. You don't have acne.

Rita: That's the reason we don't!

Mindy: If you wash your face with this stuff morning and night and do it continuously, it will reduce the chances that you'll get acne.

RF: So it solves problems *and* prevents them?

Rita and Mindy: Yes.

RF: So you need this product *one way or the other*, all the time, no matter what? There's never a time when you *don't* need it?

Rita: Yes, we always need it. [Mindy nods in agreement.]

RF: Is that logical?

Rita and Mindy: Yes.

Months later at another school, two students in the group tell me that they use an acne medication advertised on Channel One, even though they have "never broken out." If students *do* have an acne flare-up and use the ointment (and it helps)—and if it's intended to prevent another outbreak—

then it indeed seems logical to continue using the product. However, the larger context—of students not seeing any options, in the present or future, no matter what the conditions—is neither logical nor reasonable.

Overvaluing the Visual

RF: How do you know, for sure, that Chuckie [Chuckie V. of Gatorade commercials] is a "real" or serious or professional athlete?

Ian: Probably 'cause he's always doing sports on his commercials.

Beth: Yeah—he's always running or swimming or biking or something like that.

Before Ian and Beth had watched Chuckie V. in a series of Gatorade commercials, they had never heard of him—not in sports broadcasts, newspapers, or magazines; nor had their friends and families. Nonetheless, because they had seen him many times on commercials, they believed what they saw: that Chuckie V. was indeed the person whose role he played in commercials.

For most kids, the visuals in ads overpower the audio portions. The large majority of the kids in this study believed that the most important commercial element was whatever person or thing appeared on screen the longest or the most frequently or was most actively engaged. Conversely, if something appeared less often, students (such as Ian and Beth) valued it less.

At the time of this study, basketball star Michael Jordan was featured in many commercials airing on Channel One representing Wheaties, Gatorade, Nikes, and Hanes underwear. I asked three groups of students to rank their favorite Jordan commercials. All groups easily reached consensus: they preferred Jordan's Nike commercials for two reasons. First, Jordan made more Nike ads than ads for other products, because Nike sells several types of shoes. Second, kids liked these commercials best because Jordan appeared more often in each one. Moreover, all groups ranked Jordan's underwear commercial as their least favorite because "He's not in 'em much" and "'Cause he's in 'em only at the very end."

Like the kids who ranked Jordan's Nike commercials, Janet values what she sees the most while placing less merit on what appears on-screen the least.

Janet: This commercial isn't about Pepsi at all. They're just trying to help people get along with each other.

Derek: No. They're just trying to sell Pepsi, that's all. They're saying, "Drink Pepsi and you'll bond with a bunch of other people." They're just telling you what you want to hear—and then they're saying, "Drink Pepsi." That's what they're doing.

Janet: I don't think so, because you hardly ever see the Pepsi can—and when you do, it's gone real fast. I think that they care about us—they want future generations to get along better. That's what they're trying to say.

Overall, this approach is reasonable: whatever person or thing you see most often on-screen or for the longest period can be viewed as most important. However, in terms of effectively *evaluating* commercials, this outlook is sorely limited, as Derek indicates. Just because something appears on-screen a lot does not necessarily indicate that it's most important to the meaning of the entire message. Ironically, many kids interpreted the Pepsi symbol or can (displayed in the corner of the screen during a Pepsi commercial) to mean that the ad was *not* a commercial, but instead a "special program" that was "sponsored" by Pepsi!

During a conversation about Nike shoe commercials, I asked one senior why he decided to purchase Nikes. He replied, "You see 'em a lot, so there it is." I remain uncertain about what is most interesting about his reply: the fact that he values highly what he sees—or the fact that his phrase, "so there it is," directly echoes Pepsi's popular ad slogan at the time, "It's like this." Students consistently assumed that mere visual exposure "speaks for" or possesses the commercial's point of view—that it represents or embodies the ad's ultimate meaning and purpose. Simply put, kids tend to trust what they see on screen and assume that the visual shows the commercial's purpose.

Just before the following conversation occurred, a small group of ninth-graders reached consensus that the kids portrayed in the Pepsi commercial were not actors and that they were not working with any kind of script—that, instead, they were "just talking":

Allie: They say whatever they want.

RF: How do you know this?

Allie: They're like, playing around. These guys are holding girls upside down or something.

Jane: Sometimes they're at a park or a beach and just playing around. Like they're just hanging out with their friends.

RF: So, how do you know these are even commercials?

Allie: 'Cause it says "Pepsi" at the beginning and they show a can of Pepsi at the end.

RF: So—if they were actors, following some kind of directions or script—they wouldn't do that?

Allie: I don't know. . . . They speak off the top of their heads. They just say whatever. . . .

RF: How do you know they're speaking off the top of their heads?

Allie: When you read a cue card or script, you just go through it. But if they're asked a question, they have to think about it; they have to sit there for a while. Sometimes they'll sit in a circle and just start talking about it.

More than once in this excerpt, Allie and Jane trust what they see on the screen: because they *see* the people in the ad "playing around," they assume that their speech is also extemporaneous. Similarly, if these girls *see* a person pausing and thinking about a question, then they think the person's words and actions are unscripted.

The most common example of students valuing and trusting whatever appeared on-screen occurred with Pepsi's "It's Like This" ads. Most students made the following conclusions about the commercial:

1. If Pepsi cans did not appear often or for very long in the ad, then the company was not selling Pepsi.
2. If "kids like us" appeared the longest and the most frequently, then they were the ones telling the story.
3. If the audio is mostly talk about personal relationships (as it was in the ad replayed for students), then personal relationships constitute the ad's ultimate message.

Immediately after viewing this commercial, I asked students, "Whose point of view is communicated in this commercial?" or "Who is telling the story in this commercial?" The consistent answer was the person or persons who appeared in it the most, or whoever was engaged in the most on-screen action. As explored earlier, kids did not conceive of an external manipulator or creator of commercials. They observed no director calling the shots and nobody constructing a message. If kids perceive nobody *outside* of the commercial as being responsible for it, then they might also believe the authors to be the most visible, active people on the *inside* of the commercial. So what happened? In this case, kids ended up largely interpreting commercials as unmediated, direct recordings of reality, when in fact they are not. Also, students believed that Pepsi's first order of business was *not* to earn profits, but to "help them."

Making Either/Or Decisions

Early in this study, I noticed that four out of the five kids in one small group wore Nike shoes. Curiosity aroused (I knew that Nike and Reebok advertised heavily on Channel One), I said to the next group, "Let's go around the circle, one by one, so you can tell me about the shoes you own." Here is what the five girls in the group said:

Sheila: I have at least 1 pair each of Reebok and Nike.

Naomi: I don't own any Reeboks, but I own 4 pairs of Nikes.

Barbara: I have, like, 2 pairs of Nikes and 1 pair of Reeboks.

Mindy: I have 1 pair of Reeboks and 2 pairs of Nikes.

Katy: I have 1 pair of Nikes and 2 pairs of Reeboks.

This pattern of response generally held true throughout the study. Roughly, four out of five students in each small group owned Nike and/or Reebok shoes. The problem with either/or thinking is that one's options are limited to two, usually polarized, elements. Thinking therefore becomes frozen because it recognizes only two extremes; it never allows for the multiple possibilities within the large middle area. Also, of course, Nike and Reebok are very heavily advertised on Channel One.

Without mentioning any shoes by name, I asked a Nike-shod boy, "Why did you buy those?" He replied, "Because I don't like Reebok." Even though nobody had spoken the word "Reebok" during our session, this boy's thinking included only two options. Another student reported that he always tried on three or four different pairs of shoes before making a purchase. When I asked him what brands he tried on, he replied "They were all Nikes—I usually don't buy outside of that." When I asked if he knew why he did that, he replied, "No—you just see 'em a lot, so I mean, there it is."

Students were keenly aware of brand wars, such as Coke versus Pepsi, and they voiced their judgments vehemently but always in polarized terms: "I *hate* Coke! It's *terrible!*" or "I'll never, *ever* wear Reebok!" Their evaluations of products were rarely based on multiple options. Not surprisingly, most of the product pairings that students chose from were advertised on Channel One: pizza was limited to Little Caesar's or Domino's; candy to M&M's or Skittles; non-cola beverages to Mountain Dew or Sprite; fast food to McDonald's or Hardee's. When I asked one small group what my options were if I wanted to buy some medication for acne, they conferred, then quickly reported, "Clearasil and Oxy are the main ones." Both are advertised on Channel One. In addition to products, students either "loved" or "hated" the ads themselves, acknowledging no middle ground. Commercials were either "cool" or "stupid," "funny" or "boring."

Another type of polarized thinking occurred when students spontaneously categorized commercials while discussing any topic about ads. Their most frequently used labels for commercials were "old" and "new." Rarely did students qualify their judgments with phrases such as "kind of old" or "somewhat new." Of course, commercials often model and encourage this very type of polarized thinking. Advertising language and images often present consumers' options as, at best, limited to two elements. A popular deodorant commercial on Channel One effectively employed both pictures and language to communicate only two choices: "Sure" versus "Unsure." This message was repeated several times throughout the thirty-second commercial. A shampoo advertised on Channel One claims that it "never over-conditions, never under-conditions." Either/or thinking is easier than deliberation and robs students of reflection time.

Describing Intended and Obvious Inconsistencies

Students rarely volunteered explicit evaluations of commercials. When they did, they merely described an inconsistency within one commercial— usually an *intended*, *purposeful*, unreal event—mere editing ploys and camera tricks, such as flying cars or talking animals.

Heather: Let me start with commercials I *don't* like, especially commercials with animals, like ads for pet food—that cat food and talking parrot commercial. It's like the cats *actually understand and listen to a bird telling them not to eat it!* I mean—it's a natural habitat! Just the fact that the bird talks gets on my nerves. And he has an accent that doesn't even sound right!

RF: Why don't you like that?

Heather: 'Cause it's not what animals *do*. It's not real life.

RF: Do you think the makers of this commercial know that it's not like real life?

Heather: Yeah, but it's just stupid—just downright stupid and idiotic, like that Energizer Bunny commercial, which shows the bunny fighting Darth Vader and then the batteries in his laser go out, but the bunny's laser is still goin'.

RF: And this one is stupid, too?

Heather: Yes! Because you *know* they change the battery in the rabbit! They *have* to change the battery! I have *never* found an Energizer battery that has run that long in my entire life, and I've bought lots of those batteries.

RF: Why do you buy Energizer batteries?

Heather: 'Cause they last longer than everything else.

Most kids seemed to interpret intended, unreal events in commercials as adults do—with bemused acceptance of camera tricks. However, some reported that such events were impossible or unreal, articulating a naive criticism, as Heather, a senior, does here. She concluded that no batteries can run as long as they do on the commercials. Although she accepts this ad as exaggerating how long a battery can last, her criticism does not affect her consumer behavior.

Heather impressed both myself and my research assistant as a bright, articulate girl. In a world saturated with fantastic camera tricks, it is hard to understand why and how bright, normal kids would evaluate commercials in such naive ways. Following are a few possible reasons: (1) students do not know what else to focus on and talk about, having little or no experience in analyzing texts of any kind; (2) students believe their observations are safe ones, which would be accepted by the adult investigators; and (3) students can be especially irritated or disturbed by certain commercials.

Denying Commercials

Beth: I saw Fruitopia on a commercial and bought that.

RF: Did you try this drink as a result of the commercial?

Beth: Yeah. The commercial's, like, really psychedelic and they have prismatic figures. It's like a kaleidoscope. And the bottle is really cool, too.

RF: Why is the bottle cool?

Beth: It's just real colorful and has weird designs on it. It has bubble letters and little people and it has your brain and the world on it.

RF: Your brain?

Beth: Yes. It shows life and the mind. It's trying to say it's good for your mind and it's good for your body, and good for the earth. It has, like, symbols, kind of, of what this means.

RF: So, why is Fruitopia good?

Beth: I don't know. I don't pay any attention to that stuff.

Teachers, researchers, and others who work with media agree that many viewers deny watching television and film. They especially deny that media affects them in any way. Beth demonstrates a fair degree of knowledge about this product, as well as its commercials and packaging. What's more, Beth states that Fruitopia is "good for your mind, body, and earth," even though the label never states that. Rather, the words, "planet," "mind," and "body" appear by themselves, on opposite sides of the label.

Hence, Beth focuses on many specific details in the ads, as well as making a personal connection. But she denies that she would "pay any attention to that stuff."

People's initial response to media-related questions and issues often includes, "Oh, I never watch TV" or "I never pay any attention to that stuff." This pattern of response held true throughout the study. In each small group, at least one or two students denied watching commercials and/or being influenced by them, even when asked directly about specific commercials. However, when our conversation shifted to other topics (e.g., what makes a good commercial; can commercials be connected to products), the same kids would recite entire commercials, word-for-word, complete with physical gestures and imitated voices.

Donna haughtily criticized her classmates for watching *any* commercials. She scolded them when they recalled a Sprite commercial in detail. She especially rebuked the boys in the group for spending so much money on Nike shoes advertised on Channel One. But when we began talking about the qualities that make up good commercials, Donna instantly was transformed into an enthusiastic expert on commercials. She recited two commercials in a row, almost verbatim. She imitated an entire Welch's Grape Jelly commercial: "A bagel," she mimicked, "just for putting on a roof." She smiled and laughed as she re-created the ad, thoroughly enjoying herself. Donna laughed again, enjoying the commercial's replay, as one of the boys she had criticized earlier added more information to her retelling.

Like Donna, Pam also denied paying attention to commercials. "I only watch 'em if I'm really bored," she proclaimed. Pam said that her first-hour teacher had to move her because she talked during the Channel One broadcast. When I asked her what she liked to talk about during first hour, she replied, "My friends and I like to sing the Doublemint tune." I also learned that Pam phones her best friend after school and instructs her to tune in "when my favorite commercials come on."

Such contradictory behavior has long been observed by teachers and researchers. To a large extent, it's natural: the postmodern literature and media that these kids (and their parents) grew up with is often full of oppositions. However, in this study, it seemed that taking one position enabled the other to exist, that kids needed some type of equilibrium. Those who claimed disbelief (often expressed in authoritative tones) and consciously shut out some commercials in effect gave themselves permission to believe whole-hog in others. This phenomenon deserves more study.

Evaluating Only One Commercial at a Time

Beyond initial generalizations or opinions (e.g., "I hate commercials"), by far the majority of kids in this study did not criticize or evaluate commercials. When they did, their analyses were confined to *single* ads. Although any kind of analysis indicates thinking, if students don't generalize their observations and criticisms to various *categories or groups* of commercials, they severely limit their development of concepts and critical attitudes.

Students need to perform a basic sorting out of messages—placing them into categories or genres. If they do not make basic differentiations, they have little chance of making finer, more critical distinctions. For example, the kid who thinks, "These dish soap commercials only have women in them" is more likely to move toward increasingly refined and specific labels for this group of ads. The student might wonder, "Why don't these commercials have men in them?" or "The women in these commercials look like . . ."

Also, once students form even crude categories, the opposite end of the critical spectrum (i.e., the evaluation or judgment) is in place. Then, examples and illustrations or data from individual commercials can be anchored to them, allowing students to evaluate ads in a framework or context and *not* in a vacuum. When *both* ends of the critical spectrum are formed, both judgments and specific evidence will surface more easily in students' minds. If kids cannot at least broadly categorize commercials, then they will continue to be submerged in a flood of details.

Overvaluing the Newest Commercials

Kara, a ninth-grader, spoke excitedly, often giggling, when she told about "cluing in" her little brother about a new commerical.

My little brother is really funny and he has this thing about commercials. He likes to watch them. As soon as I saw the Little Caesar's pizza commercial on Channel One, I came home and told him about it and we laughed about it forever. I said, "Michael, you've *got* to see this commercial!" And it wasn't on TV at home until after it had been on Channel One for a month. I think the commercials on Channel One are more up-to-date than they are on regular TV. My brother knew "Is it on straight?" before it even came on *his* TV!

Most of all, Kara was proud that her little brother knew about the ad before his peers did and before he saw it on network television. Thanks to Channel One, Kara was able to initiate her brother into an exclusive circle.

Brent, a ninth-grader, complained about seeing the same commercials over and over. When I asked him how this situation could be remedied, his solutions did *not* include watching fewer ads; nor did he suggest watching ads for different products. Instead, Brent favored advertisers providing new commercials for the same products. Brent's response was typical of many students: new is always best. Throughout this study, the rare times that students *did* categorize commercials, they were merely "old" and "new"— regardless of our discussion topic.

Although students' recall of old and very popular ads was impressive, they never compared new ads to the old favorites. For example, students never compared Gatorade's extremely popular "Be Like Mike" commercial to any current offerings. Kids' failure to compare old and new commercials seems linked to their inability to group commercials. Getting these students to compare old and new ads could be a starting point in helping them to identify other concepts and categories of commercials.

EMBRACING COMMERCIALS

After talking with Debbie, the ninth-grader quoted at the beginning of Chapter 1, about *why* she thought professional athletes made commercials, I realized that she did not consider ads as commercials for products. Instead, Debbie (and many other kids, it turned out) viewed Nike commercials solely as advertisements for the athletes—which *they* pay for in order to bolster their own egos and their team's reputation. Hardly ever did the kids say that athletes made commercials in order to earn money. Instead of athletes endorsing products, these kids viewed the products as endorsing the athletes.

The prior examples (and many more) formed a clear pattern of student response to commercials. Throughout this study, kids wholeheartedly embraced commercials. They enthusiatically accepted and assumed the most positive motives about commercials. As mentioned earlier, they seldom perceived a creator or author behind the commercials. Even when students *did* perceive a creator, they viewed the responsible party in very positive ways. Finally, when kids embraced commercials, they bypassed analysis entirely. They took positive stances from the start, as Amy does in describing an army recruitment commercial:

One commercial that really stands out in my mind is the one where the basketball player jumps into the air, and then all of a sudden, he sits there and says, "Since I'm going to be up here for a while, I think I'll talk to you." Then all of a sudden he's in this green outfit. He wasn't just so-and-so, the basketball player—he was also Colonel Such-and-Such. This caught my eye because he just wasn't a basketball player trying to sell you something—he was encouraging you to *learn*!

All but a handful of students embraced Pepsi-Cola for its series of "It's Like This" commercials. Pepsi, which sells its products within the schools, heavily advertises on Channel One. During the two years of this study (1994 and 1995), Pepsi blanketed Channel One broadcasts with commercials that were crafted *not* to look like ads but like documentary or feature programming instead. Students trusted and admired Pepsi because of its commercials. Following is a sampling of students' positive and warm responses to Pepsi's "It's Like This" commercials:

- The most important thing in this commercial is getting along; they only show the Pepsi can a few times.
- They're [Pepsi] saying, "This is more important than what we're trying to sell you," because they don't show Pepsi throughout the entire thing.
- They say, "Love is not a color."
- They just all get along. . . . I guess Pepsi does that for them, I don't know.
- These kids inspire me.
- It's like real. It's not like TV actors.
- They're saying, "This is how life can be. It's something real."
- One of their messages is that they show kids like us, trying to fight the perception of our generation and our age group as druggies and killing everybody. They're trying to say, "Wait! There are good people out here!"

Although the following students' reasoning is not quite clear or logical, the four ninth-graders reflect their belief in the Pepsi altruism:

RF: Do you know the Pepsi "It's Like This" commercials?

Chad: Yeah. They've played 'em two years in a row. They had all those people from different high schools and they talk about important issues. They showed it when I was in eighth grade and they showed it last year, too. It's one of the older ones.

RF: What does the "it" refer to?

Chad and Sharon: [Simultaneously] Life.

RF: And what does "this" refer to?

Chad: The way they're living. [Sharon nods in agreement.]

RF: What is the one you saw today selling?

Chad: Peace.

Travis: They're trying to tell us to get along with the people around you, even though you may not—

Sharon: [Interrupting]—'Cause it's not going to change.

Ellen: They're trying to say that even if you are from a different nationality that everybody is equal. They're saying that they want the next generation not to be so prejudiced.

RF: What do you mean, "they're trying to say"?

Ellen: I mean that Pepsi is sponsoring.

RF: Do any of you see this as trying to sell Pepsi, the soft drink?

Ellen: Since that commercial reaches people, it kind of makes them think that Pepsi is a good cause—

Chad: [Interrupting]—And they care.

Ellen: And they care about people, so they want people to support Pepsi so that they can support the commercials.

Embracing Specific Values in Commercials

Ordinarily, harvesting the attention of an audience of potential consumers on a large enough scale to interest a major advertising sponsor involves considerable risk. With Channel One, that risk is virtually eliminated. The program's sponsors know the size and demographic makeup of their audience with a level of certainty unmatched by practically any other form of advertising. (Rudinow 1990, 72)

A large majority of the kids in this study expressed very positive feelings toward commercials. Many students' affection for ads and advertisers can be described as a type of blind love, where one sees no faults in another. Over and over again, kids said that they liked Channel One because "it's made for kids like us." This study clearly supports Rudinow's simple assertion—that advertisers can address their audience with tremendous certainty when the audience is clearly defined. However, as well-defined as Channel One's audience is, some ads are aimed at even more specific groups of students, tapping into more clearly defined values and attitudes. Over the two years of this study, on the basis of the ads' content—and certain students' very strong attraction to it—I identified four audience subcategories: "The Groovy Fruitopians," "The Shoe Jocks," "The Mountain Dew

Macho Men," and "The Hair Worshippers." These groups were especially sensitive to the values and attitudes communicated in specific commercials.

The Groovy Fruitopians

Several students seemed mesmerized by commercials for Fruitopia fruit drink. The ninth-graders in the following conversation spoke in reverent, awestruck tones about this beverage—much more so than kids ever spoke about any product during the entire study.

RF: Have you ever bought something that you saw advertised on Channel One?

Shaun: Yeah—these really strange commercials—they're really neat. It has all these different colors and words and stuff. I tried it once and it tasted good, so I kept buying it. In this commercial, there's some really weird music and then, like, words come up, like phrases or something, and all these fruits that are like kaleidoscoping and spinning around and all these different colors.

Melissa: There's something about "refreshing your soul."

Karen: And they end up saying, "Are you thirsty?"

RF: What's the music like? Is it upbeat?

Melissa: It's peppy, but it's not really—

Shaun: [Interrupting] No. It's not really hard. It's drums and the music is pretty soft and soothing, really.

RF: I'm not clear about what you're seeing on the screen during this ad.

Shaun: Just all those colors and everything. There's like little fruit moving around and spinning.

RF: What kind of fruit?

Shaun: There's always strawberry, and one has passion fruit in it and kiwi, grape, lemon, orange, and apple. Some have different fruits mixed together.

Karen: Like kiwi and pineapple.

RF: Does anyone say anything on these commercials?

Shaun: The words are just flashed up on the screen in white; they say "Fruitopia." There's one that says "peace and love" and one says "refresh your soul." There's six or seven different phrases on six or seven different commercials.

RF: How much time passed between the time you saw the commercial and when you bought the product?

Shaun: Probably a month before I actually bought it, because I just kept seeing it over and over.

RF: Did you ask your parents to buy it?

Shaun: Yeah. I told my mom to buy it. She went out and bought two or three different kinds of it.

RF: Do you still buy it?

Shaun: Yeah, almost every day.

RF: Can you describe the label on the bottle?

Shaun: There's usually like strange shapes on it, like spirals, sometimes—like peppermint candy. Just a bunch of different shapes. And then it's got the "Fruitopia" on the front and then on each side it's got a little phrase.

Melinda: The colors are kind of fluorescent.

RF: Do you like the name, "Fruitopia"?

Shaun: Yeah, it's neat.

RF: Can you tell me why you like this name?

Shaun: The *name*? Well . . . I just thought it was neat that they combined those two words. I had never heard those two words put together before, and I just thought it was strange and interesting. . . .

RF: What do you know about the words, "fruit" and "utopia"?

Shaun: I've read about utopias in books and stuff. . . .

RF: Why do you think those two words go together—and what does this combination make you think of?

Shaun: That it's a perfect drink. That it's really, really good—the perfect fruit drink.

RF: I guess so—that if you combine "fruit" with "utopia," you would think of the perfect, Garden of Eden, kind of place.

Tim: Fruitopia tastes just different than about anything you've ever tasted before.

RF: Really? *That* different? How?

Shaun: It's got some really strange—

Tim: [Interrupting Shaun] Have you ever tasted anything else that tastes like it?

Shaun: Like that? No! It's really weird.

Tim: It tastes completely different than just about anything.

RF: How can it be much different from any other standard, mixed-fruit drink?

Shaun: It is—it's supposed to be like natural and stuff.

RF: When you realized this product had a weird and different taste, did you read the ingredients label?

Shaun: Yes. It had filtered water and juice from concentrate and sugar.

Kaleidoscoping? Weird music and colors? Moving, spinning, colorful fruit? Refresh your soul? In the quiet, awestruck tones in which Shaun and the others spoke, this product sounded tie-dyed and drugged-out—like clips from an old film featuring former LSD guru Timothy Leary. Shaun and his classmates demonstrated that they knew a lot about Fruitopia, its commercials, and its packaging. Neither my research assistant nor I had ever heard of the product, but we were so intrigued by the kids' responses that we immediately purchased it. For us, of course, Fruitopia turned out to be just another mixed-fruit drink. According to its label, it consists of "water, high fructose corn syrup, and sugar." Also, the packaging was nondescript, if not self-mocking in its details (e.g., "totally natural, totally Minute Maid"). In the TV commercial, the bottle and pieces of fruit appear within kaleidoscopic patterns, communicating that the beverage and fruit are the same thing. They are not. My bottle of "Cranberry Lemonade Vision" labels the contents as "real fruit beverage"—not real fruit juice—which comprises only 16 percent of the contents. A bottle of "Pink Lemonade Euphoria" contains 13 percent fruit juice. The product, its packaging, and its commercials all seemed a far cry from the spiritual, mystical-experience-on-a-mountaintop relayed to us by Shaun and the others. But they are, after all, kids.

Whether Fruitopia's advertising affects young consumers directly, or whether they perceive its satire, this product is designed to appeal to a positive, unfocused spirituality that values holistic approaches to life and nature. The audience niche becomes clearer when you compare Fruitopia (the good twin) to its evil twin, "OK Soda" (which has not, as yet, appeared in Channel One commercials). Both items are produced by Coca-Cola. Both are targeted at a "Generation X" audience of young adults (Naparstek 1995). Whereas Fruitopia espouses a gentle, positive, unified, earth-mother message, OK Soda aims at the more angst-ridden, hard-edged, alienated half of the same age group. OK Soda cans are illustrated with drawings of tense-looking young adults, sketched in stark, black-and-white, comic-book style. The ad ploy seems to be that it's "OK" to be strung out. As Naparstek phrases it, "pervasive despair sells" (21). Like Fruitopia, the cans bear oblique, superficially philosophical messages (e.g., "The concept of 'OK-ness' has always . . ."). Such well-aimed messages at such specific subgroups will likely increase as advertisers continue to learn about their captive audiences in Channel One schools.

The Shoe Jocks

Although the "Be Like Mike" ad featuring basketball star Michael Jordan had ceased airing on Channel One over a year before my first visit, the kids still loved the commercial. They sang the ad's song in the hallways. Not one group failed to mention Jordan or his past and current commercials. In my written survey, kids recalled Nike and Reebok more often than any other brand name except Pepsi Cola. Not surprisingly, nearly every kid I talked to wore Reebok or Nike shoes and often owned multiple pairs.

The values of physical fitness and wellness are superficially embodied in Channel One's commercials. Kids in this study—indeed, most Americans—*say* that they value fitness and wellness. But I found very few kids who authentically linked athletic shoes with physical fitness. For example, when I asked a senior why she chose Nike shoes over other brands, her quick reply was, "Because I run and lift weights." For her, the Nike brand and serious fitness training seemed much the same thing. However, even though the majority of kids paid great lip service to fitness, I came to view it as a kind of smoke screen. In other words, physical fitness is considered a safe value because Americans have long embraced sports, fitness, and wellness.

It became very obvious in this study that physical fitness automatically connotes a cluster of *other* highly desirable values, especially for teens: attraction of the opposite sex, peer-group approval, self-esteem, and self-confidence. When I asked why they liked Nike commercials or why they wore Reebok shoes, the kids invariably replied, "Because I like sports." However, when I followed up this response, they typically said, "They [the shoes] look cool" and "All the other kids in school wear them." Hence, the strong jock factor in Nike, Reebok, Gatorade, and other ads elicited comments that flowed from the teens' "deeper" values of self-worth, identity, and peer approval.

Because Jordan and other sports celebrities (e.g., Emmitt Smith, Shaquille O'Neal, and Charles Barkley) star in Nike and Reebok commercials that dominate Channel One advertising, they are examined in many contexts throughout this report. More kids consistently valued Nike and Reebok products—and the celebrities mythologized within their commercials—more than anyone or anything else. Over the past twenty years, athletic shoes (and the athletes who appear in testimonial ads for them) have become a primary status symbol for young Americans. A British print ad for Nike shoes accurately captures this phenomenon (*Lurzer's* 1994, 103). The full-color ad depicts three stained-glass windows, each bearing the likeness of an athlete: a soccer player, a basketball player, and a tennis player. The athletes on each end (the soccer star and the tennis star) are kneeling, with their hands clasped over their hearts, as they gaze reverently upward toward the center pane—which is filled with an image of Michael Jordan, staring straight ahead, hands held together in prayer. Behind each jock's head is his respective type of ball, which of course resembles a halo. The large type at the top of the ad labels the three panes of stained glass as "The Temple of Nike." Just below that, the ad states, "Hours of Worship Mon–Sat 10–7 PM Thurs 10–8 PM Sun 11–6 PM."

The Mountain Dew Macho Men

One day I asked a group of three boys to tell me about a new soft drink commercial (which also aired on network television). The boys replied in unison: "Been there, done that. Skied that. Dewed it." Then, one boy continued, "There's a Mountain Dew machine in the middle of a jungle and . . ." Students repeated and talked about these lines just as much as they did about the commercials' images, demonstrating again how the symbol systems interrelate. These students, or "Mountain Dew Macho Men," represent another subgroup responding to specific values communicated in Channel One commercials. These values are machismo and peer-group approval, or even "male bonding."

Halfway through this study I noticed that certain students, mostly boys, were fond of Mountain Dew's commercial series featuring several scruffy-looking young men (grunge-style) who speak directly into the camera in bursts of exclamations. One group of students recalled the actors' typical lines: "Been there, done that"; "Never did it"; "Done it, did it, doin' it tomorrow"; "Skated it"; "Surfed it"; "Sphinxed it"; and "You never done do, 'til you do Mountain Dew." As these actors speak their one-liners and mug into the camera, machine-gun-paced clips cut away to the boys performing reckless outdoor stunts on mountain bikes, jumping from airplanes, and so on. Communicating an overall sense of irreverent, devil-may-care, physical and mental recklessness—in a word, machismo—these ads occur in an all-male world, outdoors, where rough-housing young men soar on mountain bikes, wrestle alligators, leap from planes, speak little but loudly, dress shabbily, don't shave, and don't care.

Notice how Mike defends the Mountain Dew commercials, against some complaints from Ann:

RF: Do any of you remember any lines from commercials?

Ann: Yes! Those Mountain Dew commercials—"Been there, done that"—I *hate* 'em 'cause they stay in my mind. I can't *ever* get them out of my mind! Those big words they use, what are they? What do those words mean? Those guys look like young college people, so how would they know those big words?

Mike: Maybe they're smart.

Ann: But those guys look like nerds, their hair is so long and greasy! How would *they* know what those words mean?

Mike: Nerds know a lot.

Ann: I mean *stupid* nerds.

Mike: Oh.

RF: [To entire group] Can you describe this commercial?

Mike: There are four guys on mountain bikes and it shows this Diet Mountain Dew machine, and they go, "Wow, never done it." Then, at the end, they go, "Been there, done that, tried this," or something like that. They skydive and—

Ann: [Quickly interrupting] Passé! *That's* the word they use! "Passé-cliché"! And I *hate* that! Ugh! They're just annoying the way they say it!

Mike: Yeah, well, they like skydive and stuff . . .

Although Mike defends the intelligence of the Mountain Dew actors, he really wants to focus on their physical prowess. The frenzy depicted in Mountain Dew commercials reflects the product's contents, because Mountain Dew contains more caffeine than other soft drinks. Another student told me that the high caffeine dosage was the reason he consumed the product daily (it was available from machines in his school cafeteria). This same boy was also attuned to the ads' macho values: he referred to the actors in the commercials as "studs."

The Hair Worshippers

When we asked students what they noticed first about certain commercials, their answer was often "hair." If boys are targeted in the Mountain Dew commercials, girls are targeted in Finesse Shampoo and other hygiene ads. One Finesse commercial fills the screen with a model's long, flowing, blond hair, swinging from side to side in slow motion. Another shampoo ad shows two similar heads of cascading tresses, which meet in the center to form a symmetrical pattern. While watching this commercial, one ninth-grade girl whispered in awe, "She's sooo pretty . . ."

Some commercials featuring hair appealed to both genders, especially the Gatorade ads featuring Chuckie V., a "triathlete" whose hair was fashioned into long, stiff spikes. These commercials actually star Chuckie V.'s hair: it's the first thing most viewers said they noticed. Viewers see it from multiple camera angles, and they especially notice it when its dark profile appears against a light background. This unique profile also appears on a tee-shirt worn by Chuckie V. during the commercial. Like the boys who appear in the Mountain Dew commercials, Chuckie V. presents himself as an irreverent, confident, nonconformist man of action.

Both boys and girls value hair because it implies a host of other, deeper values. Much like the case with physical fitness, kids seem to regard hair as a primary indicator of other qualities, especially sexual attraction, peer acceptance, and self-concept. Of course, Channel One advertisers know their audience: they know that kids are entranced by bountiful, beautiful hair; that kids are intrigued by nonconformist hair; that kids, especially girls, dislike ugly hair (remember Ann who disliked the Mountain Dew boys' "greasy" hair?); and that kids are nearly repulsed by baldness.

Indeed, Channel One seems to sequence commercials to exploit kids' strong love/hate attitude toward hair. One day a Finesse Shampoo ad featuring shimmering, beautiful locks played first. It was followed by Chuckie V. in stiff spikes of hair in a Gatorade commercial. This was followed by an ad for Clearasil acne medication, which portrayed zits as screaming, obnoxious, *bald-headed men* erupting on a kid's cheek.

CONCLUSION

Channel One succeeds in tailoring its broadcast for middle- and secondary school kids. The following indices of measurement point to this conclusion: Channel One's knowledge of its audience's demographics; its extremely high rates for advertising time; and the availability within Channel One schools of products advertised on Channel One. Overall, the four audience subgroups previously described constitute a definition of adolescence. Young adults are naturally concerned (if not downright insecure and fearful) over their sense of selfhood: how clearly they see themselves as male or female; what they look like; how other people accept them. In short, adolescents are continually struggling to find out who they are. And they often base this search upon who they are *not*.

We become individuals by separating from our parents, by valuing nonconformity. Arnold Mitchell's (1983) research on consumer audiences describes the values and attitudes of young adults as "I Am Me," which essentially means "I am *not* my parents." The Groovy Fruitopians and the Mountain Dew Macho Men tune in to commercials that communicate nonconformity. The Shoe Jocks and the Hair Worshippers favor ads communicating gender identity and sex appeal.

Sometimes, the ad messages tap into both values, as the Mountain Dew commercials seem to do. In their speech, appearance, and attitude, the ragamuffin boys on mountain bikes portray nonconformists; and in their physical stunts, they also portray macho men or well-defined genderhood. Hence, young adults' natural and intense doubts about their self-concept, gender identity, nonconformity, sex appeal, and other characteristics are directly addressed by commercials—not for purposes of helping them make the hard transition into adulthood, but for purposes of selling them soft drinks and shampoo.

In the face of this onslaught, the majority of kids in the study did not critically think about commercials. Nor did they effectively evaluate them. Most people will agree that kids need to learn how to do these things, if they are to become responsible, humane adults. However, before this issue is explored I must address those skeptical readers who ask, "Sure, most kids don't evaluate commercials effectively—but so what? It's their actual behavior—what they *do*—that's most important." Therefore, how commercials affect kids' behavior is discussed in the next two chapters.

5

How Do Commercials Affect Kids' Behavior?

I haven't seen much of Channel One because I work in the office. But I wish I had, because every morning when I went to classrooms to pick up the attendance slips, everyone was laughing about that Little Caesar's commercial.

Linda, ninth-grader

Considering the depth and detail with which kids in this study know commercials, and given the time and energy that kids think about and talk about them, it is not surprising that commercials affect kids' actual behavior—how they talk, how they act in and out of school, what they create, what they wear, what they eat, what they purchase, and even what they dream. This chapter describes *replay behaviors: any type of actions initiated by kids that repeat or reconstruct a commercial—or parts of a commercial—in some way.* Replays are repetitions or reconstructions of the original commercial. They function as prompts for the receivers, however fragmented or whole, that evoke all or parts of the original ad's message.

KIDS REPLAY COMMERCIALS

To create replays, kids can verbally imitate ads, physically act them out, or re-experience them when they dream. Images, music, language, objects, and nonverbal communication—together or separately—are used to create replays of commercials. Kids engage in replays after an ad has penetrated their consciousness. By simply conjuring up an ad's images, music, or language, we replay all or parts of an original ad's message. For senders and receivers, each replay elicits different degrees of the original, or stimulus, ad.

Replays require associational and visual thinking. Associational thinking involves the linking of symbols or signs in nonlogical ways. For example, red apples may remind us of small children or fire trucks or the old Harold Arlen song "Get Happy" or the poet Robert Frost, and on and on. Such thinking has its roots in semiotics (e.g., Eco 1976; Sless 1986). Visual thinking has roots in semiotics, too, although its influence is obvious in most arts and sciences disciplines, including literature, general semantics, cognitive psychology, and Gestalt psychology. Arnheim (1986) has argued that we think "by means of the things to which language refers—referents that in themselves are not verbal, but perceptual" (138).

Paivio's theory and research also help explain how replays function. Paivio's work demonstrates how words may elicit other words within us—or images. Conversely, images may arouse other images—or words (1990). In this study, verbal and visual associations were triggered within individual students, as well as between and even within small groups of students. For example, immediately after one student described what she remembered from a mouthwash commercial—what she called "that song about George in the Jungle"—her classmate immediately responded, "Oh yeah, it shows that bottle of Listerine swinging through the jungle on a vine!" Here, the words and music elicited the images. When I cited a line or jingle to prompt kids' memories of a specific commercial, they could recall visual (and verbal) parts of the ad that had occurred just before and after the prompt.

The replay behaviors described in this chapter are of three overlapping types: verbal, physical, and mental. First, *verbal* replays employ language, such as when kids sing a jingle from an ad ("Crave the wave!") or write a note to a friend about a commercial. Second, replays can be *physical*, such as when kids act out or imitate an action or scene from a commercial (e.g., the model in a shampoo commercial shaking her hair). Physical replays also include paintings, sculptures, or other objects that portray products and/or images from ads. Third, *mental* replays occur when kids think or even dream about commercials they've seen. All types of replay occur in a variety of contexts, from events and art classes, to phone conversations and backyard games. As the previous two chapters illustrate, most students do not judge and evaluate what they see. Instead, they tend to *use* their mental maps of

TV commercials by simply replaying or rerunning them. Replays were the most widespread type of student response to commercials that I found throughout this study. This chapter describes the following types of replay behaviors:

- Singing Songs, Jingles, and Catch-Phrases
- Adopting Jargon and Brand Names
- Playing with Language
- Mimicking Voices
- Interacting
- Matching Up Commercials with Other Ads
- Playing Backyard Games
- Eating Packaging
- Adopting an Ad Star's Name
- Choosing Clothes and Objects
- Completing School Assignments
- Entering Contests
- Cheering at Sports Events
- Competing in Sports
- Watching and Talking about Satirized Ads
- Imitating Actions
- Creating Art Projects
- Dreaming

These informal and random replays can be amusing. They are a safe topic for kids to talk about with their peers (especially while establishing friendships), their parents, and siblings. But such conversation carries a high price, because replaying commercials often flashes back the ad's original sights and sounds, again and again. The result is that popular commercials, such as the "Be Like Mike" ad, recur in varied ways thousands of times more often than they air on television.

Singing Songs, Jingles, and Catch-Phrases

My friends and I used to sing the Doublemint gum song everyday during first hour, but then the teacher moved us, because she didn't want us talking during Channel One.

Ann

Like Ann, many students reprise songs, jingles, and catch-phrases from commercials. During our small-group sessions, students often spontaneously sang songs and jingles—for myself and my assistant, even though we were complete strangers to the kids. Andy and Jim try to explain the pull that ad songs, jingles, and catch-phrases exert on kids:

Andy: Sometimes commercials stick in your head all day and you maybe want to try it . . . like "Be Like Mike" did.

Jim: Yeah, it's kind of like the last song you hear. Or, you wake up in the morning and that's the song you hear and you sing it all day.

Lana: Or like, if you see a commercial—and you see it enough, that you can say it word-for-word or sing the song they sing. And then you get to the grocery store and you see that product and all of a sudden you say, "I know that commercial!" and you start hearing the words and humming the tune.

RF: Can you give an example?

Lana: Cheerios. [laughing] It's about school—and I *love* school! It tells about how Cheerios give you energy through the day until lunch. It was about this kid who woke up in the morning and didn't have time for anything else, so he grabbed a bowl of Cheerios and his books and went to school and the bell rang for lunch and he ate lunch.

Joy: There's another Cheerios commercial with this woman who sounds like an auctioneer. She's saying all these different kinds of cereal that they could have for breakfast. And then the little bee is on his box of cereal and so, he chooses that.

Without being asked, Lana and Joy simultaneously broke into a song from this commercial, never missing a word or a beat. The mere mention of the song elicited the message and images from Joy and Lana before they quickly moved back to the tune. Again, the point is that music, words, phrases, and images evoke *other* music, words, phrases, and images—in effect creating a commercial echo chamber. Rita, a ninth-grader, fond of a jingle from an acne cream ad, frequently repeated the phrase that included the product's name. This helped Rita separate the product from its main competitor, Clearasil. Further, she knew exactly *when* the girl in the commercial said "Oxy-cute them!"—while she dances. When Jerry heard a few bars of an old Van Halen song used in a commercial, he told me that not just Pepsi appeared in his mind, but *Crystal* Pepsi.

Some replays depended on the visual for their meaning and impact. One student replayed this line from a Nike commercial into a conversation: "There—that was refreshing!" But the line didn't make much sense, because it requires the visual for impact: a basketball player suspended in mid-air above the net. I can only speculate that this line so powerfully elicited the images for this boy's classmates that they may have thought everyone else was imagining the same scene that they were.

Although some of the following songs, jingles, and catch-phrases had ceased airing on Channel One the year before our study, students replayed them in many contexts: "Be like Mike," "I love Jukie," "Obey your thirst," "Riiight now," "Crave the wave," "Like a rock," "Been there, done that," "You never done do, 'til you do Mountain Dew," "Skied it, skated it, sphinxed it," "Got-to-be, got-to-be, Dom-in-os," "Does this remind you of anyone's face?" "You've got the right one, ba-by—uh-huh," "On the road with Chuckie V." "Oxy-cute them!" "Is it on straight?" "Kiss a little longer," "Yabba-dabba-doo," "Just do it." A few groups of students listed all the places where they continue to hear their classmates sing the "Be like Mike" song from a popular Nike commercial that stopped airing the previous year: in the cafeteria; in the hallways before, during, and after school; on the bus; during after-school sports; and many more.

Jingles, songs, and catch-phrases attract students so strongly that replays occur in unique situations. One boy told me that the very small children at his brother's day-care center regularly sing the "Got-to-be Dominos" jingle. Another boy disrupted class time devoted to SSR (Sustained Silent Reading) by loudly repeating the cola jingles "Yee-hi!" and "Like a rock." During a conversation about Cinnaburst gum, one girl volunteered the following comments: "Whenever you go to the store, I mean, and you don't buy a regular stick of gum, you buy Big Red, you know, because it lasts longer. It's not like you've ever tried it or anything, because everybody *knows* that Big Red lasts longer. It's like one of those common sense things." Twice, this girl mentions that this gum "lasts longer," which she believes is a "common sense thing." However, the actual commercial states several times that this gum "lasts a little longer."

Adopting Jargon and Brand Names

Using jargon and brand names is an abbreviated or condensed form of replay, which is more selective than merely rerunning an ad's content. One boy used the term "flavor crystals" to describe Cinnaburst gum (indeed, it seems that every student I talked to over the two-year period knew what flavor crystals were). When I asked him what flavor crystals were made of, he replied, "bursts of flavor"—another empty phrase from the same commercial. Kids sometimes picked up pseudo-scientific jargon from commercials and integrated it into their own explanations. When a group of girls discussed shampoo commercials, they used terms such as "hair follicle," "hair shaft," "hair cuticle," and "pro-vitamins"—all of which occur in Pantene and Finesse shampoo commercials.

Such hollow jargon sounds impressive and technical to the students, thereby legitimizing the product for them. Several girls had used a shampoo because its commercial promised that it "never over-conditions, never under-conditions," a line they had memorized. Although the girls had watched this ad many times, memorized its claims, and bought and used the product, they remained unclear about what the claim meant.

Brand names also serve as an abbreviated way of replaying commercials. We had been talking in generic terms about products and commercials, until Sherry invoked a specific brand name: "I never buy anything that I see on commercials, except candy, because that's one thing that, if you see it on a commercial, you buy it, because it's like Nutrageous: it looks good!" Nobody prompted Sherry to be specific about her topic. Nor had any of her peers mentioned brand names before her. Hence, even under circumstances not requiring brand names, students often mentioned them readily and effortlessly. By referring to products (shampoo) by their brand name (Finesse), students seemed to equate the two.

One boy told us, "If I'm sitting at home and I'm hungry, and like, a Taco Bell commercial comes on, I'll go out and get some Taco Bell." He *doesn't* say he'll "go out and get some Mexican food." He states that he'll eat some Taco Bell. When one girl was explaining how everyone in her family only buys Reebok, she enthused, "My whole family lives on the Reebok." She was referring to this shoe's ad phrase, "Planet Reebok." Melinda used a brand name of one commercial (and brand-name product) to jog her memory of another ad for a different product. When I asked her to tell me what the people say at the end of a certain Pepsi commercial, she replied, "It happens really fast, like on the Sega commercials. Let's see, now . . . Sega! Sega! Sega!" These examples of brand-name replay seem especially condensed and potent. In the first case, the actual product (Mexican food) is fused with its brand name (Taco Bell). They become the same thing. And the girl who told me that her entire family "lives on the Reebok" has simply abbreviated the catch-phrase through intense familiarity with the product and its advertising. In the last instance ("Sega! Sega! Sega!") a brand name invokes a completely *different* product and commercial, illustrating its ability to cross-over and be used in very different situations—a kind of all-purpose chant that replayed the brand name three times. Such replays of brand names and other ad language help kids internalize commercial messages. One ninth-grade student internalized them so thoroughly that he insisted he knew that the shoes worn by Chuckie V. in a Gatorade commercial were Nikes. However, the commercial shows Chuckie's feet from a considerable distance as he furiously pedals a bicycle! Finally, brand names even appeared in kids' dreams:

Phil: I'm sure I *have* dreamed about commercials, but I can't think of one right off hand. Because you *have* to. I mean, if you see your clothes in a dream, usually they're going to be a name brand. I know I do that.

RF: You notice your clothes in dreams?

Phil: Yeah, sure—if you see yourself in a dream, you'll see your clothes.

RF: I've never noticed my clothes in a dream—or at least never remembered them.

Phil: You've never seen your whole body in a dream?

RF: Sure I have, but I couldn't remember what I was wearing, unless it was somehow important to the story.

Phil: Huh!

Phil said "Huh!" with utter incredulity. To him, clothes—and their brand names—are an integral part of everyone's lives. When Phil sees the "Levi's" patch on his jeans in his dreams, he is replaying an ad message, validating it for himself in a powerful, private, unique way.

Playing with Language

Meaningful, intelligent replays of commercial material that fit the context at hand include student-generated puns and coherent replies and answers to questions. When I asked some kids if they talked about commercials outside of class, Lindsey said, "The M&M commercial." Her friend answered, "That's all Lindsey ever talks about!" Evidently in character, Lindsey responded, "At least I'm friend-leh!"—imitating the exact line and voice from the M&M's commercial. Lindsey meaningfully integrated the ad's line into her *own* response, which fit her context and intent.

When one girl reprimanded her classmate, John, for not being aware that today was their teacher's birthday, he innocently replied, "Bo didn't know!" Here, John appropriates the Bo Jackson ad line, "Bo knows . . ." to fit his own circumstances. Of course, even when students creatively play with ad language, it still largely has the same effect—rerunning, to varying degrees, the original ad's message.

Mimicking Voices

RF: What candy advertised on Channel One is sold in the candy machines here in your school?

Bob: Skittles.

Maggie: Yeah, and Starburst and Snickers and—

Dan: Yeahhhhh! 'Cause it really satisfies!

Maggie: And Reese's, M&M's, Peanut M&M's, Pepsi, Mountain Dew, and . . .

Here, Dan interrupts Maggie by imitating the voice from the commercial. He fits his comment into the overall meaning or context of this situation, albeit loosely. Kids often imitated commercial voices for little or no reason. Of course, their immediate listeners often shared knowledge of the commercial being replayed with the replayer, but not always. Most of the mimicry I observed occurred while kids were *not* watching TV. Imitating voices is fun, and commercials strive to provide as many irresistible morsels as possible. Such sound bites consist of a few words, mainly one-syllable with long vowel sounds (e.g., "Crave the wave"). Highly memorable and easy to replay, these lines elicit the ad's visuals, music, and message. Kids replay the voice's content but also strive to capture its vocal intonation, emphasis, and subtleties of dialect. The more the kids hone their imitations and inject them into different situations, the more attention and acceptance they garner from peers. Cartoon voices (and what *sound* like cartoon voices to kids) are especially tempting to imitate. Some voices—such as that of a small child who enthused on one commercial, "It's shake and bake, and I helped!"—become exaggerated during students' replays.

Irresistible voices have to be mimicked, just as pent-up energy has to be vented. One night while listening to the tapes of a small-group discussion, I heard one girl whisper something while all the other kids were talking: a barely audible, "pizza-pizza." Evidently the little cartoon man from the Little Caesar's boxes and commercials could not be silenced.

Interacting

Very few students directly talked back or answered commercials *as* the ads were playing. Such talking back usually requires strong disagreement with what is being watched, and students seldom demonstrated this. Also, the school setting of Channel One inhibits speaking aloud during air time, because many teachers would consider it disruptive to other students' viewing. However, a few kids *did* interact directly with commercials by imitating ad voices *simultaneously with the commercial*. For such parallel or synchronized mimicry to succeed, kids must key the audio to the visual parts, which requires them to memorize the complete commercial.

I watched in awe as one ninth-grade boy replayed a commercial's lengthy audio just seconds *before* it happened on the screen in front of us. Kids seemed to derive pleasure from engaging in this parallel mimicry—it was a kind of game for them: if they "beat" the ad voices to the punch, they won at a more advanced level. This kind of interaction is certainly less "confrontational" than talking back to a commercial, which is a habit most of us associate with older, more experienced viewers. Finally, the less confrontational approach seems consistent with the students' warm regard for commercials.

Matching Up Commercials with Other Ads

Several students simply matched up one ad with another—and then immediately abandoned this pairing, making no specific or critical comparisons of elements. I call this "matching up"—and not comparing—because comparing suggests some degree of critical thinking by inspecting one element against another, and then verbalizing similarities and differences. These actions, however, never occurred in this type of replay. Instead, match-ups provided a brief replay of two commercials. For instance, one senior girl said that the series of Gatorade ads featuring Chuckie V. reminded her of the old Dave and Dan commercials in which two athletes trained for the Olympics. Then, like the other students who made match-ups, she stopped cold. When I followed up her observation with questions, she merely replied, "Both commercials are about athletes." However, when students made match-ups that were not pursued with questions from someone else, they immediately abandoned the paired ads regardless of the context of their group's conversation—which, by the way, was usually an appropriate and safe one for offering any such comparisons. These match-ups, then, mainly provided a brief replay of two commercials.

Playing Backyard Games

Dale: Everybody talks about those "deranged referee" commercials. Usually someone will see a new one and then everyone else will find out about it from them.

Marnie: And make fun of it!

Dale: Yeah! And I've seen the new commercial and it seems like everyone's got their own favorite deranged referee. There's a bunch of 'em. There's one on

Barry Sanders, Bruce Smith, Troy Aikman, Mike Gardner, Artie Nickerson, and Sterling Sharp—that's the best one.

RF: Why is the Sterling Sharp ad the best?

Dale: He just goes up to the security gate and he like, "What's your name?" and just takes off running toward the field! [At this point the other four students in this group could not contain their laughter; they obviously knew this commercial well, which accounts for Dale's gaps and abbreviated style of language.]

RF: The referee does?

Dale: Yeah, the referee does. And he's telling about Sterling Sharp the whole time. And he gets to him and then Sterling Sharp just hits him and runs him over. So he grabs Sterling Sharp's face mask and says, "Choo-choo, choo-choo."

RF: So what's that all about?

Dale: A train—he runs the ball like a train. [As Dale says this, two girls near him are whispering. The microphone nearest them picks up their voices: "choo-choo, choo-choo."]

RF: What does he look like?

Dale: He's always wearing an overcoat, he's not shaven, and looks like a bum, and he's always got the referee hat on. I think it's Dennis Hopper. Like in one of 'em, he's down in the parking lot, playing this tape recorder. And then a car starts up and he's like, "just act normal," or something like that. The whole time he's talking to the audience.

RF: Has this commercial shown up in other ways?

Dale: Yeah—I've seen this one in the backyard, when we've just gotten together to play football. When this one kid tackled others, he'd run over like four or five people, while he just kept sayin', "choo-choo, choo-choo" and all this stuff. And then other times in backyard football I've heard kids say, "I hear the footsteps; I don't hear the footsteps." It's from that same Nike commercial.

These kids were so involved in the commercials that acting one out during a backyard football game seemed entirely natural to them. However, the fact remains that the ad's basic message was felt again by each kid playing in the game, by those watching, and by those who heard about what happened at the game later—creating, in effect, echoes of replays.

Eating Packaging

RF: Have you ever bought something because you saw it on a commercial?

Alissa: Yeah: *"The Gum!"* [Imitates same line and voice used in one actual gum commercial.]

Tom: I don't remember their commercials, but Cinnaburst comes to mind first.

RF: Do you buy Cinnaburst?

Tom: Yes.

Alissa: And Mintaburst. I was buying those because it was something new.

Brit: And *everyone* was buying it. I mean, *everyone* had Cinnaburst!

Alissa: Definitely. It was like a great big fad.

Lisa and Dana: Yeah!

Alissa: It was!

Tom: It's *"The Gum!"* [Everyone laughs at his imitation.]

RF: Why was this so popular last year?

Brit: I don't know . . .

Dana: Ooh! You can chew the wrapper!

Alissa and Lisa: Yeah! You can chew the wrappers!

Eating gum wrappers was the most curious type of replay I found during this study. Several students reported regularly eating the inner, tissue-paper wrapping on sticks of Cinnaburst and Mintaburst gum. Sometimes they ate it with the gum itself, swallowing both, and sometimes they consumed only the wrapper. Out of 13 students I asked about this, 9 had eaten wrappers. One student estimated that she had eaten about 40 gum wrappers. Although I don't understand this action, I at least recognize it as *physical* engagement with a popular, heavily advertised product. It is an action that replays the original commercials for students in a visceral, unique way.

Knowing a little more about these gum commercials may help you understand this action. When the students mimicked the commercial by saying, *"The Gum!"* they were replaying part of the actual Channel One ad, in which parents meet in a therapist's support group for adults who have children "addicted" to this brand of gum. The ad treats this gum like a dangerous drug—complete with over-anxious, hovering parents who exclaim in distress, "I didn't think *my* son would ever do this! Not *my* son!" In short, the commercial satirizes nervous parents who equate this gum with hard drugs.

For kids, the commercial was a delicious romp on what they see as overprotective, paranoid parents. I believe that kids ate the gum wrappers for two reasons. First, eating wrappers became a fad—the "in" thing to do in a small town. As one student said, it became "the great thing to do."

However, students told me about friends in adjacent towns, about fifty miles away, who had also eaten wrappers. Second, by consuming the gum wrappers, kids pushed the TV commercial parody one step further: it became, for them, *another* humorous move, one step beyond what the commercial satirized. Eating wrappers continued the same theme of shocking parents with nonconformist behaviors. Like the original ad, eating wrappers became an outlandish way of ingesting the "dangerous drug"—of mainlining the product. When I asked one girl if she had ever talked to a parent or teacher about eating gum wrappers, she said, "They'd just look at us like we were stupid." Although students creatively "appropriated" these commercials and even extended the ads' tone and intent, doing so still qualifies as a replay of the original ads—a very physical, involving replay, which generated more talk about the product and commercial than many other replays accomplish.

Adopting an Ad Star's Name

I talked to (and heard about) kids who assumed the names of people featured in Channel One commercials. One girl observed, "They did that all last year. They like signed their name with somebody else's name. It's fairly common. It's mostly the guys that do it." One boy was called "Chuckie" for two reasons: (1) some kids felt he resembled "Chuckie," the main character in a popular horror film (*Child's Play*), and (2) because of "Chuckie V.," who was featured in current Gatorade commercials. This same student vowed to fix his hair into several stiff spikes, as the Gatorade star did. Other boys signed their first names in yearbooks as "Shaq," after Shaquille O'Neal, the basketball star currently endorsing products in Channel One ads.

Choosing Clothes and Objects

Karla: The Mountain Dew "Doin' it, Did it" commercials! I mean, we used to recite those all the time. . . . The senior tee-shirt for this year has a type of logo that came from Mountain Dew.

Alan: Yeah, Josten's, the company that we're working with, had to get the rights from Mountain Dew.

RF: Did students here design this tee-shirt?

Karla: No, the company designed it. It says, "Seniors 95" on it, so it's kind of our unofficial senior tee-shirt. It has a graduate's cap and tassel on the front. The back says, "Saw it, heard it, done it." They've got a picture that goes with each saying. "Saw it" has a picture of an eye; "Heard it" has a picture of an ear, and then "Done it" has a picture of a cap and tassel.

Alan: When Josten's was showing us the tee-shirts, mugs, and other stuff, they said they would have to get permission from Mountain Dew, because of copyrights.

RF: Isn't it hard to say that Mountain Dew owns the rights to a phrase like, "Did it"?

Karla: It's kind of like, "Did it, done it, doin' it again." It's not something that we came up with. We got it from watching the Mountain Dew commercials. And the shirt we're talking about is derived from Mountain Dew commercials.

RF: Can you think of other examples when you've repeated something from a commercial?

Alan: Sure, but I can't remember specific commercials.

Karla: You know you'll do anything for a laugh, if it's on a commercial.

Jeannie: Yeah—they tend to stick in your head, especially if you see it everyday.

RF: Any examples?

Alan: "Just do it."

Karla: Then there are church signs that say, "Just pray it," and one that goes, "Unbutton your faith," which is from a Levi's commercial.

Shirts, sweatshirts, beach towels, and hats with ad messages on them are nothing new. I do not know if the students proposed the Mountain Dew replay to the company, or if the company offered it to them. The point is that Mountain Dew commercials were currently very popular in that school and had been for the past two years. Also, students could purchase Mountain Dew from machines inside their school. Every time those shirts are worn, Mountain Dew commercials will echo.

In the short *and* the long run, students' memories of graduation will be entwined with memories of beverage ads. Karla and Alan (who seems impressed with copyrighted ad phrases) place a high premium on what they view as *Mountain Dew*'s creative language—a creativity that they suggest is far from the abilities of mere mortals like themselves.

Completing School Assignments

Last year we acted out commercials in Spanish class. We could either make up our own product and commercial, or just do one that's already on TV. . . . I think that all of us used commercials that we already knew about—things like dog food and Cheerios, and then we videotaped

them, so they'd look even more like real commercials. I even brought
in my own dog to use in my Kibbles N' Bits dog food commercial.

Emily

Emily proudly remembers her Spanish class assignment. I'm sure that
she learned Spanish in an active, purposeful, and engaging way. She may
even have picked up something about the persuasive techniques of TV
advertising. However, when advertising is not the course topic, teachers and
students focus on what *is*—in this case, Spanish. In these situations, neither
teachers nor students have the time or motivation to analyze an ad for its
persuasive techniques. Hence, in addition to what Emily learned about
Spanish, and in addition to what she *may* have learned about advertising
along the way, the assignment remains a replay of a Kibbles N' Bits
commercial—in this case, a literal and physical re-enactment of the entire
commercial for herself, her teacher, and the other students. Emily's video-
taping of her commercial deepened her memory and knowledge of this dog
food brand. (She valued the look of real commercials enough to video-tape
her ad in the first place.) Again, students chose to replay existing, professional commercials over creating a new message of their own.

School assignments occur more commonly as replays in the following
manner: "Last year we made a commercial for Social Studies class, when
we finished the book at the end of the year. We also watched old commercials and talked about the economic stuff." Here again, this *could* have been
an excellent lesson; but it's clear that the study of commercials was treated
by the teacher as a kind of treat or dessert that students were allowed to
consume only *after* they had finished the book. Given the extent, complexity, and seriousness of the issues involved in media manipulation, schools
that trivialize this study as curricular add-ons provide new meaning to the
old saying about straightening deck chairs on the *Titanic*. Although production of media is usually included in definitions of media literacy, professionals must always ask themselves, "How much of this school experience
teaches critical detachment and analysis of media—and how much merely
reinforces students' current attitudes and values toward media?" The issue
is neither simple nor easy.

Entering Contests

Cathy: I bought Gatorade that I saw on a commercial and—
Donna: [Interrupting] Chuckie V. The biker! The swimmer! The runner!
Cathy: You can, like, call him!

Donna: I called the number—1–800–CHUCKIE! I got a recording [disappointed tone]. It was like [imitating recorded voice]: "We will enter you in the sweepstakes, but too many people have called for you to get your free tee-shirt."

Cathy: We thought Chuckie V. was cool. But that was last year when we were in eighth grade. Now he's just a veert. The only good part about that commercial was that if you called the number you might get a free trip to Hawaii, but someone from Indiana won.

Channel One commercials abound with contests and toll-free telephone numbers. Cathy and Donna are talking about the "Chuckathon," a contest promoted by Gatorade's Chuckie V. commercials. The title of this contest blurred the star's name with "marathon" and "triathlon"—words from the Gatorade ads. When talking about this commercial, kids often used the terms interchangeably. Pizza Hut advertised a toll-free number that kids could call to receive directions to the Pizza Hut franchise nearest them. When kids obtain, read, and fill out contest forms; make phone calls; and collaborate with others in such tasks, they are involved in another form of replaying commercial messages and re-presenting products. Such replays induce some students to take action:

Darrin: Sometimes I buy Gatorade 'cause it says you can win something on it.

Lana: Yeah, that's why I buy Dr. Pepper.

Cheering at Sports Events

Replays can even involve hundreds of people engaging in spontaneous, unofficial group cheers at school sports events. During a couple of high school football games with neighboring small towns, bleachers full of people chanted in unison, "Got-to-be, got-to-be—Dom-in-os!" This huge group inserted, at just the right time, the actual commercial's punch line, "Crunchy thin crust!" The fans were accompanied by the school band, playing the commercial's music. The fans did not even insert their own team's name into the jingle; they merely repeated the identical line from the commercial. The very same scenario occurs on a Domino's Pizza commercial that aired heavily at this time, on both Channel One and network television. In the ad, football fans chant the same line to an old rock song by the group "Queen," which goes, "We will, we will—*rock* you." With people chanting, clapping, and stomping to the beat (accompanied by the school band), this spontaneous replay mirrored the actual ad's setting, music, and language. The large number of participants in the rerun were viscerally and intensely engaged with all elements of the original ad's message. Participants faithfully copied the original commercial. This team's pep squad and band does indeed have an *official* cheer modeled after the same Domino's commercial. The message from the bleachers that afternoon was *also* replayed to everyone within earshot, including those people who chose not to participate. The main beneficiary of the spontaneous re-enactment was, of course, Domino's Pizza Corporation (which, in fact, sold pizza at these games).

Competing in Sports

> I like to do the Foot Locker commercial where they show all the sports for the fall, and then they do the cross-country part, where they say, "Oh—just three more states to go!" I'll be out there and say that while I'm running a race!
>
> Paul

Paul and a few other students reported using commercial lines to "psych themselves up" while competing in school sports events. Part of Paul's motivation for replaying this line may have been to entertain (as well as psych up) his fellow runners. Fusing ad messages with the mental focus and physical demands of sports competition creates an unusual form of replay, which here seems related to the growing number of coaches using mental imagery techniques to teach athletic skills (e.g., shooting free-throws in basketball). Again, the main difference is that Foot Locker has a commercial motive.

Watching and Talking about Satirized Ads

Sara: I like the commercial that says, "Obey your thirst." I just like that one. I don't know why.

Tammy: Yes, I know that one, too: there's a group of singers and they're wearing those Madonna cones. They're like body suits, only the chest part has these cones up here [holds hands to chest and others laugh]. And they're bad singers—like weird!

RF: What are they singing?

Sara: "Just one sip."

RF: Where are these people? What's in the background?

Sara: I don't know. It's on a TV show in black and white. A guy is watching TV and he sees these singers. He's telling about how different commercials for different products advertise. He's watching a whole gob of different commercials, and he says, "Sprite doesn't have to do this, because you just have to obey your thirst."

Replays of essential ad messages occur when students watch and talk about media texts that satirize *other* commercials. These occur not just in Channel One ads, as in the prior example, but in other media as well, especially movies (*Wayne's World*) and regular television programs (*Saturday Night Live*). When the network TV program *Saturday Night Live* broadcast a comedy skit about "clear gravy," for Sam it simply elicited memories of real commercials (i.e., replays) he had seen on Channel One for "Crystal Clear Pepsi" (which he purchased from the machine in his school). Consider the following exchange between Belinda and Terry:

Belinda: In the movie *Stay Tuned* they have a commercial for Thigh Master and the Energizer Bunny.

Terry: In *Wayne's World* when they talked about, "Oh, we will not promote certain stuff." Then all of a sudden, they hold up a picture with Garth in it—but then they say, "But we're not like that! We will not promote this—um, the new generation."

The fact that Belinda remembers the satirized products in this film, and that Terry recites relevant dialogue from *Wayne's World*, tell me that these kids considered the ad satires to be important parts of the films. In essence, these are "replays of a replay." Kids never lost sight of the original ad message being parodied. When one girl was trying to describe an ad and she kept referring to the product as "Jukie," her classmate corrected her three times, insisting that she use the precise brand name. Similarly, the conversation quoted at the beginning of this section begins and ends with "Obey your thirst," the ad's slogan that evokes other elements of the message (e.g., music and visuals) that merely reinforce the point. Again, what students are "obeying" most is not their thirst, but the soft drink ad.

Imitating Actions

When I asked Lavanna to describe her favorite shampoo commercial, she said nothing. But then she and her friend swung their hair from side to side. "They've been doing that all morning," observed Resa, seated next to them. When I noted Lavanna tossing her head forward and then to the left, I asked her if that was exactly the way the model did it on the commercial.

"No, it's this way," she replied, sweeping her hair straight back. Although this was not hugely different to me, it was significant to Lavanna. I observed or heard students physically act out specific actions or scenes from their favorite commercials, often as a kind of pantomime:

RF: Do you ever talk to teachers or parents about commercials?

Don: If I do, I act 'em out for my parents. I remember going home when the Little Caesar's one came out and telling my parents about it. I thought that one was pretty amusing.

RF: How do you act out that one?

Serena: [Laughing] He gets out the lipstick!—"Is it on straight?" [exact words from commercial]

Don: I tell 'em what I can remember from it and tell 'em the funny part. When I act it out, I just imagine that I'm using the lipstick.

RF: Do you act out any other commercials?

Don: I describe a lot of 'em to my parents, if I find 'em funny or something. We'll be sitting at the dinner table and this commercial will click in my head, and I'll say, "Oh, you should've seen this commercial; it was really cool," or something like that. I can remember the Emmitt Smith Reebok commercial really well. Running right at you, like he's going to run right over you. Then he says, "Some people work a little harder in the preseason."

Serena: [Interrupting] "All men are created equal." [exact words from commercial]

Don: Yeah—I like that one a lot.

RF: And you physically acted this one out?

Don: Yeah, sure.

Serena: [Laughing] He runs right at his parents!

Serena cannot resist supplying the sound bites that accompany this commercial. When she interjects the ad line, "All men are created equal," it seems elicited by Don's previous replay of the image of Smith running at the camera—or by Smith's line, "Some people work a little harder . . ." or, more likely, by both the verbal and visual prompts. In other words, our conversation about Don's replays elicited *other* replays from Serena. And so it goes.

Creating Art Projects

Replays of commercials even appear in students' art projects, such as painting and sculpture. I discovered this manifestation purely by accident.

One day in a school's hallway, I noticed huge panels (about $4' \times 4'$) above the student lockers—paintings of Pepsi cans, Mountain Dew cans, and other products. My research assistant and I took a closer look at other student artwork on display, including some small sculptures in a glass case. Surprisingly, these too were partly made of advertisements. So we began interviewing the student artists and their teachers. The following subsections discuss three students who created the art projects illustrated in Figures 5.2–5.4. These student artists depended on specific and current Channel One commercials and products, not only to conceptualize their artwork, but to construct it as well. Their personal artwork depends on (and functions as) replays of commercials.

Max and the Pringles Can Man

When an art teacher in a Channel One school received sixty empty Pringles potato chip cans, she asked her students to fashion them into three-dimensional self-portraits. The teacher explained that her students "enjoy this kind of self-portrait more than just doing a drawing or a painting [because] this is more of a personal kind of thing." The teacher instructed her students to "somehow represent their face on the sculpture." The projects had to be "representative of them in some way." Max, a ninth-grader, created a face that looked exactly like the mustachioed cartoon character portrayed on the Pringles can—which did not resemble Max at all. (See Figures 5.1 and 5.2.)

Even with small details, Max copied the can: Max's eyes are green, but he chose to make his sculpture's eyes black (like the eyes on the can). What's more, Max's sculpture holds a tray with an ever-so-tiny can of Pringles chips on it. At least for this assignment, Max's mental image of himself turned out to be a three-dimensional replay of the Pringles product, which advertises on Channel One.

Max's teacher attributed the heavy dose of advertising images in students' art projects to the source material they often work with—old magazines. Although this may be partly true, kids do not have to choose ads to cut out and incorporate into their work; nor must they select *whole* pieces of ads. They tended to select ads for products that *also* aired regularly on their school's Channel One monitors. Max talks about his sculpture:

RF: Tell me about the assignment.

Max: It was supposed to be something about us. We were supposed to put ourselves into it. See, I came from a Butler family—our name used to be Butler, so I just decided to put a butler on there. I put him in tight clothes with old paint spots on him, with an artist's type tray with paint spots and a brush and a Pringles can by his foot.

RF: Why did you place a Pringles can by his foot?

Max: To make him eat Pringles.

RF: So you chose to make him into a butler because your mother's maiden name is Butler—and on the tray, you made him carry a Pringles can. How'd you think of that?

Max: I thought I'd make a little Pringles can so he can take it up to a person who wants Pringles.

Figure 5.1
Pringles Potato Chip Can

Photo by author.

RF: Do you like Pringles?

Max: A little bit.

RF: Have you seen their commercials on Channel One?

Max: Yes, last year.

RF: Can you remember one?

Max: Those commercials say "20 percent less fat" and they wipe their hands off on their shirt after they've touched Pringles and they leave less grease. They also sing outside about Pringles and dance around, but I didn't pay much attention to them.

RF: Can you describe what a Pringles can looks like? [No Pringles cans were in sight at this time.]

Figure 5.2
Max's Sculpture

Photo by Laura Beattie.

Max: The man on it has dark hair, mustache, and a flat nose. The can also has a big ear of corn, very yellow, with the words "corn chips" on it. And from the ear of corn, big 'ol chips are falling out, sort of stacked. The guy on the can looks just like the one I made.

RF: Were you looking at the can while you were creating this?

Max: Yes. I drew it from the can's label and pasted it on.

RF: Since you made this Pringles man holding a tray with a Pringles can on it, do you notice this product more?

Max: Sort of.

Although Max has his own reasons for making a Pringles can replica (e.g., his mother's maiden name), the overriding influence seems to be the Pringles commercials and packaging. Max placed the Pringles can near his sculpture's foot to "make him eat Pringles"; he copied the black bow tie from the actual can, even inscribing the word "Pringles" in red on the bow tie (why not "Butler"?). Max even included the flavor, "Sour Cream 'N Onion," his favorite. Finally, Max describes the can almost as if it were a *moving* image, much like what happens in an actual Pringles commercial. Overall, even though Max's sculpture reflects a little about himself and his family, it remains essentially a replay of a commercial and product.

Suzie and the Sturdy Jack Rabbit

Suzie and Jason completed a different assignment—a large, flat collage, using two media, one of which had to be paint (see Figures 5.3 and 5.4). Students also used old magazines from the library and whatever they brought from home. The project had to be done in a surrealistic style mimicking the art typified by Salvador Dali, best known for his melting watches. Suzie explained her understanding of the assignment: "To make something surreal. Put things together that don't make sense, but have a background. Surrealism has a meaning, but uses different forms of things in the picture that wouldn't ordinarily go there."

Suzie's artwork (Figure 5.3) shows the Energizer Bunny from the battery commercials (which also air on Channel One) heading down a desert highway. An overstuffed chair, with human lips on it, flies above the bunny, while the tip of a Campbell's soup can peeks up from the opposite side of the road. Suzie talks about her artwork and how she got her ideas for it.

RF: Tell me what you did for this surrealism assignment.

Suzie: On TV, they're always trying to destroy the Energizer Bunny, so the couch is flying over him.

RF: How did you select the Energizer Bunny?

Suzie: I started with the desert and the Energizer Bunny was already in it, so I left him in, because you don't usually find bunnies in the desert. And the chair is just kind of hanging over him, flying down in front of him, because they always miss the Energizer Bunny. They never get him.

RF: So this idea came to you from a commercial?

Suzie: Yes. They always try to destroy the bunny.

RF: Who is "they"?

Suzie: Whoever is in the commercial.

RF: How do they try to destroy the bunny?

Suzie: They always try to take his battery. Like Luke Skywalker, on one Energizer Bunny commercial, but his laser goes out because he doesn't have the Energizer battery. They never get the bunny's battery because their battery goes out.

In describing her art, the first thing that Suzie does is to replay this popular commercial: "On TV, they're always trying to destroy the Energizer Bunny." In her collage, Suzie places the bunny in a more central position than anything else. Also, the white highway lines, the chair, and the soup can all point to the rabbit. Most important, Suzie carefully positions the

Figure 5.3
Suzie's Surrealist Collage

Photo by Laura Beattie.

airborne chair so that it would appear to fall and miss the rabbit, allowing him to escape once again—to keep going and going—exactly what the rabbit does in the actual commercials.

In sum, the visual composition of Suzie's artwork, its central action or plot (the chair about to squash the bunny), as well as its meaning (batteries that never die), all focus on directly replaying a popular commercial. Suzie was obviously very engaged by these ads. When she told us about the entire ads she had used to clip out the other images—weeks earlier—she recalled many small details about them. The lips, she reported, were cut from an Annabell Makeup ad in *Seventeen Magazine*, and the model "was applying blue eye shadow, while looking into a mirror." The hands were clipped from a facial cleansing product ad. Suzie described the hands as "cupping the cheeks, ready to wash her face with the cleanser." Suzie explains more about how and why she relied on the Energizer Bunny ad to construct her project:

RF: What do they say on these commercials?

Suzie: They say, "I'm going to get that bunny" and "It keeps going and going and going."

RF: Do you use Energizer batteries?

Suzie: Yes, because I think they last longer than Duracell and all the others.

RF: Why do you like the Energizer Bunny?

Suzie: Because he's cute.

RF: When you know that one of these ads is on TV, do you stop what you're doing and watch it?

Suzie: Yes. I want to see what's after him.

RF: How did you choose this desert background in your piece?

Suzie: I was going through a magazine, looking for a background, and I saw this desert and then I saw the bunny. And they looked like they'd fit in the project. I already had the couch, the earth, the wings, the lips, the sun, and the other things. So I had to come up with an idea to fit them all together.

RF: So, how'd you get the idea?

Suzie: Well, I had the bunny and the couch and the lips and the wings and the earth and the can and the hands, so I thought of the commercials and putting these things on top of the bunny.

RF: What about the soup can?

Suzie: I thought it would look neat coming out of the ground.

RF: What does this piece mean to you? What are you trying to say through it?

Suzie: I suppose nothing.

Suzie later explained that she preferred the Energizer Bunny over an earth she had clipped much earlier and arranged so that the hands held the earth. However, Suzie selected the bunny to take precedence over everything else—including hands holding Mother Earth. Suzie stated, "I had to fit the bunny in with everything else." The Energizer Bunny wins again.

Jason and the Mysterious M&M's

Like Suzie, Jason created a surrealistic collage (Figure 5.4). Jason understood surrealism in this way: "It *could* be real, but the way you put it together is unrealistic." Jason said that his piece was about "the horrors of society."

The following conversation focuses on Jason's reasons for including specific images in his project.

RF: Why is the barrel there—and the apple and snake?

Jason: The guy in the barrel of nuclear waste is trying to get away from society. This hand holding the apple and snake represent people rebelling—like anarchists and Neo-Nazis. And not just those groups, because we're all doing

Figure 5.4
Jason's Surrealist Collage

Photo by Laura Beattie.

something that we shouldn't do. In the Garden of Eden, Adam and Eve were going against God's rules and soon we'll all be punished for that. And President Clinton is there because he's not doing as good as everyone thought he would.

RF: And what about that lemon?

Jason: The lemon is there for the fertilizers and herbicides outlawed in the U.S. but being used in other countries that ship their fruits here, that still have toxic chemicals.

RF: What other things in your piece can you tell me about?

Jason: Well, the trees are there because the rain forest is going quick, which could have some cures for today's diseases and viruses. And if those get wiped out, we'll never know if some of the plants and trees could actually cure some people. Those are being lost quick, by farming in the last three years. I used Kareem Abdul Jabar there because I was going to use Nixon's head, but I lost it, so a friend suggested I use Kareem. . . . The mushroom with the eye was originally a costume, to stand for people hiding. This guy [pointing] represents all the evil people, like Jeffrey Dahmer, who grew up in a strange environment.

RF: What about the lizard—and Kermit the Frog?

Jason: The lizard represents war, because all this stuff is going on, but war is creeping up. Like Bosnia. And eventually, more war is going to break out and we'll be stuck in another world war. And America is like the world's policeman. And Kermit the Frog is for the children's shows, which make, like, if you've got manners, then you'll get everywhere; but it's not like that. Manners help out but that's not what always counts.

RF: What about that big M&M piece of candy?

Jason: I don't remember why I put that in there. I don't know.

Jason provided specific reasons for choosing most of his artwork's images. The thoroughness, number, and detail of his justifications for decisions (regardless of their accuracy or wisdom) set him apart from most other students. These facts, however, flew in the face of his final observation—that he could not remember why he chose something as large and simple as the green M&M, which he had placed in a dominant position. Because M&M candy has long advertised heavily on Channel One, I pursued the commercial with him:

RF: Do you remember the M&M commercial that's playing on Channel One?

Jason: Yes. It's about this guy who has a bowl of M&M's and they go up and ask him if he's going to have any, and he says, "Yeah, well of course." And then he talks about how good the M&M's are.

RF: How many M&M's are talking to him?

Jason: Two.

RF: What color are they?

Jason: Yellow and red.

RF: Do you remember anything about the bowl that the M&M's are in during this commercial?

Jason: It's clear glass or plastic.

In considerable detail, Jason reconstructed the Channel One commercial for M&M's currently playing in his school. Further, the M&M's ad that Jason recounted fits well into his *own* criteria for effective commercials, which he described as ads in which "something that couldn't really happen is made to *look* like it really could—like that Coca-Cola commercial where they have those bears drinking Coke. That's neat the way they did that." Because of Jason's sharp recollection of the M&M's commercial, as well as how snugly it fit his own criteria for effective ads, his artwork seems to have been replaying the ad/product.

Another commercial representation that Jason selected for his project (and displayed prominently) is an AT&T credit card. AT&T was airing commercials on Channel One during the same period. I viewed only one of these ads. One morning, in the midst of setting up microphones, an AT&T ad caught my attention because it contrasted so starkly with the action, loud sounds, music, and fast-paced editing of the other commercials. This one was extremely quiet. It did not try to sell anything or make any claims. Instead, it was a soothing, feel-good, "just-want-to-let-you-know-we're-here-and-we-love-you" type of commercial—something that marketers use to establish trust and brand-name identification. Jason offers a glimpse into his reasoning:

RF: Why is the AT&T card here?

Jason: That has to do with belittling other companies. AT&T tries to get its prices lower than the other companies, saying that you'll get more savings than MCI. But MCI says the same thing about AT&T, but even more.

RF: What does your family use?

Jason: AT&T.

RF: Would *you* switch to MCI?

Jason: Probably not. We're satisfied with AT&T.

RF: What does MCI offer that AT&T doesn't?

Jason: Nothing. They're pretty much the same thing.

The AT&T commercial I watched neither belittled nor mentioned MCI or any other competitors. Even though Jason saw no differences between the companies—and even though he thought they "belittle" each other—he nonetheless preferred AT&T. Why? We can speculate that the reasons are (1) because that's the brand he's heard about at home, and (2) because that's the brand he's heard about at school. His statements suggest at least a more positive feeling toward AT&T.

Jason is a knowledgeable, articulate student who can describe the contours of his own thinking. Commercial messages seem to surface in his artwork and thinking in complex, indirect, even obscure ways. The point is that replays occur in many colors and shades, for all types of kids, for an infinite number of reasons.

Dreaming

Replays of commercials occur in subtle, private ways when kids dream about them. Several students described dreams they had about Channel One's commercials. Because I never dreamed that anyone would dream about commercials, for the first half of this study I did not even ask the question. Out of approximately 100 students, about 8 kids reported having dreamed about commercials. In these dreams, kids made commercials and starred in them. Each dream we investigated featured the products in some important way. The following sections describe a few of the dreams.

"This Could Be You"

Although Amy and Sandra later agreed that the commercial they describe was probably selling potato chips, it was the promise of stardom, framed in a hot new baseball card, that enabled Amy to replay the ad in her dream.

Amy: I had this dream that me, Emmitt Smith, Kirby Puckett, and my boyfriend were all in my boyfriend's van. I don't know why we were there, but I think I'd seen Emmitt Smith on a commercial that day. It was something about—it was either Kirby Puckett or Ken Griffey Jr.—something about their baseball cards—that you got to be on that edition of their baseball card.

RF: Are Puckett and Smith on Channel One commercials?

Amy: Yes.

Sandra: Was it the Reebok commercial with Emmitt Smith?

Drew: Ken Griffey Jr. is on commercials, too.

Amy: I remember always thinking about that on that day. I was telling my dad and boyfriend about it, about how the commercial said if you won something, you were on that baseball card. One of them things.

RF: So you not only watched and remembered the commercial, you talked about it that day with your father?

Amy: Yes. I remember saying, "I can't believe that everything I dreamed was from a commercial."

RF: What was this commercial advertising?

Amy: I don't know. I just remember thinking how much my brother would like it. I think it was a promotion for something else. You had to buy the product and send in your little proof of purchase, and then you got to be in his next baseball card with him.

Sandra: I think I remember the commercial you're talking about, because it shows a baseball card and there's a little head cut out and they say, "This could be you!"

Amy: Yes! "This could be you!" *That* one! It had the baseball card and a little picture of a kid cut out. It's like a little, dotted line, and it said, "This could be you!"

RF: And *that* card was shown on the commercial? It was advertising a contest to be on a baseball card?

Amy and Sandra: Yes.

RF: Let's back up a minute. You were in the van with Smith, Puckett, and your boyfriend—doing what?

Amy: Just kickin' back—scrunched up. Then we were out at the ballpark and I remember they were in this van and pulled up and I was on a motorcycle and then got off and got into the van with them.

This commercial penetrated Amy's consciousness deeply enough for her to replay it in a dream. This commercial acutely affected Amy for several reasons. First, she thought about how much her brother would be interested in the ad's contest. Second, she talked with her father and her boyfriend about the ad. Third, after some prompting, both Amy and Sandra recalled the exact phrase and visual of the baseball card and dotted line. Fourth, in her dream, Amy was on intimate terms with the baseball superstars as they were all "scrunched up" and "kickin' back" together. Also, Amy chose to abandon the glamorous motorcycle in order to hang out with the stars at the ballpark—and, we assume, pose with Puckett for his new card. Amy's dream fulfilled the promise on the commercial: "This could be you!"

"I Want a Big Mac and Large Fries"

DeAnn told us about a dream she had three years ago (Channel One was airing in her school, then, too).

DeAnn: A long time ago, there was a McDonald's commercial about a girl at a piano recital. And she's up there playing—I think the song is "Fleur De Lis"—and while she's playing, she's singing, "I want a Big Mac and large fries." And her little brother is over there eating her fries while she's playing and she gets so mad!

I *loved* that commercial, 'cause I play the piano, too. I went home and dreamed that I was at a piano recital, and I'd just gotten done eating at McDonald's, and my brother was throwing his fries at me, while I was playing the piano! [laughs]. It's an old commercial, but it's my favorite!

RF: You dreamed that you'd just eaten at McDonald's?

DeAnn: Yes, and my brother was throwing fries at me.

RF: Did the dream actually begin at McDonald's—or did you just know that you had been there?

DeAnn: It started out that we were at McDonald's and then we were in a rush to go to my piano recital, and then I was sitting there, with millions and millions of people watching me, and I kept messing up because my brother kept throwing fries at me, and I didn't know where they were from.

RF: Were you singing that same song?

DeAnn: Yes, "Fleur De Lis," I think it is. That commercial wasn't on very long, maybe about a month, and when it went off I was *so* mad, because I *loved* that commercial because I could play that song on the piano and sing along because I loved that commercial!

RF: Was your dream the same as the actual commercial?

DeAnn: Yes. The girl in the commercial is up on a stage, too, in front of people. She was playing when her parents got to the recital late. They had stopped at McDonald's, and her brother had the fries with them and he was eating them and she got mad because she couldn't have any. I don't dream much, anyway, but this one was cool!

DeAnn's dream closely replayed the original commercial, down to the same tune on the piano. Later, DeAnn carefully sorted out a few discrepancies between the real commercial and her dream. However, in both texts, the french fries starred.

"I Was Filming Cindy, as She Looked at the Little Box"

Jodi: Cindy and Katy and I were bored one day—and it was when that Glints commercial came out. And then Katy called me and said, "Did you see that new Glints commercial? I wanna try it!" And I said, "Yeah, let's call Cindy and try it!" So they came over and we all went out and got the three different colors and tried it. And then I dreamed we were all in this commercial about Glints. I don't know why.

RF: What is "Glints"?

Jodi: It's this hair stuff and it says, "Give your color a little kick." We were bored and none of us had to go to work, so we went to different places to get all three colors and did our hair, and then I dreamed we were all in this little commercial. I got in trouble with my mom for using that stuff.

RF: What was the commercial in your dream?

Jodi: The girl is sitting on the couch and she's got this little box of Glints in her hand, and she's got this gorgeous hair!

RF: What were the differences between the commercial in your dream and the real commercial?

Jodi: The people in it.

RF: Were you the girl sitting on the couch?

Jodi: No, Cindy was. I was taping it and Katy was sitting behind me laughing at her.

RF: What were you taping?

Jodi: I was filming Cindy, as she looked at the little box.

RF: Were your friends saying or doing anything—were they repeating the real commercial?

Jodi: It was so long ago [four months] that I can't remember exactly, but they were sitting there and doing what I think was the same commercial.

RF: How much time passed between when you saw the Glints commercial and when you and your friends bought this product?

Jodi: About a half hour.

Five months after this incident, Jodi still recalled the hair product's slogan ("Give your color a little kick"). In her dream, Jodi was in control: she was the person behind the camera. But she did nothing different from the actual commercial and hence seemed firmly wedded to that text. Also, she filmed her friend holding the box and gazing at it. As in the actual ad, all eyes were focused on the product.

Like DeAnn's dream about the McDonald's commercial, Jodi's dream closely paralleled the original Glints ad. The dream and the ad were so much alike that we could even say DeAnn had blurred one type of text for another—in this case, commercials for dreams. Of course, unlike the many instances of blurring, these kids were fully aware of which text was which.

"Jonathan Asked If They Could Do a Movie"

Andrea, a ninth-grader, explained how commercials for a network television program prompted her to dream about a date with its star as well as an appearance on the show.

Andrea: I don't watch the series *Seaquest,* but I always dream about Jonathan Brandis, because he's always in the commercials for *Seaquest*—so I watch more of the commercials for that show than I watch the program itself!

Patsy: It's stud!

RF: Who is Jonathan?

Andrea: He's the young, blond-haired dude. He's cute!

RF: Tell me about the commercials for *Seaquest.*

Andrea: Jonathan is always acting like everything's real scary, but he can take care of it. There's always lots of running around and screaming.

RF: What did the actual commercial consist of?

Andrea: Shots of the next episode coming up. Jonathan is in almost every scene. The commercials will show things like water seeping through the roof, or like, somebody kidnapped the dolphin.

RF: What happened in your dream about this commercial?

Andrea: Jonathan came to my house and asked if they could do a movie because they liked my house and needed it for the next show. And I wouldn't let them because I was afraid my family would be pushed out. And then the people he worked for offered a whole bunch of money. And then I said, "Oh! Give me a date with Jonathan, and I'll let you use my house!" Then they made the show and I got to be in it.

RF: What was the show in your dream about?

Andrea: Like the commercials, it was scary, a thriller, like running around and screaming because somebody was after me. The girl who was supposed to play this part got sick at the last minute and Jonathan said, "Hey, she'll be good for this role," so I got it.

RF: So—what makes you connect this dream with the commercials for *Seaquest*— and not the program itself?

Andrea: Because I saw that commercial and I thought, "Oh, I gotta watch that show 'cause he's on it!" Also because every single commercial is scary, and they're always running around and screaming. And all you remember are the people you saw on it.

RF: Would you say that these *Seaquest* commercials advertise Jonathan just as much as they do the program?

Andrea: Well, for girls my age, it is, because a whole bunch of girls in my class think he's fine, so we watch them.

In Andrea's dream, she became the apple of Johnny's eye as well as the star of an episode—even forsaking her family for a "whole bunch of money" and a date with Jonathan. Other than Andrea functioning as a replacement character, nothing about the commercial fundamentally changed in her dream. By Andrea's own admission (and what I gleaned from our entire conversation), she was far more familiar with the commercials than she was with the actual program. Indeed, her dream of the program sounded very much like a commercial—another replay.

Andrea's dream is like the previous dreams explored in this section: Cinderella stories that fulfill the promise, "This could be you." Again, this illustrates (1) the lack of critical distance and (2) the sheer intimacy that kids feel between themselves and commercials on the small screen. Indeed, in their dreams these kids portray themselves as buddies of superstars such as Kirby Puckett and Jonathan of *Seaquest* fame, hanging out together and dating each other. Of course, we are all much more likely to replay messages to which we feel closely bonded.

When kids dream about commercials and products, they validate ad messages for themselves in intensely private, emotional, powerful ways. In all the dreams explored here, the products from the actual commercials maintain their primary, active role. DeAnn must perform her music and resist eating the delicious McDonald's french fries that are teasingly flung at her; Cindy holds the box of Glints hair coloring while Jodi films her gazing at it; and Jonathan remains the object of desire in filming *Seaquest*. In essence little or nothing changes, because the dreamers do not become the stars, as we might expect. None of the human beings eclipse the products.

Finally, in these dreams of commercials, kids participate in television and movie production. Like many adult Americans, kids prize this *process* for its glamour and excitement. Kids may value the celebrity process of being gazed upon and valued by others more than anything else that is relevant to commercials. You will recall that kids in these dreams (1) controlled the camera and filmed (and appeared in) the hair coloring commercial, (2) were photographed next to Puckett on his baseball card, (3) appeared on stage in what probably was a McDonald's commercial, and (4) starred on a *Seaquest* TV program.

None of the kids, though, starred as themselves, or even as individuals who might deviate from the original commercial's script. Instead, in their dreams the kids exist only as instruments for delivering products and product messages. In these dreams—perhaps the most intense and private of human activities—products star more than the dreamers.

CONCLUSION: ECHO CHAMBERS OF PROFIT

First, student replays directly imitated the original commercials. Students did little or nothing to reshape the messages or to appropriate them in any way. Whenever kids engaged in the replays described throughout this chapter, they somehow decided that certain information, attitudes, and values were important enough to be retrieved from memory. Almost spontaneously they decided how to modify, if at all, the original information. All these replay decisions require that students possess at least some mental groundwork or previous processing of commercials.

Second, replays never "slowed students down" so that they had a chance to reflect on the message, debate it, or think about it critically. It's useful (and ironic) to consider the differences between the replay behaviors enacted by kids and the actual video replays employed by television sports directors (when, for example, a baseball player slides into second base and the umpire makes a close call). A video replay can engage viewers in critical thinking by encouraging them to look closely, sometimes again and again, while talking out their observations with fellow viewers in an informal debate—much like two game announcers might do (by also supplying more information about player statistics, etc.). Even if no other people are around, viewers can mentally debate the situation observed on the video replay.

Actual television replays slow down the action and allow time for viewers to observe closely, and then to analyze the play and call. On the other hand, whenever kids enacted a replay, this did not happen. Never once did any of the replay behaviors described here motivate kids to slow down, reflect on, or debate the message being rerun. On the contrary, the time and energy devoted to the replays by students merely displaced time and energy needed for academic, cultural, or personal learning. The frequency and variety of replays also validates the presence of commercial messages in schools. This validation is reinforced—again and again—with each replay, turning schools into echo chambers of commercial messages, echo chambers of profit.

Third, replays occurred frequently inside and outside school—in the cafeteria, hallways, gym, and parking lot; on the bus and in the classroom and at the football game. The replay behaviors described throughout this chapter illustrate just how easily and frequently the basic messages of television commercials are transformed into different media, while still retaining most of their original plot and meaning.

Replays reinforce commercials and their products. They create an environment in which ad messages—in all their varied forms, shades, sounds, shapes, and echoes—become as common as the air we breathe. Replays constantly replenish and stir the flood of advertising symbols in which students are immersed. It's difficult for kids to resist these glitzy, high-voltage ads. But when the sophisticated messages are replayed—by all kinds of people, in different ways, over and over—then it's nearly impossible for kids to resist buying the things they see.

The activities, information, attitudes, and values that make up replay behavior are linked to products or services being sold for profit—not to kids' *own* personal thoughts, not to family stories, not to academic principles, not to cultural concepts, not to spiritual needs, not even to practical information. In other words, in replays the kids' independent thinking—as well as their personal, familial, and community cultures—dissolve into a life based on appearances.

6

How Do Commercials Affect Kids' Consumer Behavior?

It's Captain Crunch. He started it all. In the first commercial, Captain Crunch has this little pirate, who had this big jar of peanut butter. And then they run into each other, or into someone, or something like that. And they both merged together [laughs], and it became "Peanut Butter Crunch" [laughs]. That's why I bought it.

Pam, ninth-grader

If Channel One commercials affect students' thinking, evaluating, and other behaviors (from choosing clothes to creating art projects to dreaming), then it seems inevitable that they also influence students' consumer behavior.

Throughout this study I was amazed at the number of kids who, like Pam, reported purchasing an item because they had seen it on a specific commercial. The number averaged from one-third to one-half of the kids in each small group. They could describe the exact commercial they saw, why or how they were attracted by the ad and/or product, how much time passed before purchasing the item, and how they bought it.

One school sold the following products advertised on Channel One: Twix, Skittles, M&M's, Pepsi, Crystal Clear Pepsi, Starburst, Snickers, Mountain Dew, Ocean Spray cranberry juice, and several others. One girl related how her first-hour teacher allowed students to take a snack break immediately after the Channel One broadcast. That morning she had bought M&M's immediately after viewing the M&M's commercial.

By the same token, kids who engaged in the replay behaviors described in the previous chapter did not necessarily run right out and buy the product (though many did). Kids who actually bought items they saw advertised on commercials did not necessarily engage in replays beforehand (though many did). It's not that simple. The cumulative effects of different commercials, recommendations from friends, personal needs and tastes, and combinations of these reasons all affect our decision to make a purchase. However, such other reasons were not investigated here. This chapter explores only those kids who connected specific ads to specific purchases. Each of the following vignettes, however, represents an approach to consumer behavior observed in other students. Also, the written survey reflected my findings from the focus groups: 62 percent of students were neutral, agreed with, or strongly agreed with the statement, "My family or I have purchased products advertised on Channel One's commercials."

"THEY FLEW OFF OF THE BUILDING, SO I *HAD* TO HAVE THEM SHOES!"

Pam, quoted at the opening of this chapter, purchased cereal because she was amused when she saw two cartoon characters "merge together." She was not alone in her attraction to camera techniques. Other students reported that they bought an item because of some fancy footwork from behind the commercial's cameras. Long after seeing the ad and purchasing the product, Shannon, a senior, was still amused by it.

RF: Does anyone else remember buying something because they saw it on a commercial?

Shannon: The Fila tennis shoes [laughs]. I bought some Filas because . . . I don't know who makes 'em, but I bought 'em because they was having, [pause] I don't know who this basketball player was, but he was jumping. Anyway, the shoes have like, little flaps on the sides of 'em. They're velcro. They come off, and started flying [giggles]. They flew off of the building, so I *had* to have them shoes! And they was cute! So I bought 'em. I mean, they're very expensive, but they was cute!

RF: What made them cute?

Shannon: Because they was red and black and . . . I don't know . . . they was suede. And they just . . . flew around [giggles]. I liked the little flaps that they had on the side that made the shoe tighter to fit and . . . I don't know! They was just really cute! I mean, I wasn't interested in the basketball player; I wasn't even paying attention to him. I was just looking at the shoes.

RF: Because they were flying?

Shannon: Yea! But they didn't really show him! What made it so bad was . . . I know they paid him a lot of money . . . I mean, they showed him puttin' the shoes on, and he had a basketball in his hand. And that's the last time you seen him in the commercial. The rest was just based on the shoe itself. Flying through New York!

Although Shannon may lack academic skills and background, she seemed to be a bright, independent senior. She lived alone and seemed mature beyond her years. Yet she giggled and laughed every time she mentioned the "flying shoes"—a commercial that fit her criteria for effective ads: "vivid colors, loud music, entertainment, people." Shannon had great fun watching the commercial's flashy camera stunts—a feeling that she transferred to the expensive shoes. Of course, unlike Shannon, most students attracted to glittering color, loud music, quick cuts, and action in commercials do not seem quite sure why or how the ads attract them. When I asked Dana if she had ever seen a commercial that motivated her to buy a product, she said, "Yeah—that Levi's commercial shows people doing flips and flying through the air, which kind of made me want to buy Levi's, but I don't know why."

"I HEARD ALL KINDS OF RAMPAGE ON THE SCREEN, SO I LOOKED UP"

Ryan: I saw that Donkey Kong Sega game on Channel One, and I'm gonna go buy that 'cause it looks cool.

Sonya: It's a cool game. I've got that one.

Ryan: I'm gonna buy it this weekend.

RF: Can you tell me about the commercial for Donkey Kong?

Ryan: It just had Donkey Kong bouncin' all over the screen, hittin' people and stuff. My little brother'll like it. It has good, realistic graphics. I like the graphics. It shows someone playin' the game on the commercial, so it previews the game.

RF: How much does it cost?

Ryan: About 65 or 70 dollars, but my brother will like it and Christmas is coming up.

RF: How will you pay for it?

Ryan: Money I save up from my job.

RF: How many times have you seen this commercial?

Ryan: Once. I think it was last week.

RF: Usually the same commercial runs more than once a week, right?

Ryan: I usually don't pay much attention to Channel One. I think it's kind of dull, myself.

Sonya: I agree.

RF: So, if you don't pay much attention, why did you watch this Donkey Kong commercial and decide to buy it?

Ryan: I heard all kinds of rampage on the screen, so I looked up and saw Donkey Kong—and it was like, "Oh, aw riight!"

RF: Describe the rampage you saw on the screen.

Ryan: I don't know. I think Donkey Kong was like, swingin' through the trees and beatin' people over the head or something.

Shannon and her flying shoes embody the gentler side of TV's commercial sensationalism: camera tricks, music, colors, and action. On the other hand, Ryan represents the harsher side of this coin: he likes the same bells, whistles, and flashes that Shannon does, only he prefers it a little louder, a little faster, and, mainly, more violent. Ryan appeared to be less interested in school and less articulate than the average kid in the schools I visited. He stated he is bored by Channel One, which places him in the minority. (Numerous kids voiced this opinion about Channel One's news offerings, but not with much conviction.) In short, Ryan seemed like one of the hard-to-reach students. Even television didn't seem to be reaching him.

However, three things might "steel" Ryan against the TV's commercial influence (1) he was not interested in school and seemed disconnected from it; (2) he denied watching Channel One *and* its commercials; and (3) he denied buying the video game for himself. But Ryan planned to purchase this game after seeing the commercial only once. Therefore, only one exposure to a commercial can influence a decision to buy.

"THAT'S THE COMMERCIAL I WATCH, 'CAUSE I DRINK IT DAILY"

Brad: I saw Skittles on TV here at school and at home, and I thought one day I'd go try it. Then they started showing Skittles commercials here every day and now it's getting boring. That's why I hardly ever pay any attention to commercials—because they don't mean anything to me.

RF: But you tried Skittles as a result of a commercial?

Brad: Yes

RF: And you mentioned another product earlier that you had tried because of a commercial?

Brad: Yes, Mountain Dew. I drink that every day. That's good, that's necessary! I seen it on TV commercials here, but they don't bother me as much as the Skittles commercials, because they haven't played as long as Skittles has.

RF: Can you describe the Mountain Dew commercial?

Brad: One has three studs, as you could say, who have done everything. They've jumped it, they've sky-dived it, and stuff like that.

RF: What was it about these guys and what they do that made you buy the product?

Brad: Well . . . mainly because it made 'em—I guess you could put it this way— they do all kinds of stunts. And after their stunts are done, they go to the Mountain Dew, and they just make a little rhyme of it.

RF: Can you recall some of their exact words?

Brad: Like, "dude." And I guess you could say it's a fifties and sixties attitude, that kind of slant. Their hair's long. That statue that's part human and part tiger—the Sphinx—yeah, that's it; they jumped off the head of it—all kinds of weird stuff. It's a funky commercial.

RF: What do you mean by "funky"?

Brad: As in "cool"—it gets me to where I like to watch *that* kind of commercial. That's the main commercial that I watch—the Mountain Dew ones, 'cause that's what I drink daily. I have to have at least one Mountain Dew a day.

RF: Why is Mountain Dew so good? Isn't it just like Seven-Up and Sprite?

Brad: No. It's totally different. Seven-Up and Sprite are more for upset stomachs and stuff.

RF: You mean, kind of a wimp's drink?

Brad: [Laughs] Yeah! There ya go! Yeah! But they're okay. I drink them whenever I'm sick, but most of the time I drink Mountain Dew because it's sweet, it tastes good, and it has more caffeine.

Although Brad quickly assures us that commercials "don't mean anything to me," Channel One ads have nonetheless induced him to purchase two products, one of which he buys every day. Enamored of the daredevil, macho antics of the boys on the commercial, Brad recalls some of the stunts ostensibly performed by the actors whom he refers to as "studs." Overall, he views these commercials as "funky," which he defines as "cool." Brad seems to have connected the commercial's portrayal of macho hyperactivity with the fact that Mountain Dew contains more caffeine than other soft drinks. He also recalls a specific word from the ad, "dude," which reflects the ad's overall tone. Further, Brad's *own* language echoes the exact wording of Mountain Dew commercials: "jumped it"; "sky-dived it," and "they go to the Mountain Dew."

The world of this commercial, which Brad seems to have bought into, holds a can of Mountain Dew as the reward awaiting you after performing a series of daredevil stunts. But that's not all. Because of Mountain Dew's caffeine, you are then primed to do it all over again. Now *that's* macho—albeit in a never-ending stream of Mountain Dew. Brad also said that he watched Mountain Dew commercials more than any other, because he drank it every day. He never explained why he *had* to have "at least one Mountain Dew a day." Like other kids I talked with, purchasing a product seen on a commercial focuses Brad's attention *back* to the same commercials. This creates a "loop effect" that takes kids from commercial to product, from product to commercial, and so on. When I talked with one girl who seemed to be revolving in such a loop, it became a "chicken and egg" question:

Lee: I bought the Reebok Cliffhangers because I saw them on a Yabbadabbadoo commercial.

RF: What attracted you to this commercial?

Lee: Because I had the shoes. I had them before I saw the commercial, so that's what drew my attention to the commercial.

RF: Uh . . . how did they show the shoes in this ad?

Lee: When people were doing things, like climbing a mountain or riding a bike, they would show the bottom part of their body and then their feet. You can't tell what kind of commercial it is at first, because you just hear the Flintstones' theme song and see people riding bikes and flying through the air and everything. And at the end, they just show the shoe. At the end they showed "Yabbadabbadoo" on the screen while the commercial was going on.

I never confronted Lee about her contradiction. It happened so quickly that I was too surprised and fascinated to "turn her off" with a correction. Instead I merely asked about details of the shoe commercial, hoping I'd find out what really happened in a more natural way. I did not. However, Lee does reveal a firm knowledge of the ad. My only conclusion here is that just as ads lead kids to products, products lead them back into commercials, where the cycle begins again.

"I ALSO BOUGHT THE MUSIC THAT WAS PLAYED ON THAT COMMERCIAL"

Casey: I already had the system itself, and then I saw some commercials for games on Channel One and they looked pretty neat, so I went out and bought one—an NHL hockey game.

RF: Can I ask how much it cost?

Casey: Sixty-four dollars. I also bought a CD of the music that was played on that same commercial. In the commercial, as this guy played different games on a TV, this music group played the whole time in the background, but it never actually showed them.

RF: How did you know who this band was?

Casey: I'd heard that song once, but in the commercial they played more than I'd heard before, so I knew who it was.

Rock music is so effective that Casey purchased not only the product advertised, but also the ad's musical soundtrack. I talked to only a few students who had sought out the music heard on commercials (but I didn't ask this question, either). Rock music with commercials is now marketed for schools to play in the hallways between classes. Star Broadcasting, which broadcasts rock music and commercials into 400 schools across the country, advertises its services in this way: "By filling a school's hallways, lobby and lunchroom with rock music and commercials, some administrators bring in up to $20,000 a year in extra cash" (Consumer's Union 1995, 25).

"IF I HAD THE MONEY"

Throughout this study, most kids were eager to talk about commercials because (1) they regarded them as entertainment; (2) they enjoyed them; (3) they had extensive experience with commercials and many of the products advertised; and (4) they were in small groups with their friends, away from their teachers and the usual classroom routine. However, a few kids, like Evan, were simply not talkative by nature and had to be drawn out. I'm glad that I did, because Evan revealed several attitudes and behaviors common to many other kids.

RF: Have any of you ever bought something because you saw it on a Channel One commercial?

Evan: [Pointing to his feet] I bought these.

RF: What are they?

Evan: Air Max Two's.

RF: Who makes them?

Evan: Nike.

RF: Why did you buy them?

Evan: Saw 'em on a c'mersh'l.

RF: When did you buy them?

Evan: This year.

RF: Can you tell me about it?

Evan: It had Charles Barkley in it. It shows the air pockets in 'em; that one area has twenty-five pounds of pressure in it and the other has five. It helps in basketball, like when you jump up for a rebound and come down. It doesn't like, shock you, and stuff like that.

RF: And you saw this on a Charles Barkley commercial.

Evan: They've got all kinds of them. They've got Air Max Two's for Michael Jordan for baseball and some for running and some for track and stuff.

RF: Do they have any just for walking?

Evan: Yes.

RF: So you've seen several commercials about these shoes?

Evan: No—these are all in one commercial—and at the very end they've got this guy running and he steps in a puddle and it splashes on the screen, or uh, the camera lens. And it acts like it shorts out the screen and it goes fuzzy—and then it says, "Air Max Two."

RF: What happens after that?

Evan: They just put a big Nike on the screen.

RF: And then what happened?

Evan: They went to another commercial.

Teresa: Then what did you do?

Evan: I wanted to get some.

RF: So why did you decide you wanted some based on this commercial?

Evan: I don't know.

Teresa: "Because Charles Barkley had 'em" [laughs slightly].

Evan: I don't like Charles Barkley.

RF: Then what did you do? Did you tell your parents?

Evan: No, I told my grandma.

RF: What did you say to your grandmother?

Evan: I asked if I could get some for my birthday.

RF: And what did she say?

Evan: She said she'd pay for all but fourteen dollars of it.

Teresa: How much did they cost?

Evan: A hundred and fourteen dollars.

Teresa: Oh my God! [laughter from group]

Evan: They were on *sale*!

RF: I would've sold you a car for 114 bucks.

Evan: I can't drive yet.

RF: Okay.

Evan: And they were on sale, too.

Teresa: I would never buy shoes that cost that much.

Mary: That's how much my shoes cost in one year—*never* would I buy that much.

RF: When you went to the store, did you try on brands other than Nike?

Evan: I just picked 'em out.

RF: Okay, but did you try on *other* brands?

Evan: Uh, no, because I don't like Reebok.

RF: Okay—you've tried those other brands before?

Evan: No.

RF: So—how do you know you don't like Reebok?

Evan: Because, it's kind of like, uh, most of the kids wear Nikes and you should, you wanna wear Nikes.

Teresa: Yeah, lots of kids wear Nikes, so you wear Nikes.

RF: So . . . you don't want to wear a brand that says, "Bob's Running Shoes" on them?

Several Students: [Incredulously] What? No way!

Evan: That's why they can charge so much for them, because most kids like them. I think it's a rip-off.

RF: Why?

Evan: I mean, some people only prefer Reebok. And not all the companies raise prices. Reeboks has these "Insta-Pumps" that use CO-2—and I saw in a magazine that they cost $229.

Teresa: Oh my God!

Evan: It's for track and that's it.

Joel: They've got some Shaq shoes for basketball and they cost about $230.

Teresa: That's stupid!

Evan: And they sell 'em, too.

Joel: Uh huh.

Katy: I wouldn't pay that for shoes! If I pay that much I'd wanna take off in 'em.

Jane: I'd expect them to fly!

Teresa: Yeah, if they cost that much, I'd wanna go somewhere with 'em.

RF: Have you seen any Nike commercials recently?

Evan: Like every other one.

Teresa: Yeah, they play 'em over and over again all the time. We get sick of 'em!
   [Whole group vigorously agrees.]

RF: Well, Evan, how have your shoes worked out?

Evan: Ummm . . .

RF: Were they worth the money, or better than another kind?

Evan: [In a very low voice] Umm . . . I don't know.

RF: Would you buy them again?

Evan: If I had the money.

   Evan expressed two opposing views: on the one hand, he called the price of such shoes a "rip-off." But on the other hand, he said he would buy them again if he had the money. Evan's uncertainty about his purchase was not unusual. I observed this sort of contradiction—you could even call it tension—in many other students. This strain also surfaced when Evan justified his purchase by repeating that the shoes were on sale. Evan and his classmates agreed that "most of the kids" wore Nikes, yet his voice sank to a murmur when he said he wasn't sure if his shoes were worth the price. In this conversation, the other kids had teased him for spending so much money on shoes. Evan felt some peer pressure to buy them, and now he was feeling peer pressure against the decision (which might not have happened if I had not asked questions).

   Also, Evan and his classmates believed these shoes were popular because so many kids wore them, never linking the shoes' popularity to the flood of Nike commercials airing on Channel One and network TV. Further, Evan recalled the Nike commercial in good detail, and he never considered any brand of shoe other than Nike and Reebok—the two that saturate Channel One. Evan's purchase of the high-priced shoes was a family affair—a joint effort between himself and his grandmother, who paid most of the tab. This familial involvement is reminiscent of how kids often buy their first car, indicating the high premium placed upon such items.

   Evan is short for his age. Unfortunately, later in this conversation, three girls in the group teased him about his size (e.g., "You're so little!" and "He gets swallowed up in that jacket!" and "You need to grow up!"). Evan did not respond to these comments. But the girls' taunting—along with his attraction to the Nike ads and his need for peer acceptance—helped me understand why he paid so much for basketball shoes, when he never played basketball.

"'CAUSE EVERYBODY WEARS 'EM AND STUFF"

One morning, my first group consisted of five ninth-grade boys. Because I had talked with Evan during the previous visit (in the prior section), I began by asking, "Are any of you wearing Nike shoes right now?" One by one I went around the circle, listening to each response, double-checking each boy's feet. Four of the boys were wearing Nikes and one was wearing Reeboks. I continued to ask this question throughout the remainder of the study and found the ratio to be typical. For example, in another random group of four girls and one boy, shoe ownership broke down in this way: the first girl owned 4 pairs of Nikes; the second girl 3 pairs of Nikes and 1 pair of Reeboks; the third girl 2 pairs of Nikes and 1 pair of Reeboks; the fourth girl 1 pair of Nikes and 2 pairs of Reeboks; and the lone boy 1 pair of Nikes and 1 pair of Reeboks.

I also found that the reasons the boys in the following conversation reported for buying these shoes were typical. In this session I asked David if he had picked out his Nikes.

David: Yeah.

RF: Why?

David: I like the name. That's it.

RF: Is Michael Jordan's name on your shoes?

David: Yeah [laughs]. His autograph is stitched into the shoe.

RF: Did you try on other brands before you settled on these?

David: Yes.

RF: What were they?

David: Nike and Reebok.

RF: Why do you think you only looked at those two?

David: Because I never buy outside of them.

RF: Why not?

David: I don't know. You see 'em a lot.

RF: How come you didn't try other brands—like Asics or Converse or Schmidt?

David: Schmidt? Never heard of 'em! I got Nikes 'cause I like 'em, and that's what everyone else gets.

RF: Can you remember why and how you bought them?

David: I thought they were cool.

John: Yeah—that's what everyone else gets.

RF: Why?

David: Because they last longer.

John: They're cool.

RF: Did you buy them or someone else?

David: My mom bought 'em, but I picked 'em out.

RF: So she didn't prefer one over another?

David: No.

RF: John, you said Nikes were "cool." What did you mean?

John: 'Cause everybody wears 'em and stuff.

RF: How many students here wear them? Ninety percent?

David: More than that.

RF: Jim, could you tell me about how you bought your shoes?

Jim: We were out shopping for school clothes, and I told my mom the pair of shoes I wanted and she bought them.

RF: So why did you pick out Nikes?

Jim: Because I like Nikes and everybody else wears 'em.

RF: And Rich, how'd you buy yours?

Rich: My mom bought them for me for school. I didn't go with her to pick them out.

RF: Did you tell her what to get?

Rich: She knows I like Nikes 'cause I always tell her about 'em.

RF: And why do you always tell her about 'em?

Rich: Because I like 'em, I guess. Like he said, everybody wears 'em.

RF: Shaq does Reebok commercials—but you don't like those?

Rich: I don't care for Reeboks, but I like those commercials. I like Shaq and basketball commercials—they make cool commercials, like when they're slammin', dunkin', or breakin' the backboard or something like that.

RF: Okay. Now, Larry, how did you buy your shoes?

Larry: I saved money from birthdays, Christmas, and stuff like that.

RF: May I ask how much you spent?

Larry: One hundred dollars—but they were on sale from $130.

RF: Did that wipe you out?

Larry: Kind of—I had twenty bucks left.

David's estimate that more than 90 percent of the kids in his school wear Nike cannot be far off. When I asked him why he didn't consider other brands of shoes, I tossed in the "Schmidt" to see his reaction, which was incredulity, because he'd "never heard of 'em!"

I began this session (and a few others) by focusing on buying the shoes—not on the commercials. Hence, even when commercials were not the focus of conversation, kids' main reasons for choosing Nike and Reebok were that they liked them and that everyone else wore them. I never learned why the kids "liked" these shoes so much. Other than a few mentions of durability, kids seldom offered specific, logical reasons for limiting their purchases to these two brands. And when I pressed them to explain why these shoes were "cool," they usually answered "because everyone else wore them." In short, when we did not focus our discussion on commercials, nobody attributed Nike and Reebok's massive popularity to their extremely heavy advertising on Channel One. Nor did students attribute these shoes' popularity to advertising when the topic of conversation was indeed advertising.

However, sport shoes are advertised heavily on Channel One, and sports heroes such as Michael Jordan appear in commercials not just for Nike but for a gaggle of other products—from Gatorade to Hanes underwear. One girl said, "One time I bought Gatorade 'cause it had Michael Jordan drinking it on the label. I thought that was cool." Kids repeatedly demonstrated their love for celebrity-laden, action-packed, sports-oriented commercials. As Rich stated earlier, "They make cool commercials, like when they're slammin', dunkin', or breakin' the backboard or something like that." A ninth-grader explains how her attraction to such ads influenced her purchase:

Pat: I went out and bought some Reebok shoes when I saw 'em on a commercial. And also with Jordan Nike shoes and other products, like Pert Plus.

RF: Can you describe this Reebok commercial?

Pat: It flipped around to like, Nancy Kerrigan and Jackie Joyner-Kersey and another person. And they were like, doing it, for like, around the world. And there were like, these tennis shoes my sister and I got. And the colors were like, these really, like, a little darker than light blue, but it's white and got this pink . . .

RF: This was on a commercial?

Pat: They were showing it and Jackie Joyner-Kersey was running up a mountain or something and Nancy Kerrigan was skating.

RF: And you liked this commercial?

Pat: Yeah. I just like to see the famous people who go to the Olympics and stuff like that and do those commercials.

In this conversation, Pat later said that her entire family "loves" Reebok and that they "live on the Reebok." Given that Pat had some difficulty describing the commercial, I thought that her phrasing, "we live on the

Reebok," was odd. I then realized that she was merely repeating, verbatim, an advertising slogan. After all, as one print ad states, "That's the way things are worn on the Planet Reebok" (Naparstek 1995).

"I'M NOT GONNA RUN OUT AND BUY IT"

Alan firmly denied buying products he saw advertised on television. However, the more we talked, the less convincing his claim appeared.

Alan: I know of a lot of people who saw the Crystal Pepsi commercial and said, "I'm gonna go out and buy that." But I've never had Crystal Pepsi in my whole life! Also, there's like, name-brand shoes—but those are just advertisements—like Nike or something. But if I see that shown on TV, I'm not gonna run out and buy it.

RF: You've never bought Nike shoes?

Alan: Yeah, I have. In fact, I have some on right now [group laughs]. I like them—they're one of the better quality shoes, I think. . . .

RF: Why did you buy them?

Alan: Well, uh, actually, I didn't buy them. My dad went to Columbia and he came home with a pair of these.

RF: So, why did he choose Nikes?

Alan: I guess he figured out that I like them.

Twenty minutes later in this same conversation—after the topic had changed a few times—I asked the group if they watched commercials differently from the ways they watched regular programs. Alan immediately volunteered, "If it's something I don't really care about, I won't pay attention. I'll just try to do something else until the show comes back on. I mean, I like the Nike commercials that have a man dressed up as a referee and he talks about people and the NFL, like Barry Sanders and, uh, Sharkie, or something like that, who plays for Green Bay."

Neither Alan nor any of the kids in his group noticed his contradiction. People seem to naturally deny watching commercials and admitting to being influenced by them. However, many times during this study the kids' denial or disavowal of commercials apparently functioned as a kind of green light for them to pay attention to and like *other* commercials.

"THEY SAID IT WOULD GIVE YOU BOUNCE AND SHINE AND THINGS, BUT IT DIDN'T— AT LEAST NOT FOR ME"

Hailey: I bought Finesse Shampoo after I saw it on a commercial, because it was supposed to give me all this *bounce*. And I didn't see any bounce! Their hair had bounce and it was shiny and curly and everything. But mine didn't have all that bounce and body. The box said to wash and rinse and condition and then repeat. But it over-conditioned my hair . . . so it like, had nothing.

RF: Why did you choose Finesse?

Hailey: Because on TV they said it would give you bounce and shine and things, but it didn't—at least not for me.

RF: Did you go to the store and buy it yourself, or tell your parents you wanted it, or what?

Hailey: I told my mom to buy it for me, because I didn't have any money. I went to WalMart with my mom that night and pulled it.

RF: Why?

Hailey: Because she wouldn't have remembered it. She would have gotten the wrong kind. They have two different kinds of Finesse: one's pink and one's blue. Pink is for extra body and bounce, and blue is for hard-to-hold and hard-to-style hair. Blue is for dry and bristly hair and pink is supposed to condition it just enough.

RF: Why did you go with your mother to WalMart?

Hailey: Because I like putting stuff into the carts when she's not looking! But I had to get other things, too. But I walked with her down the aisle to make sure she got the right one.

RF: What kind of shampoo did you buy?

Hailey: I got the pink Finesse. But I tried the blue kind, too. I didn't like it.

Hailey left nothing to chance. She wanted this product so badly that she went far out of her way to obtain it. Because she had no money, she accompanied her mother to WalMart, walked down the aisle with her, and "pulled" the correct product. She was even prepared to place the shampoo in the cart when her mother wasn't looking. Hailey's description of how the pink and blue types of shampoo differ echoes several phrases from the commercial and the packaging: "extra body and bounce," "hard-to-hold," "hard-to-style," and "dry and bristly." Also, Hailey's frequent repetition of the word "bounce" indicates that the visual portion of the commercial was extremely effective. And the Finesse commercial does indeed show long, beautiful hair that flows and bounces. The ad uses a mirror image so that

"I THINK THEY'RE SO *CUTE!*"

One ninth-grade girl glared at two of her classmates in astonishment and said, "Man! How do you *know* all of this?" Mickey and Sharon, close friends, had just finished spontaneously reciting a commercial for Kick soft drink. They executed this replay in tandem, word for word. They told me that they had purchased Kick because they liked the ad so much. Sharon then explained that she used to dislike Dr. Pepper, another soft drink. However, Sharon said she had tried the product again after she saw its commercial featuring a "cute guy" who, with a large cast of other people, wore jeans and tee-shirts, danced, and held Dr. Pepper cans. Because she had such a "crush" on this guy, Sharon reported that she "made myself like it." Throughout this conversation, Sharon giggled with embarrassment and enjoyment. She had formed a kind of relationship with the commercial character and communicated her affection through purchasing and "making" herself like the product. I talked with many other students who seemed to form such informal, personal bonds with characters they viewed on commercials. Indeed, many students answered, with no hesitation, that they could be "friends" with the people they watched on commercials.

For instance, one student told me that a boy on a Pepsi commercial "knew a lot" and "had a good outlook on life," even though this boy had spoken only a few lines of dialogue and appeared on-screen for only a few seconds. (The student, of course, had seen this commercial, as well as others in the same series, numerous times.) Becky and Mora seemed to have a similar relationship with animated characters:

Becky: I buy Skittles and M&M's 'cause I like their commercials—the one when they're at camp and two M&M's say, "Rise and shine," and another one is writing home.

Mora: They're earning their M's—their letters.

RF: Had you tried M&M's before this commercial?

Becky: Well, yes, I had. But I didn't eat 'em very often—and now I eat 'em every time I can. I think they're so *cute!*

At this point in the conversation, Becky and Mora giggled, clearly charmed by the little M's. Other students developed a similar emotional fondness for small children and animals in commercials. The kids I talked with who demonstrated such warmth toward a person, character, or animal from a commercial seemed to like commercials in general and to have had considerable experience with ads. Also, both Sharon and Becky were uninterested in the product until they developed some sentiment for the people or characters in the ads.

CONCLUSIONS: PROFIT AND NURTURE

Corporations and advertisers have long known that young adults are a highly desirable group at which to aim commercials. They have several reasons for "targeting" kids, some of which are supported by this study's findings, and some of which are not. These issues will be examined first. The final part of this section explores the human implications of this study, not the business ones.

How Do These Findings Relate to What Advertisers Want?

First, advertisers' most frequently cited reason for targeting kids is that kids spend lots of money—what market researchers refer to as "disposable income" (an interesting phrase, which treats money as trash to get rid of quickly). In 1992, "children ages 4–12 spent about $9 billion, and adolescents ages 12–19 spent $57 billion of their own money and $36 billion of their family's money" (Bowen 1995, 1).

Second, in the advertising business it's common knowledge, that young adults have long been a difficult "target" for advertisers. The findings of this study agree that students in grades 6–12 are indeed hard to reach—outside of school—because they are pursuing the things that most typically interest adolescents: each other, sports, jobs, cars, family, church, clubs, scouts, band, homework. The list is endless.

During my interviews most kids said they watched very little television outside of school. Therefore, in-school commercials have very little competition. Also, at home, kids need only press the remote control's mute button to block commercials—something they cannot do in school. Ironically, the school—traditionally the protected bastion of democracy—has become the most pure or controlled environment for studying the effects of propaganda.

Third, considerable research reveals that brand loyalty is established at an early age. For instance, a University of California study (Newsweek 1994a) reported that right when cigarette advertisers began targeting women (1967–1973), the number of twelve-year-old girls who smoked increased by 112 percent.

Throughout this book, kids have demonstrated their unshakable loyalty over and over to certain brands: from Evan (and many others) and his Nikes, to Pat and her Reeboks, to Shaun and his Fruitopia, to Brad and his Mountain Dew. Some marketers believe that the earlier in life a child becomes familiar with a brand name, the better. Nipple-topped baby bottles are now adorned with Pepsi logos (Harper's Magazine 1994).

Fourth, conventional wisdom holds that young adults have short attention spans and therefore cannot hold still during commercials. "Short attention spans" afflict all of us at one time or another, and it's highly debatable whether this represents a "constant" condition in most kids. Actually, Channel One commercials help *create* and feed short attention spans, providing abundant jolts-per-minute (JPMs). This approach, borrowed from Music Television (MTV), seems to have contributed to students' shrinking and embedding of TV texts (see Chapter 3). The approach works. You need only recall Shannon's attraction to her flying shoes, Ryan's looking up to see what all the "rampage on the screen" was about, Dale's delight at the deranged referee, or Rich's fondness for ads in which basketball players are "slammin', dunkin', or breakin' the backboard."

Fifth, conventional wisdom states that young adults buy products on impulse—that they randomly erupt into a purchasing frenzy and fork over cash for no reasons whatsoever. I found little of this behavior. But I did find many students buying items because they had first seen them on commercials—hundreds of times, which they and others had replayed and replayed. This constitutes anything but impulsive behavior.

How Do These Findings Relate to What Parents and Teachers Want?

Using persuasive techniques and audience demographics, advertisers target teens because of their vast "disposable incomes," their brand loyalty, their short attention spans, their habits of impulse-buying. Advertisers want to get people to buy things and increase their profits. This book explores the human costs that a captive audience of kids must pay when they are systematically conditioned to be consumers. The conditioning is intense, and it occurs over a long period of time. When kids buy things they see on commercials, they pay with more than just dollars and cents. They pay with their minds, hearts, bodies, and spirits. They pay in time, learning, language, thinking, creating, and maturing. These are the processes and values that shrivel in ad-saturated environments.

We see this psychic waste in boys like Evan, who, when stimulated by commercials and lack of peer acceptance, try to achieve popularity, athletic ability, and even sheer, physical height by spending $114 on basketball shoes. In girls like Hailey, who blame themselves and not the product when it doesn't deliver bouncy, shiny hair. In girls like Suzie, whose art project imitates both the form and content of an Energizer Bunny commercial. In girls like DeAnn, who dreams she stars in a McDonald's commercial in which the product still takes top billing. And in kids like Mindy and many others, who cannot tell the difference between public service announcements and Pepsi commercials.

The diminishing of such values and processes are not always easy to see, but that doesn't mean they are unimportant or, worse, nonexistent. In this book I try to make them visible, through the words of kids, with the hope of reclaiming them.

7

Conclusions and Recommendations

If we redefine young learners as "young spenders," are the young really to be blamed by acting like mindless consumers?

Benjamin Barber, 1993

This chapter summarizes the major conclusions of the study— "answers" to the questions posed throughout previous chapters. These conclusions lead to another conclusion, namely, that the context of commercial television in the schools can most accurately be described as propaganda. Finally, recommendations are made for reclaiming the harvested minds described throughout the book.

KIDS AND COMMERCIALS: CONCLUSIONS

Commercials Play Significant Roles in Kids' Lives

Although it is seldom acknowledged, commercials are a vital part of kids' lives. They provide a means for kids to socially interact with others. Indeed, kids talk about commercials with friends and peers, at home and at school— in the hallways, during sports and band practice, on the bus, and in the cafeteria. To a lesser extent kids talk with teachers, siblings, and parents about commercials. Throughout my conversations, the *way* that kids talked about commercials surprised me: they talked—often all at once—with animation, energy, and interest. Consequently, early on, I had to switch from using one microphone to using five separate ones.

Kids enjoyed commercials as entertainment and as a way to relieve stress. When we talked about or viewed commercials, they smiled and spontaneously talked about who and what they knew about the ads, as if they were seeing old friends. Jenny "watched and waited for months" for a commercial that she had seen at school to appear on TV at home, so she could update her younger brother and parents. This made her feel proud and cutting-edge.

Many kids approached commercials as if they were "regular" programs. "Good commercials" were seen as including elements of regular programming such as humor, action, and interesting plots. Overall, kids talked more frequently and intensely about commercials than about news or feature programs. Among a few sets of "best friends," interactions about commercials seemed to be a basic part of the relationship, almost a means of bonding. Together the kids repeated memorized lines, acted them out, and shared laughter. After school, when one kid was watching a commercial that she thought her friend "had to see," she called her on the phone so they could talk while the commercial aired. Using commercials as a means to bond with others was the most positive effect observed in this study. On the down side, such interaction usually involves many "replays" of ads, which further reinforce ad messages and corporate ideologies.

Kids Accept, Value, and Embrace TV Commercials

In spite of how often and how long some ads aired (a year or longer), kids remained amazingly tolerant of commercials. They rarely questioned the dominant presence of ads in their lives. Today's kids have grown up with commercials—and many are further bombarded with them when Channel One broadcasts become part of the school day. Heavy exposure to anything, over time, can lead to greater tolerance. But what surprised me was the kids' positive, often warm regard for ads. Many kids *embraced* commercials. They stated this warm regard directly (e.g., "Pepsi is trying to help us") as well as indirectly. Anna, a senior, said she could "relate to" and "communicate with" characters in one commercial. Kids didn't look for ulterior motives in commercials; they assumed that commercials were altruistic. For instance, Debbie, a ninth-grader, thought that professional athletes such as Michael Jordan paid the Nike Corporation for the opportunity to make commercials.

To some extent, these warm feelings are generated by simple familiarity with ads—their sheer volume and high repetition. But there are other reasons. One is that kids often did not recognize a "creator" or "maker" of commercials. I found very little evidence that kids were conscious of someone "outside" the commercial's internal story constructing the message. Instead, they often identified the person or persons who appeared on screen the most often (and for the longest period) as constructing the message. Moreover, in commercials, the people on-screen the most are likable folks. Hence, kids' limited awareness that someone else constructs ad messages helps them to accept commercials as direct, unmediated representations of reality.

Another reason that kids felt so warmly about commercials was due to "blurring." Kids sometimes confused a commercial with a news program or with a feature program. However, they frequently blurred regular commercials (e.g., those for Pepsi) with public service announcements (PSAs) that warned against drunken driving and taking illegal drugs. This blurring occurs primarily when ads are constructed to resemble the documentary style of PSAs. Even one of my student teachers (a mature, bright, knowledgeable former editor) could not tell the difference between the two types of messages. It's little wonder that kids, too, were confused. As a result, the kids thought *both* messages were concerned with "doing good," and not with selling. Overall, most kids did not regard TV commercials as fundamentally different from other forms of television, such as news and features. Rather, the most common distinction kids made between the types was each segment's length of time.

Kids Know TV Commercials, Products, and Packaging

Kids know commercial texts extraordinarily well: they quickly identify and recall commercials, products, and packaging. They often know the relationships between and among manufacturers, commercials, products, and packaging. Most kids consistently linked actors and actions to products and commercials. During every small-group session, if one kid said, for example, "Gatorade," then others would jump in with, "Chuckie V.!" (who currently starred in Gatorade commercials). If someone said that a commercial was about "cinnamon gum and people kissing," then others would immediately counter with, "Big Red!" (the product's name). One magically elicited the other.

Kids also know the structure of commercials. Even after seeing an ad for the first time, they could label and describe its main parts and correctly sequence its events. They could do the same for a series of ads featuring the same character, such as those for the Energizer Bunny. A few kids could even explain the intricate web of relationships among commercials and products: which company owned which items, and which products spawned which competitors.

Further, kids could recall a commercial's most minute details. This impressive recall proved true for ads that kids had seen only once, as well as for those that had stopped airing over a year ago. Kids recalled many dialogue lines (sometimes the entire script) as well as visual details about setting, such as the color and pattern of the seats on the inside of an airplane. They remembered phone numbers presented within commercials, as well as how the product was packaged. For instance, Paul explains some differences in Gatorade products and packaging:

They've also got two-gallon jugs and those are different from the bottles. Because on the two-gallon jugs, some of the print is a different color. On the bottles, it can be fruit punch flavor, but the label will be red and the print white. But on the two-gallon jug, sometimes the letters might correspond to the flavor, and the background will be a different color.

Clearly, kids viewed a product's packaging as an integral part of the product itself.

Kids Simultaneously Believe and Disbelieve in Commercials

Kids insisted that they "don't pay any attention to commercials." However, even those who said, "I hate commercials!" could reel off extensive details about ads and could describe how certain commercials influenced their purchasing decisions. Such schizophrenic behavior, demonstrated in a variety of situations throughout this study, has long been observed by teachers and researchers. On the one hand, kids emphatically denied watching commercials and claimed to shut them out altogether. On the other hand, these same students were very willing to believe whole-hog in other commercials.

To some extent this is a natural response, because the postmodern literature and media that these kids and their parents grew up with contain contradictions and oppositions. However, throughout this study I often got the impression that taking one position allowed or enabled the other to exist—as if the kids needed some kind of equilibrium.

Kids Use Restrictive, Nonreflective Strategies to Think about Commercials

In addition to thinking strategies (e.g., seeing no authorship, blurring), kids used numerous other strategies to think about and respond to TV commercials: shrinking and embedding, generalizing, confusing, substituting, contradicting, and fluctuating. Most of these approaches inhibited kids from further reflecting about commercials. For example, numerous students considered flashes of Pepsi cans (each lasting for one or two seconds) as "commercials," because they were surrounded by what *appeared* to be noncommercial text (the ad was crafted to resemble a PSA). When advertisers "embed" one ad within another, kids often regard the text surrounding the flashed ad as *noncommercial* in purpose. And if kids don't define the ad as a commercial in the first place, they cannot possibly analyze it as persuasion. Other strategies included substituting, without realizing it, a desirable value or action for an advertised product's name. One student used the phrase "washing your face" synonymously with the product name, "Clearasil," an acne medication he'd just viewed on a commercial.

Probably the most common and restrictive thinking strategies observed in kids were associating and mirroring. Both approaches inhibit kids from further thinking about commercials, albeit in different ways. Associating occurs when one symbol quickly and easily triggers memories of *other* symbols or products. When viewers associate (when they relate one ad to others; one ad to other TV programs or print texts; one ad to life experiences), they make linkages on the basis of simple and random similarities. For example, a student might say, "That shampoo commercial reminds me of the new girl at our school." In this study, students engaged in associational thinking more often than any other type. But once associations were made, kids instantly abandoned them, cutting off any opportunity for further reflection or critical evaluation.

Although making comparisons is crucial to most types of thinking, unless they are pursued they become relatively dead-end observations. In this study, kids assumed that making the link was sufficient in and of itself. They saw no reason to take the comparison further or in a different direction—that is, to elaborate on it or to critically test or examine it.

There are lots of reasons for students stopping dead in their tracks after observing a connection. First, they don't regard media as a legitimate subject of study. It's seldom modeled to them, and they seldom read or write about it. Second, students are merely behaving like the medium itself, which never explains why, for example, a news story about a liquor store robbery occurs right after a story about this year's cucumber crop.

Mirroring, one of the most common behaviors observed, occurs when the main (and often only) way of interacting with commercials involves stating the message again, usually word-for-word. Kids commonly parroted the exact lines from ads, complete with vocal intonations; sang jingles from ads (e.g., the "Be Like Mike" song); and physically demonstrated how a commercial's character behaved. This mirroring was evidenced not only in kids' language but in other ways as well, such as replays.

Kids Use Restrictive, Nonreflective Strategies to Evaluate Commercials

About six of the two hundred kids in this study clearly demonstrated reflective, analytical thinking about commercials by (1) mentally "distancing" themselves from commercials; (2) selecting appropriate elements to respond to in the first place, before closely inspecting and comparing them; (3) connecting observations, ideas, and concepts from commercials to other texts, events, and experiences; (4) hypothesizing why the makers of ads made certain decisions; and (5) describing an ad's overall tone and pointing to specific evidence from the text to support their assertion.

However, by far the majority of kids did *not* evaluate commercials effectively. These kids were thinking, of course, but in ways that quickly dead-ended. For example, if kids believed that their only options for buying athletic shoes were Nike and Reebok (which was usually the case), then they shut themselves off from considering other options. Such polarized thinking forced kids to arrive at conclusions quickly, which restricted further and deeper analysis.

Following are a few ways in which the large majority of students did not effectively analyze commercials: (1) they overvalued the audio or visual portions of a message, thereby ignoring one or the other; (2) they seemed to place most value on whatever ads were "newest" and forgot about earlier ones, which prevented them from making connections to previous ads and experiences; (3) they drew "boxed-in" conclusions about commercials and products, which usually led them down a one-way street where they had no choices except to buy and use the product advertised. As noted earlier, kids could not gain critical distance from ads because they seldom considered commercials to be *constructions* of reality, that is, texts crafted by someone "outside" the ad. Of course kids knew on one level that commercials were not "reality." But when I asked them who was "telling this story," they almost never identified a director, manufacturer, marketing agency, or other type of author or "maker." Instead, they identified an ad's point of view as being expressed by whomever appeared on camera for the longest period of time—usually a likable character. And, of course, when kids liked the person they liked the commercial, and hence felt warmly toward the ad and product.

The most powerful element in commercials that prohibited kids from gaining critical distance was the presence of a specific value—a value that certain kids were evidently ready and eager to embrace. One group of ninth-graders seemed mesmerized by the "New Age" nature, unity, and "whole earth" values expressed in ads for Fruitopia fruit drink. This product's commercials and packaging featured exotic drum beats and "kaleidoscoping colors." Another group (mostly males) identified with the macho, daredevil action values expressed in Mountain Dew soft drink ads. Such kids deeply identified with commercials, products, and packaging that expressed particular values—so much that they seemed blind to everything else.

Kids Replay Commercials in Many Ways

Although kids in Channel One schools are exposed to about seven hundred commercials per year (Honig 1993), they receive *additional* sales messages through "replay behaviors." Replays occur whenever kids mimic, act out, sing, dream about, or otherwise repeat and reconstruct the original commercials. The content and delivery of the original ads are repeated with little change from the original messages broadcast on television.

Research into how we respond to literature and film indicates that readers bring experience to the reading of any text, what Gombrich calls "the beholder's share" (1982). In short, the act of reading involves (1) the text itself, (2) the situation and environment in which the reading occurs, and (3) the reader herself—her experiences, background knowledge, mental schema, attitudes, and values. These three elements interact, or "transact," with each other in order for readers to construct meaning (Rosenblatt 1978).

However, the majority of kids in this study showed little or no evidence of constructing their own meaning from commercial texts. Instead, they mirrored and replayed commercials in a variety of ways. Replays involve language, music, images, objects, and nonverbal communication to elicit the original ad's images, music, and language. Each replay elicits different degrees of the original, or "stimulus," ad.

The replays observed in this study consisted of three related types—verbal, physical, and mental—that involved single kids, small groups, and even large crowds. *Verbal replays* employ language (e.g., when kids sing or say the ad line, "Crave the wave!"). *Physical replays* occur when kids act out or imitate actions or scenes from a commercial (e.g., when a student shakes her hair like the model in the Finesse Shampoo commercial, or when kids act out a "Deranged Referee" commercial while playing football at home). Physical replays also include actual objects created by kids—paintings, sculpture, or other objects that re-present products or images from commercials. Finally, *mental replays* occur when kids think or dream about an ad they have seen, or dream about making a commercial for a product with which they are familiar. One girl, for example, dreamed about a McDonald's commercial that was similar in all respects to the original ad, except that she and her family appeared in it.

Kids Buy the Products They See in Commercials and Replays

Kids in this study purchased the items they saw advertised on Channel One commercials (and often replayed by kids themselves). My questions focused only on one type of consumer behavior: kids who connected specific, recent purchases to having seen the products advertised on a specific commercial. Approximately 40–50 percent of the kids in each small group reported having bought a specific product because of a specific commercial. The time lapse between seeing the commercial and buying the item ranged from one hour to several days. Typically, these kids could (1) describe the ad in question; (2) explain why or how they were attracted by the ad and/or the product; (3) specify how much time elapsed before purchasing the item; and (4) describe details about *how* they purchased it (e.g., one student said, "I put the package into my dad's shopping cart, without telling him").

I began this project assuming that kids spend money for as many reasons as adults do (e.g., the cumulative effects of advertising, recommendations, needs, timing, personal taste). However, I soon found so many kids who could "trace" single purchases to individual ads that I focused on this behavior only. Realizing the limitations of self-reporting, I closely questioned students and examined their responses for believability: Did their stories about seeing a commercial and then buying the product sound convincing in their details and presentation? In most cases, they did indeed. Also, what I found in the focus groups was reiterated in kids' responses to the written survey, completed weeks before the group sessions took place.

In addition, the kids who reported buying specific products as a result of their attraction to certain commercials did not differ from the kids who did *not* report this link: both types of kids evaluated commercials in restrictive and nonreflective ways (e.g., becoming enchanted with camera techniques). Shannon, a senior, reportedly bought a pair of athletic shoes after seeing them fly in a commercial: "They flew off of the building, so I *had* to have them shoes!" After buying an advertised product, students reported watching the product's commercials with much more interest. The commercials and the products generated a circular process: (1) kids would buy the product as a result of the ad's influence, and then (2) watch the ads for that product (and others) more frequently and intensely, and then (3) buy again and repeat the process.

Kids purchased products for many of the same reasons that the rest of us do, but for them it's especially important to be like their peers. Over and over, kids reported that they bought something because "you see it a lot" or because "everybody else does it." They also said it was "cool." But when pressed, they usually defined "cool" as "everybody does it." The commercial may also have convinced students that the product could relieve some "deficit" or fear. For example, Evan, a ninth-grader, explained how the Nike commercial for Air Max Two's had convinced him to purchase them. Evan had other, more personal reasons for buying these shoes; but the effective Nike ad served as a concrete motivator. During one small-group session, Evan was teased by the girls for being short. Although Evan was not on the basketball team and didn't play outside of school, he nonetheless saved up a large amount of money (with the help of his grandmother) to purchase the expensive basketball shoes and a warm-up jacket. Stimulated by a lack of peer acceptance—and by commercials—Evan tried to gain popularity and stature through his purchase.

KIDS AND PROPAGANDA: CONCLUSIONS

> I mean, they give us free TV's and the whole thing's being paid for by the sponsor.
>
> Linda, ninth-grader

Discussing her school's contract with Channel One, Linda expresses a common attitude about the commercials kids watch at school—that benevolent "sponsors" provide something for nothing. Most of the previous conclusions demonstrate that students are oblivious to the fact that vendors and advertisers benefit far more than anyone else. In fact, throughout this study, students continually expressed the opposite viewpoint—that vendors and advertisers were dedicated to "doing good." Therefore, the most accurate label we can apply to the Channel One school environment is *propaganda*, plain and simple.

Given the high-budget, high-tech, persuasive nature of Channel One TV ads and the closed environment in which they are transmitted, students behaved and responded exactly as expected. All societies propagandize. All people engage in persuasive communication. But there are significant differences between, say, convincing one's boss to change computer systems and being exposed to authentic propaganda. The sinister and negative connotations of the term "propaganda" do not apply to everyday instances of persuasion. Rather, propaganda applies to persuasive communication *contexts* wherein many messages, repeated over time and in different ways, shape the attitudinal *climate* or *environment* (see, for example, Ellul 1965 and Sproule 1994). Certain conditions must be in effect before an authentic propaganda environment can exist. Channel One meets these conditions.

Propaganda Occurs in Ideologically Neutral Places

America's most politically and ideologically neutral institution has always been the public schools. Indeed, the public schools were intended to be a bastion of freedom, an open marketplace of ideas. But this is not the case under Channel One, because any private corporation (or other institution) invariably communicates its own ideological and political agenda through its selection, arrangement, presentation, and style of symbols used. When commercials are shown during the school day, the students are led to believe that their school endorses those products, which bestows on them a special credibility and value. Although the most obvious examples of ideological bias occur within Channel One's ads, such persuasion also occurs in news and feature programming. According to *U.S. News and World Report*, in a profile of a Los Angeles juvenile jail: "an inmate's description of his joy at stabbing people trails off into an ether of soft music and slow-motion images—with no comment by Channel One" (Toch 1992, 88). This portrayal may have been intended for dramatic effect, but it also persuasively communicates certain values and ideologies.

Propaganda Involves Many Captive People Exploited by Few

Propagandized people rarely have control over anything. Others make decisions for them. This criterion easily fits commercial television in the schools. School district administrators and boards of education decide to pipe in the Channel One broadcast. A single, private corporation controls the messages beamed daily to millions of kids. By signing a contract, the schools are obligated to show the broadcasts on 92 percent of all school days (Celano and Neuman 1995, 444). Kids control nothing: they cannot adjust the volume or mute the commercials. They must quietly watch and listen. Because the law requires attendance, students must watch an endless stream of TV commercials (an estimated 700, plus replays). Advertisers have the advantage of precisely defining their audience and studying its demographics, attitudes, and values so they can more effectively persuade kids to buy their products. In fact, Channel One's founder, Christopher Whittle, began his career in 1969 by publishing "Knoxville in a Nutshell," a specialty magazine targeting college freshmen. By 1988, Whittle was crafting "Special Reports" for patients waiting in doctors' offices. The *New York Times* called Whittle the "impresario of captive-audience marketing" (Kozol 1992, 274).

Propaganda Involves an Orchestrated Delivery of Multiple Messages Communicated in Many Ways

When propagandists orchestrate multiple messages and communicate them in many ways, they promote special interests over the public good. Channel One orchestrates sales messages—for products as well as for itself—in a variety of media, genres, formats, and styles. Throughout its history, Channel One has infused its programming and publications with sales messages. This communication qualifies as the "massive and self-serving outpouring of symbols" that is characteristic of real propaganda (Sproule 1994, 3). It's important to remember two characteristics of such messages. First, they manipulate people without appearing to do so. Second, the infusion of symbols creates an *information environment* by establishing a *climate of acceptance*. Success is nearly guaranteed for the propagandist if the information environment is constructed within an actual or host environment that appears neutral and safe (as public schools have been perceived). Channel One creates a complete information environment by constructing messages crafted in many different ways—all necessary to change an individual's attitudes, values, and behaviors. A few examples follow.

First, Channel One commercials range widely in content and style—from soothing, "feel good" commercials for AT&T, to the splashy graphics and loud music of Sega video game ads. The variety and volume of ads help one commercial to sell another. For instance, values and messages identified with basketball star Michael Jordan are easily transferred to other basketball stars who are pitching different products. Values and messages are easily trans-ferred to other products when the same person, such as Jordan, sells several different products, from Nike shoes to Gatorade to Hanes underwear.

Second, covert manipulation occurs when Channel One "blurs" genres: commercials are made to look like public service announcements, features, and even news stories (e.g., Pepsi's "It's Like This" commercials). By the same token, news and feature stories have been blurred with commercials. One genre leads into and overlaps with others. For example, after a news story about teens who were on death row for committing murder, the "Pop Quiz" segment—which is part of the news program—asked viewers, "How old were teens, on average, when executed?" The announcer's voice was festive and upbeat, sounding like a game show host. Next, viewers saw a small group of students from a "Channel One school" as they went into an intense huddle. When this group guessed correctly, they exploded in euphoric screams, smiles, and high-fives all around. Under the guise of "news," viewers received an image of "clubbiness" for Channel One schools—in effect, an ad for Channel One. Even worse, the news story about teens on death row was trivialized. Blurring has also been used as a lead-in to ads. Halleck (1992) reports on a Channel One feature called "Now That's Art!" that ended with a segment on the French painter Georges Seurat and his painting technique of pointillism. Seurat's pointillism was immediately followed by a Sprint commercial showing how the network's "points of light" had helped to end Soviet communism.

Third, Channel One employs a variety of technical and structural propa-ganda devices. Because many of these are examined in the context of students' responses to commercials in Chapters 2–6 (e.g., association, testimonial), I will mention only a few more here. For example, viewers cannot switch channels. They cannot control the audio volume of Channel One broadcasts, or the frequency of ads, or the "muting" of ads (commer-cials are often broadcast in higher decibels of sound). Also, Channel One relies heavily on repetition. Not only are students exposed to hundreds of commercials each year, but popular ones are repeated for weeks and months. In a publication for school administrators, Channel One even argues that schools should show the same broadcast several times each day:

Most of the schools implementing this plan say the multiple viewing opportunities allow them to make sure that every student sees Channel One at least once, even those (students) who have unusual schedules or who have been absent for part of the day. In addition, multiple showings give students the opportunity to see the program more than once, if they wish. (Whittle Educational Network 1989)

Of course, such viewing "opportunities" would exponentially increase the number of commercials and student replays.

Fourth, timing of communication is important to propaganda. In most schools, Channel One is broadcast first thing in the morning. A signal operated in Los Angeles is beamed to schools in every state and turns on a signal that activates the program and commercials. Kids are most open to receiving communication during morning hours. Also, scheduling morning broadcasts allows kids to talk about and replay commercials for the remainder of the day.

Fifth, Channel One has manipulated program structure for maximum effect. Its news program was designed so that the thirty-second commercials had more impact on viewers' attention than the news segment. The news was divided into three parts (separated by commercials), which contained approximately three, one-minute news stories. Added to this were other features, each lasting ten to twenty seconds (called "Fast Fact," "Pop Quiz," and "Flashback"). Added to these were previews and promos for upcoming news and features. In short, within this fragmentation the commercials became the most dominant, complete, and coherent text (Rudinow 1990, 71).

Sixth, like the program itself, Channel One's printed materials sell products and programs. *Teachers' Guide: Whittle Educational Network News & Programming* leads readers to expect an emphasis on curriculum and teaching strategies; this is not the case. Appearing at the beginning of the October 1993 issue is "SAT Flash." What *appears* to be a feature or news article explains a new video course sold by Channel One (Whittle Educational Network 1993, 4). Also, on the facing page of this article is the first page of a two-page, tear-out type ad promoting a contest sponsored by Mountain Dew soft drink, in which students are asked to send in videos for possible use in future Mountain Dew commercials called "Doing the Move" (5). Students are asked to make videos of coaches, players, and fans doing "spectacular or funny things." The ad's fine print states that Pepsi-Cola Company has complete control over using the videos in all future commercials. Following this ad is a "news article" (7) that urges teachers: "Have your students check out *Teen* magazine (October, page 102) for a look at what it's like to be a part of *Channel One's* Student Produced Week." The next article explains how students can enter three different contests, each of which solicits student-made videos for use on Channel One.

Seventh, even though it is titled a "report," Channel One's publication for school principals and superintendents, "Scheduling Channel One in Your School" (Whittle Educational Network 1989), is actually a thick advertisement. It is full of splashy graphics promoting not only itself but also books penned by supporters of Channel One, such as Lamar Alexander, E. D. Hirsch, and Chester Finn. After making dire comparisons of America with Japan and Europe, this document concludes with an ominous, McCarthyesque warning: "Continued failure to address America's educational problem could ultimately weaken the country's security."

While establishing Channel One in the New York state schools in 1989, Whittle's oral language and newspaper ads employed a variety of propaganda devices. Whittle often relied on zingers and sound bites, including the line, "Kids believe that 'Chernobyl' is really Cher's full name." One Whittle ad cited a student who thought that Jesse Jackson was a baseball player and that silicon chips were snack food (Barry 1994, 106). Other propaganda techniques included "denial of controversy, subtle criticism of existing institutions, and projections of a rhetorical vision" (Adams 1991). Whittle intensified his own "good" and others' "bad"—while simultaneously downplaying his own bad and others' good. For example, in "An Open Letter to Members of the New York State Board of Regents," Whittle associated himself with "pioneering educators." In the same ad, members of the Board of Regents were labeled as "these critics" who oppose "alternative solutions" (Carmody 1989, A28). Also during this period, Whittle's media blitz employed another propaganda technique, "projection of a rhetorical vision" (Adams 1991, 6). Whittle created a "fictional, faceless scapegoat" because, to create a positive image as an educational revolutionary, he could not directly attack the institution he was trying to convert (6).

Propaganda Reduces or Removes Competing Sources of Information

Because propagandists do not want competing or conflicting messages to counteract their own line ("noise"), they try to control intrusions. Control over students' options is achieved in the following ways: (1) students are required by law to attend school and hence to view commercials; (2) students cannot turn off the TV, switch channels, or turn down or mute the broadcast; (3) students cannot leave or disrupt the room in which the broadcast occurs; (4) satellites receiving from Channel One can only pick up Channel One signals; (5) students cannot control how or when the program is broadcast (although they *can* record the broadcast to watch again!); and (6) students are not required to view any other competing or alternative broadcasts. Moreover, Whittle commissioned a three-year research project on the effectiveness of Channel One—but he banned researchers from evaluating the effects of advertising on students; and published summaries of the research reports employ boxed information and other techniques to intensify Channel One's successes. Barry (1994) offers a detailed critique of research investigations into Channel One, especially those paid for by Whittle.

RECOMMENDATIONS

The following recommendations are offered in the spirit of recovering the harvested minds described in this book. If nothing else, I hope these suggestions encourage debate, which in turn will generate better solutions.

Ban Electronic and Print Advertising in Schools

We could reduce the exploitation of students who must watch commercials in their classrooms by providing each school with the same budget that is required to create each commercial shown. Each school would also receive payment for each time a commercial is repeated. This would total billions of dollars in revenue for each school. Only then would the playing field level out. I mean no exaggeration here; I only point out the obvious truth about disproportionate resources.

Johnston (1995) suggests that the federal government purchase Channel One and integrate it into the Public Broadcasting System (PBS). Although this is not a bad suggestion, I doubt it would ever happen: it's too expensive (Whittle sold Channel One to K-III Communications in 1994 for $300 million). Anyway, it would *add* to the woes that PBS has continually experienced with obtaining federal funding. If Channel One were added to PBS and its programs were broadcast to schools *without* commercial advertising, then it would be the first thing cut from the budget.

A more reasonable alternative would be to enact federal legislation banning all forms of electronic and print advertising in schools. Such laws would protect American education as a democratic enterprise—as a bias-fee marketplace of *ideas*, not as a locus of high-budget, slick, packaged ideologies wrapped in the guise of entertaining TV ads and programs. Enacting legislation to ban advertising from schools would enable them to once again be places where all ideas are debated and tested and explored in an unfettered context. Free and democratic education is the bedrock of a democratic society. It is crucial that we define public school students as citizens, not as consumers.

Tax Advertising and Subsidize Students

Although an outright ban on all forms of advertising in schools is the best option, Edwin Baker proposes the second-best alternative: a hefty tax on advertising. These taxes should be returned to education and to the press, for purposes of subsidizing readers—to educate and retrain teachers and readers; to purchase technology and training for schools; to establish graduate degree programs in media literacy; and so forth. The program's rationale and constitutionality are detailed in Baker's *Advertising and a Democratic Press* (1994).

Baker argues that advertisers and corporations control information more than anyone else; that "advertisers, not governments, are the primary censors of media content in the United States today" (99). He proposes to change the law because, he warns, "individual efforts . . . cannot succeed adequately given the existing economic and legal framework" (136). I would add that taxes on advertising should be based on the length and frequency of commercials. The longer the commercial and the greater the frequency of its broadcasts, the higher the tax. Such taxes should escalate, so that the most popular commercials pay the highest amount. Baker proposes other laws, such as requiring that films created by corporations and used in TV newscasts carry identifying source information throughout their running time. He also recommends restrictions on *when* commercials can appear, limiting them to scheduled blocks of time—not as interruptions in programs.

Establish the American Mediacy Project

Even if advertising were to disappear from classrooms, helping people to become more media-literate should remain a top priority. After all, in America media literacy lags behind many other countries such as Australia, Canada, England, Finland, France, Norway, Scotland, Sweden, and Switzerland. In these countries, media education is a well-established part of regional and national curricula (Bazalgette et al. 1992). To some extent, in developing a media literacy movement America should "go its own way" (hence the word "American" instead of "National" in the title of this section). Other countries' models and approaches may not work as effectively here. American media—and especially Americans' relationships to media—may significantly differ from that of other countries. For the past several years, America has been deepening its "love-hate" relationship with media. Throughout history, Americans (including this writer) have loved media; but it's increasingly easy to blame it for all our social ills. The greatest challenge to media literacy professionals may be perspective—the maintenance of balance in our perceptions of media and media issues.

America needs a major public movement to counteract its pervasive, powerful corporate media. First, how best to sustain and develop the media literacy movement needs to be a more central and lively debate than it has been in the past. Without doubt, America's media literacy movement must continue growing from the roots upward. The past twenty years have seen an encouraging growth of media literacy organizations (e.g., the Assembly on Media Arts of the National Council of Teachers of English; the Cultural Environment Movement; the National Telemedia Council; Strategies for Media Literacy; and Citizens for Media Literacy). The sprouting of these small organizations suggests that it's time to consolidate efforts. The best way to do so is to form an American Mediacy Project, which would emulate the National Writing Project's model of "teachers teaching teachers"—during intensive summer institutes and in-service work throughout the school year. In such workshops, teachers of *all* disciplines and grade levels (K–college) come together for intensive collaboration and sharing of their most successful teaching strategies.

In an American Mediacy Project, media literacy teachers would not only read and interpret media but compose it as well. Also, just as writing teachers now work with authors and other literacy professionals, media literacy teachers would work with local TV news directors, writers, editors, and producers. Teachers would return, reinvigorated, to their own classrooms and "spread the word" by teaching their colleagues.

An American Mediacy Project would articulate a much-needed central mission or mandate, as well as provide a central database and network. This would lend a more coherent image to media literacy than it currently enjoys. Of course, enhanced faculty development and community education in media literacy would require support—through research into what kids do and do not know about media, as well as how best to address their needs. Increased research and faculty development would also require more graduate programs in media literacy.

Use Media to Teach Print and Use Print to Teach Media

An important focus of faculty development must be on the use of media literacy to teach print literacy and vice-versa. Electronic media texts are often hypnotic—seamless messages of music and pictures and words that militate against "viewing" them actively and analytically. Therefore, teachers, parents, and researchers must better understand the relationships between verbal and visual literacy. If we continue to isolate verbal from visual literacy (along with other "literacies," such as musical), then we doom any efforts at developing authentic literacy for the coming century.

The widespread assumption that print literacy and media literacy reside at opposite ends of the spectrum prevents us from using one to teach the other. As a result, we fail to learn both print and media literacy as effectively and efficiently as if they had both been valued and taught equally. Currently, if media literacy *is* taught, it is a "tag-on" to print literacy. With students raised on intense exposure to media, secondary and college teachers must face the fact that we should teach media literacy first—and then transfer those skills to writing and reading print (e.g., see Costanzo 1992; Hovanec and Freund 1994). One symbol system helps us understand and communicate in another. We need to become literate in "synthesized" messages—communication that speaks to all senses and employs all symbol systems simultaneously.

Treat Media Issues as Public Health Issues

Other issues affect the harvesting of minds examined in this book. Kids' health, for example: their mental, social, physical, and emotional health. Several health issues are summarized in recommendations made by the American Academy of Pediatrics (Schwed 1995), which estimates that kids are exposed to 20,000 TV commercials each year. The Academy believes that this volume of commercials—especially the 2,000 beer and wine ads that kids watch each year—explains kids' increased liquor consumption. Also, the Academy expresses concern about kids' watching so many commercials for sugary, salty, and fatty foods. Pediatricians feel that these correlate with an increase in children's obesity.

Consequently, the Academy recommends (1) banning all beer and wine ads; (2) banning all "passive advertising [of tobacco and alcohol] in sponsored sports events (i.e., banners, logos, etc.)"; (3) reducing by half the number of commercials aired during kids' programming; (4) collecting a 10 percent surcharge on advertisers targeting adolescents and children; and (5) classifying all toy-based programs as infomercials, so that the Federal Communciations Commission can more effectively regulate them (Schwed 1995, 20). These recommendations, which do not address other health issues such as media violence, come from America's pediatricians. They have nothing to gain, except better health for kids; their recommendations are reasonable and responsible. Media should be considered a health factor that affects our mental, social, physical, and emotional well-being.

Return Media to Its Rightful Owners

A final recommendation is to oppose media monopolies. Small groups now own most television and radio stations, newspapers, magazines, and many other channels of public discourse. Too few control public discourse. The public media in America is an extremely private enterprise. The fault must be shared by everyone. Average people have long felt powerless about matters of public discourse—that we cannot infringe on free speech, that we lack the business expertise or technological know-how. But public matters belong to the public. Because the public is most affected by media—including the kids interviewed for this study—the public should exert the most control.

Not so long ago, Native Americans could not fathom the white settlers' concept of "ownership of land." After all, something so huge and undifferentiated as nature *had* to belong to everyone. It could not possibly be parceled out and sold in small units. Today, we are in much the same state with information. The territory where we live and travel is made more of symbols than of earth. These symbols should belong to everyone.

8

What Can We Do Right Now?

A democratic civilization will save itself only if it makes the language of the image into a stimulus for critical reflection, not an invitation to hypnosis.

Umberto Eco, 1976

AN INVITATION TO CRITICAL REFLECTION

After briefly reviewing the richness and complexity of media messages, this chapter summarizes crucial issues in media literacy and provides specific ideas, approaches, and strategies for teaching people how to become more media-literate. "Media literacy" (or "mediacy") means thinking critically about media—connecting media content to daily life, interpreting and analyzing the economic and political ideologies in media, and even constructing media messages. The following strategies are intended for parents, students, teachers, administrators, community leaders, and others who want to help people use both print and media to understand (and better control) the world around them.

WHY MEDIA IS SO RICH—AND SO COMPLEX

Waiting in a long line in a hotel lobby, I mindlessly leafed through a chamber of commerce brochure—one that "sells" the host city on glossy paper, with bright photos of toothy couples smiling over plates of red lobster. One whole-page ad depicted a woman's bare legs standing spread-eagled over the city's night skyline. The tallest building (and the antenna that sits atop it) point to (and nearly touch) her crotch. The large caption promises, "We'll show you Atlanta's most interesting parts" ("Atlanta Quick City Guide" 1990). This ad doesn't directly lie, but few readers would doubt what it *suggests* or implies visually. The visual subtext is the primary message. Distinguishing the crude promise of "interesting parts" from the human being whose legs fill the page is a tough assignment in separating the dancer from the dance. But so is separating *that* image from an enculturated attitude toward women. And so is separating these things from our own perceptions and lives. In short, media texts *look* simple. They are not.

Because the words, pictures, motions, and sounds of media are meticulously synthesized to elicit emotions, they are hard to deny or ignore. When a commercial about old friends hearing each other's voices on the phone brings a lump to our throat, who can deny that what we are *feeling* isn't there? Moreover, because our perception naturally gravitates toward wholeness and not fragments, we accept most pictures as complete truths. Even if we *were* skeptical of images, technology presents them in a flash and robs us of needed time for reflection.

We also have trouble negating images because our culture equates seeing with believing. How many kids could gaze at a photo of their favorite rock star and say that what they experience is something *other than* the surface image? Moreover, images cannot be refuted because they are so close to reality. We've all experienced a time when something that really happened blurred with the fluid, imagistic ways in which we represent reality to ourselves.

Even isolated images can wield unlimited power: a single photograph (Jackie Kennedy waving from an open car) or other image (McDonald's golden arch) can become a national icon that communicates volumes to millions. However, when technology fuses layer upon layer of sounds, motions, images, smells, and words—and then multiplies them with each other when creating new messages—the intricacy of the message itself (and the difficulty of understanding it completely) increases exponentially. In the face of these overwhelming odds, media literacy must be our first priority.

The following teaching strategies address many of the problems examined throughout this book, ranging from gender stereotyping, to making either/or decisions. Although these approaches focus on television commercials, they are easily adaptable for other kinds of media and print texts.

They are also adaptable to most age groups and levels, at home or in school.

CREATE AD-FREE ZONES—EVERYWHERE

If you wait in line at a theme park, TV monitors placed about every twenty-five feet blare advertisements. If you stand at a urinal in a men's restroom, you must often stare at an ad. When you sit at a restaurant table, a clutter of ads—some enshrined in free-standing, clear plastic holders— greet you. At some gas stations, while you pump gas into your car a TV monitor "entertains" you with commercials. And Channel One TV commercials are not the only advertising in schools: "We found that thousands of corporations were targeting school children or their teachers with marketing activities ranging from teaching videos, guidebooks, and posters to contests, product giveaways, and coupons" (Consumer's Union 1995).

Another study on advertising in schools concluded that many corporations communicate their special interests to schoolchildren through "free" posters, magazines, book covers, folders, and other items they refer to as "learning tools." Examples include a school magazine from McDonald's that extols the environmental virtues of its styrofoam packaging and a booklet from Procter and Gamble called "Changing" that provides instructions on how girls should use its brand of sanitary napkin, "Always" (Washington Office of the State Superintendent 1991, 1–2). Such corporate propagandizing can be even less subtle. Bowen (1995) summarizes the following examples from the Consumer's Union 1995 report "Captive Kids":

- Clear-cut logging is good for the environment, reads a Proctor & Gamble curriculum called "Decision Earth," which claims the controversial practice "mimics nature's way of getting rid of trees."

- Eating meat makes people taller, says the "Digging for Data" study guide from the National Live Stock and Meat Board. The guide asks students to use data to learn why early American settlers were short in stature.

- "Power from Coal," an environmental study program from the American Coal Foundation, dismisses the greenhouse effect and claims that "the earth could benefit rather than be harmed from increased carbon dioxide." (Bowen 1995, 1)

Ad-free zones should be designated in schools, parks, cities, hospitals, restaurants, theaters, office buildings, neighborhoods, historical districts, and most other spaces where Americans spend time. America was founded because colonists wanted freedom from intrusions into their lives. Today, ads influence more people and actions than anything Thomas Paine and

Thomas Jefferson could have imagined. Insisting on and working toward ad-free zones is a simple yet comprehensive way to raise awareness levels of commercial intrusions. Following are some more specific suggestions for creating ad-free zones.

Protest Imposed Advertising

When paying for specific services or products (e.g., meals, movies), complain to managers if you are forced to view advertising or to complete marketing surveys. Couch your objection in the fact that you paid to watch a movie—not to be held captive for commercials running before the film (not to mention "product placement" ads within the film). Ask that the theater print a warning line that informs customers that commercials are part of the price for the feature film. Also, when eating out, point to the ads on the table and ask if your companions have finished reading them. Then gather them up and place them on another table or someplace out of sight. If someone asks why you did this, explain your right to ad-free zones.

Count Ads with Kids

Like the old game of counting license plates, ask kids to count ads. Kids will often not identify as ads those commercial symbols (a golden arch) and photos or illustrations that are devoid of print (Joe Camel or Colonel Sanders). Explain to them how such symbols are actually ads. Especially try to do this in ad-saturated environments and places that are relatively free of ads. Also ask kids to name places that are completely devoid of ads. Help them understand that advertising is *not* part of the natural or functional landscape.

Encourage Before and After Photographs of Ad-Free Zones

To visually document the impact of advertising in specific places, sponsor "Before and After the Ad-Free Zone" creative photography contests. Students and other amateur photographers can use computer manipulations and air brushes to remove advertising from photos of ad-soaked areas. Each entry should consist of two photos: one depicting the place "Before the Ad-Free Zone" and another portraying the same area "After the Ad-Free Zone." Such photos can be powerfully persuasive. Winning entries should be widely distributed.

Communicate the Benefits of Ad-Free Zones

School administrators, teachers, and religious leaders can help in creating and promoting ad-free zones. Ask local teachers, writers, and church leaders to speak to classes and other groups about what they see as the effects of commercialism. Consider an essay contest: "Which rooms in Smithton Middle School should be officially designated as ad-free zones, and why?" Letters to the local newspaper editor could persuade readers which areas of a city or town should be officially designated as ad-free zones. Sponsor and create illustrated brochures or tour guides to ad-free and minimal-ad zones within a given building, neighborhood, city, or county.

UNPACK INITIAL RESPONSES TO MEDIA

Before doing anything else, viewers should voice their initial, emotional responses to media texts. Commercials and other media are often crafted to elicit emotional responses. When this happens, a door opens into viewers' attitudes and values. Ads that link a product to an emotion and value create dramatic, internalized experiences that help viewers remember and purchase the product. Because emotions play such a large role when we process media, it's important to "place them on the table" so viewers can begin to gain critical distance from them. If this doesn't happen early on, then such emotions distract and preoccupy viewers, preventing them from analyzing.

This advice does *not* mean that emotions are isolated from critical analysis. On the contrary, emotional responses are an integral part of effective critical analysis. But there are two main reasons for "giving voice" to emotions immediately. First, it legitimizes emotions as a necessary part of understanding, because viewers need the raw data of personal responses to examine the text that helped create them. Second, giving voice to initial and personal responses helps us as viewers to objectify them—to examine them *apart* from ourselves. If this doesn't happen they remain hidden inside, where they are more prone to confusion, misinterpretation, or wholehearted belief. Following are some methods for beginning with emotional responses. Whenever possible, record these responses on tape or in writing.

Talk Back to Your TV

Some teachers ask students to read something and stop periodically to think aloud—to state the images, ideas, and questions the story, up to that point, is creating for them: what Peter Elbow calls "movies of the mind" (1973). The same approach works for media. If the text is taped, stopping the action is no problem. Students can try such think-alouds on their own, then with a partner. The sessions can be audio- or videotaped and then replayed for an entire group, for discussion. Also, they can be transcribed or summarized in writing, or they can be completed as freewriting.

Freewrite

Freewriting involves writing—lickety-split—whatever comes to mind about a commercial or program. It can be done by hand or on computer. Also called "rush writing," "intensive practice writing," and "nonstop writing," freewriting should occur within a specified time, usually three to ten minutes; viewers write nonstop about what they are thinking and feeling as the program or commercial unfolds. Such writing can also occur after a text is viewed once, twice, or even three times. Kids are not allowed to stop writing. If they get stuck, they should repeat the phrase "I am stuck" until they get moving again. Freewriting is excellent for capturing initial, personal responses to media because it prohibits writers from censoring themselves, from editing out feelings and emotions that are powerfully stirred by images and music.

Describe Emotional Flows

Using tapes of commercials or programs, viewers write down every change they detect in their overall attitude or emotional response to a text (or character within a text). Viewers then describe these changes in writing or create a simple graph, noting *when* each change occurred. An option is to list all mental images that are *suggested* by the text. Here, viewers should be careful not to merely describe what's already there. For example, when Mary views a commercial for cereal that features a talking chimp, she might record that one scene suggested within her an image of her cousin. Next, viewers can work with a partner or small group in (1) comparing descriptions of emotions or images suggested; (2) comparing shifts in emotions or differences in the types of images suggested; and (3) drawing conclusions.

Talk to Kids about Attention-Grabbing Ads

Even five-year-old children are capable of talking with adults about advertising. If your children want toys they have seen on TV commercials, ask them why. Have them tell you what they expect the toy to do or what it will be like. Clarify their comments by adding (and making sure that they agree with) phrases such as, "That's what the commercials *say* it will do." Then ask them, "Do you think it really will?"

If they answer yes, explore with them how they know and why. If they say "no," ask them how they can find out. Avoid purchasing items for them, sight unseen. Go to the toy store with them and examine the product together: look at the packaging and read the fine print to them. Ask the child if he or she thinks the toy will deliver what the commercials promised. If you buy the item, be sure to follow up on what the ad promised and what the product actually delivered. Such discussions with children should never be lectures. Commands only make them want the toy even more. Instead, make kids feel responsibility for paying attention to both the ad and the product, matching one against the other. Kids will benefit if they *participate* in making purchasing decisions.

VIEW MEDIA WITHIN ACTIVE, SMALL GROUPS

Media, especially television, is at its hypnotic best when we watch it alone—as an escape from work, children, and other daily stresses; when we want to avoid thinking. In fact, this may be television's greatest benefit. However, the pattern becomes so rewarding, so easy to slip into, that it's hard to avoid. The escapist mind-set can become such a familiar, automatic response that it spills over into those times when we *do* want to think about what we're watching. But when the phone stops ringing, the lights dim, and the blue tube flickers, it's all too easy to turn off our minds and drift into the TV-scape. This is harder to do when we share the living room with a few other people who will speak openly about what they're watching. A small media group can work much like informal book groups, where friends select books to read, and then get together to discuss them.

When watching television becomes a social process, we will hear perspectives that differ from our own. When we watch it with others, we can ask, "Is this real? Does it match my own experience and what I know to be true about the world?" In small groups, response, interpretation, and criticism of television become a collaborative and enjoyable process.

Another good reason for watching television in groups is that it enables us to (in context) apply our *own* language to a visual medium. Listening to what Dan Rather has to say about the debate we just watched doesn't count; what's most important for critical thinking is that the words about the pictures come from us. And our words will be affirmed, challenged, or qualified by our cohorts sitting next to us. Making media viewing an *active and social process* helps us receive feedback about our ideas. This, in turn, allows us to adjust and refine them, making us more perceptive, accurate critics. We will be less prone to manipulation; less likely to become confused over a program or ad; less likely to blur one element with another; less likely to draw boxed-in conclusions or to make either/or decisions; and more likely to become aware of authorship. Following are additional ideas for home or school viewing of media within small groups.

Predict Outcomes

One group member records a commercial, program, or film and previews it to determine a few crucial stopping points—places to ask the others to guess what will happen next, and why. Next, the group finishes watching and discusses each prediction in light of the actual text. People making accurate predictions of the program—or those who supplied scenarios that the group thinks are even *better* than the actual one—should win something (including the opportunity to organize the next "Prediction Party").

Predicting outcomes during crucial points in a media text is a quick and enjoyable way to expose for examination many important elements of media—from plot and character development, to values and point of view. Also, discussions arising from predictions often elicit *natural* inquiry and questioning. Such within-context inquiry is crucial for critical viewing.

Ask Each Person to Focus on a Different Element

Each person selects (or is assigned) a single different element to observe. Notepad in hand, one person might view an evening news program for the uses of its soundtrack, such as voice-over narration, music, and other background sounds. Another person might observe transitions, noting what kinds of breaks occur between one news story and another, or between a news story and a commercial. Someone else might watch for the sequencing of stories. Finally, people report to the group about what they observed, and the group responds.

Analyze Television Flow

Closely examine a television segment that contains the following parts: (1) the final commercial from a familiar program; (2) the opening or closing minutes of the program; (3) the ending credits of the program; (4) the station breaks and commercials that follow the program; (5) the opening of the next program, which group members should also be familiar with; and (6) the first commercial of the second program. Try to make connections between these segments. How does one lead to another? How are they related?

Evaluate Questions and Answers

After viewing a commercial or program, each person writes his or her most pressing question on an index card and passes it to another person, who answers or responds to the question. Next, cards are passed again, with the third person reflecting on the strengths and weaknesses of both the question and its answer. Cards can be passed again, read aloud, and discussed.

SLOW DOWN MEDIA AND YOUR RESPONSES TO IT

Fifteen- and thirty-second commercials are the fastest media texts around. Much of the thinking and behavior described in this book can be thought of as nearly instantaneous responses to the speediest texts within a quicksilver medium. Many of the thinking and evaluating strategies that kids used are partially due to the sheer speed and volume of TV commercials. When kids mirrored and replayed ads, they were probably demonstrating the quickest way to respond because they involve no active or personal intervention. (They do, however, demand deep absorption within the commercial.) Making an association may be the second-fastest way of responding to ads. Fast stimuli force fast responses.

Many types of thinking and behavior about commercials seemed influenced by the sheer volume and speed of commercials: shrinking and embedding, seeing no authorship, confusing, substituting, contradicting, fluctuating, and blurring. The speed of television also forces kids to make quick judgments, resulting in more polarized or either/or decisions. So, too, speed and volume help kids most value that which is newest.

Rapid responses usually lack critical distance, specificity, and sharp distinctions. A more critical reflection is only possible with more time. Hence, texts and viewers need to be s-l-o-w-e-d d-o-w-n. That's why simple acts of cataloging and/or objectively describing commercials are powerful tools for analysis. Following are suggestions for slowing down the narrative flow of media texts, which will also slow down our responses to them.

Rerun Media

Rerun portions of a taped media text two or three times to stimulate analysis and discussion of a difficult or intriguing segment. This approach imitates a type of critical thinking. As a model, use a clip from televised sports—such as when an umpire makes a close call and announcers talk it over as they review the action several times, often supplying additional relevant information (e.g., a player's record for safely stolen bases). Viewers are often thinking right along with the program and sometimes even "talk back" to the screen—which is what students must do.

Stop Media

Stopping tapes of media texts allows time to think: viewers can gather their thoughts, reflect, question, pose problems, and predict outcomes. They should also brainstorm answers and solutions. Select key stopping places: parts in the story just before the plot turns, a character realizes something, or the tempo or mood shifts. The ensuing discussion can be oral or written. Some kids should be assigned note-takers (if not everyone). After the viewing is complete, return to these notes so that kids compare their *own* thinking with the text's creators.

Delete or Substitute Media's Visual/Audio Elements

Using tapes of films and TV programs, ask students to *listen* to a television program while not viewing the screen. Next, ask them to write or discuss what they think is displayed on the screen during certain parts. Do the opposite by watching the screen with the sound muted. Here, ask students to write out a summary of the plot, complete with names, conflicts, and resolutions. Also, supply radically different music to familiar film scenes that effectively use music to create moods (e.g., the runners on the beach in *Chariots of Fire*). Explore with kids how the meaning of the scene also changes. Processing media texts in these ways helps kids to better understand how audio and visual tracks affect each other.

View Media from Other Countries

Show students TV commercials and programs from France, Spain, Japan, and other non-English-speaking countries. Stop the tape or delete parts from the ads that identify the products being advertised. Ask students to figure out what the products are. Ask them what types of cues or evidence they used to arrive at their answers. This approach forces viewers to figure out meaning from context, because they have to pay greater attention to characters' vocal inflection and tone, facial and other nonverbal gestures, music, setting, and so on.

Respond to Written Transcripts of Media

Using written transcripts of media texts before and after viewing a program provides a vivid and concrete way for viewers to become aware of what elements are changed by each medium—what, for example, television intensifies, distorts, and downplays; and what print intensifies, distorts, and downplays.

Log Viewing Habits and Media Content

Ask kids to record what they have watched and how often. Include specific examples of behaviors or other phenomena, such as how many acts of physical and psychological violence occur within a thirty-minute episode. Keeping a record of media-viewing habits and counting various actions help viewers to *delay* judgments about programs, because they must take time to collect a different type of data before they arrive at conclusions. Gathering observations and drawing conclusions shows students that television study is just as legitimate as other disciplines.

Write Objective Descriptions of Media

Ask students to write descriptions of ads without evaluating or judging them. They should reconstruct, as objectively as possible, exactly what happened on the screen (e.g., how an investigator writes up a science experiment). For an example, see "Cavorting on the Farm," in Chapter 1. Such writing slows down viewers, and forces them to re-see the commercial, using a different symbol system (print language), a different purpose, and a much slower time frame. These differences are crucial for counteracting quick responses to fast texts. After looking for patterns within their viewing habits and written descriptions, return to the students' original responses and compare them.

Write Detailed Analyses of Media

Students should regularly deconstruct single-media texts, each time focusing on a different medium or genre. Teachers can adapt tools from literary analysis, including binary oppositions, which ask viewers to reconceptualize a text in terms of its reversals. For example, if viewers perceive Scarlet O'Hara in *Gone with the Wind* to be cold and selfish, who within the narrative might we call her *opposite*? And if Rhett Butler is dashing and daring, is there a counterbalance to him? In dissecting texts, students can also employ tools such as Rank's Intensify/Downplay schema (1976) and traditional propaganda techniques (Fleming 1995). Writing detailed analyses of media texts should never be a one-shot deal. Students must systematically compose such analyses in order to begin developing critical thinking about media.

EXPLORE VALUES COMMUNICATED IN MEDIA

It's nearly impossible for any text—print or media—*not* to communicate values. In TV news programs, talk shows, and documentaries, values are often communicated explicitly and directly: the senator being interviewed can wave her arms and state emphatically into the camera, "Abortion is every woman's right—I value freedom of choice!" There's no mistake about what she prizes. However, values can also be communicated indirectly in this type of text. The same senator can appear on television and make no direct statements at all, as the camera follows her on a tour of an abortion clinic. Here, the text *suggests* that the senator values freedom of choice.

Fictional media texts usually communicate values implicitly and indirectly (although they sometimes state them directly). For instance, mainstream Hollywood cinema and dramatic television shows usually only hint at values through the type of people the main characters turn out to be. By story's end, viewers can generally determine where the values reside simply by asking themselves, "Which character do I feel most warmly about or identify with the most—and what does this character stand for?" Also, values are communicated implicitly through the text's setting; gender, race, age, and social-class dominance; motivation of characters; choices made by characters; and smaller elements such as dialogue, gestures, nonverbal behavior, and soundtrack music.

The same principles about values hold true for media advertising—except that we can always count on ads to imply, however subtly, one dominant value: money, materialism, and consumption of products and services. However, as we've seen throughout this study, kids often don't see commercials as selling something. Also, many observers believe that materialism now dominates *all* media texts, not just commercials. Therefore, the following activities will help kids explore the presence or absence of values in media, as well as how these values might relate to materialism and consumption. Exploring media for the values represented gets kids to see beyond the specific characters and actions—to interpret media and not merely react to it.

Identify Values in Media

Ask kids to examine and discuss Table 8.1, which illustrates how traditional American values may be evolving into new ones.

Next, have kids examine a commercial, program, or film for these values. Ask how and why the text communicated these values. Work with students (allowing them to collaborate with each other) so that they can point to specific characters, actions, dialogue, and the like to support their assertion of specific values occurring in the text. Also, each of these sets of values can be used not just as old and emerging values but as a continuum of values. Hence, kids could rank the television program *Beverly Hills 90210* on a numbered scale, with "Traditional sex roles" as a 1 and "Blurring of sex roles" as a 5. Such nonverbal scales can help initiate a more detailed, verbal analysis.

Compare Traditional and New Values in Media

Using Table 8.1, ask students to view one media text (preferably one that the teacher has selected for its clash of values) and note all instances of

Table 8.1
Changing Values

Traditional Values	New Values
Self-denial ethic	Self-fulfillment ethic
Higher standard of living	Better quality of life
Traditional sex roles	Blurring of sex roles
Accepted definition of success	Individualized definition of success
Traditional family life	Alternative families
Faith in industry, institutions	Self-reliance
Live to work	Work to live
Hero worship	Love of ideas
Expansionism	Pluralism
Patriotism	Less nationalistic
Unparalleled growth	Growing sense of limits
Industrial growth	Information/service growth
Receptivity to technology	Technology orientation

Source: Plummer 1989.

conflicting values, ranging from new versus old, to how one value might hinder, contradict, or somehow interact with another. For example, the film *Ghandi* may communicate self-denial; but another value, such as hero worship, may interfere. Also, ask students to compare and contrast two media texts from different eras for the same values. For example, the values in *Mr. Smith Goes to Washington* (1940s) could be compared to the values in *Born on the Fourth of July* (1960s–1970s).

Examine Materialism in Media

Use the chart in Table 8.1 again and ask students to analyze a media text in terms of how the action, character, plot structure, and monologue relate to materialistic values and attitudes. Viewers should look for issues of money, competition, greed, acquisitiveness, status based on money, and consumption of products and services. For another approach, ask students to tease out the roots of the main actions and plot turns (or the values they identify) and then determine the degree to which materialism is involved. For example, in the classic film *Treasure of Sierra Madre*, the main actions and conflicts can be traced to the gold prospectors' lust for wealth. In other texts, materialism may not be the main force, but it still might play a large role. The idea is for students to examine the degree to which all media components may be affected by the value of materialism.

Analyze Media for Spirituality

In discussions and writing, ask students to explore a media text's actions, characters, and values for the degree to which spirituality plays a role. Help students develop a broad definition of the term "spirituality." It should not be limited to a literal belief in God, although this might be part of it. Rather, spirituality should also include a belief in any "higher entity" than the self and materialism—a belief in or value of *nonmaterial things* such as nature, community, family, or philosophical ideas. The following questions may help students approach this abstract and difficult analysis:

- If you think the main character is not materialistic or motivated by a desire for money, what *does* motivate her?
- What does the character *do* or *say* that makes you think he values something other than (or in addition to) material objects?
- Identify a character who exercised control over his or her life (or a lack of control). Who or what enabled that control to happen? Largely the character

himself? Other people? Random circumstances or luck? A belief in God or religion or other ideas and principles?

Examining media for evidence of spirituality (obvious or suggested) is the opposite of looking for evidence of materialism.

FOCUS ON THE MISSING CONTEXT IN MEDIA

One day in 1979, the *Washington Star* published three photographs of Senator Edward Kennedy, in three editions. Each photograph created an entirely different impression, even though they were cropped from the same photo (Ritchin 1990, 86). The first picture showed Kennedy leaving the Washington, D.C., Kennedy Center with a young woman. It clearly suggested that Kennedy was cheating on Joan Kennedy, his wife at the time. The photo in the second edition showed Kennedy alone; the third photo in the paper's final edition captured Kennedy with a monsignor, an old family friend. This image suggested the opposite of the first one—that Kennedy was religious and family-oriented. The photo that did *not* appear at all was the uncropped original print, which revealed Kennedy leaving the building flanked by several people—the young woman, the monsignor, and a few others. The fuller context of the larger photo illustrated nothing as dramatic as the first two implied, and certainly nothing as simple.

Media messages cannot present the complete context: they do not and cannot show everything. Students seldom think about what has been cropped out of a picture, or consider that something very different could have been occurring in the picture. Kids, especially, perceive pictures as being *whole*, when in reality they are mere fragments that have been selected by someone else. This is why students need to ask of media messages, "What's missing?"

Media is highly intertextual because it often borrows from other sources. The reading of one text requires a knowledge of many others, current and past. The TV program *Beverly Hills 90210* may employ a character whose appearance, name, dialogue, and attitude are very similar to those of a character on an earlier program, such as *Designing Women*. Borrowing occurs when Bart Simpson makes a joke about his town's mayor, which, for viewers to fully understand, depends on their knowledge of former president Richard Nixon. Or, Bart's mayor could be giving a speech that contains no references to Nixon, but he could be imitating Nixon's vocal, facial, and nonverbal gestures. Such echoes take many shapes: allusions, references, imitations, similes and metaphors, editing style, format, and so on. Following are strategies for focusing on the missing context of media messages.

two heads swing their hair, which merges in the center of the screen. The effect, of course, is a lot of bounce—but it's also twice the amount of hair.

Finally, Hailey invested considerable time and energy in obtaining this product. (In another group of four girls, for example, three had purchased Finesse after seeing its commercials on Channel One.) However, after Hailey tried it and it didn't work, she blamed the product very little. When she stated that it didn't work—after she had tried *both* types—she immediately and emphatically qualified it with, "at least not for me."

"THEY DON'T SAY YOU'RE GOING TO HAVE A PERFECT FACE"

Skin care products are heavily advertised on Channel One. Although the majority of kids at the schools I visited did not have blemishes, they reported buying the products. For example, one small group of ninth-graders had purchased Clearasil, Clearastick, Oxy, Sea Breeze, and Noxzema. Another group agreed that they liked the Clearasil and Clearastick commercials because "it has kids of our age who have the same problems." When I asked them to describe a good or realistic commercial for a product they would like to purchase, Christy spoke first: "There's a boy on that Clearasil commercial that said he had real bad acne and then he used Clearasil and his face is all clear and everything."

Asked about the commercial's exact words, the group went into a huddle. They agreed that the ad claimed it would get rid of 54 percent of their acne in three days or their money would be refunded. This ad raises many questions: How do you measure acne? Who determines if the product reduces acne by 54 percent? Will acne be eradicated forever, or will it return? However, the ad claim impressed Luke very favorably. "The good thing about Clearasil is that they don't say you're going to have a perfect face. Instead, they say that you won't have as many zits. I like them better because they're honest in telling you that you're not going to have a perfect face."

Most adults would view this claim of "54 percent success" as very suspect—as pulling a specific number out of the air in order to be more believable. However, Luke sees only the positive side—that *at least* Clearasil is not claiming 100 percent success! Luke is normal. Most of the kids I talked with were similarly naive and trusting because, well, they are kids.

Examine Media for Echoes of Meaning

To increase kids' awareness of media's intertextuality, show them a media text laden with references to information outside the immediate story—information from politics, movies, commercials, and the like. Then ask kids to write down everything they see or hear that refers to something beyond the immediate storyline. Make sure they include examples that they know and examples that they don't recognize. A crucial part here is pooling what everyone observed, because viewers often don't catch references that are completely foreign to them. Finally, compare and discuss findings.

Guess What's Missing—And Then Find Out

Using lists of words and phrases or freewriting, ask students to brainstorm all the possible elements that might be absent from specific media messages. Show students only portions of messages, such as a newspaper photo without its caption, and ask them what they think the actual caption would be. After supplying the caption, ask them what elements might have been left out of both the caption and photo. Once, I showed a captionless photo to college freshmen that depicted a few couples dancing; most students thought that the "whole story" probably focused on people like their grandparents, who might be celebrating their golden wedding anniversary. Their responses were benign.

I then showed the students the actual caption: "California Governor George Deukmejian dances with singer-actress Shirley Jones and Idaho Gov. Cecil Andrus dances with an unidentified friend." At learning this, these Idaho students' responses took a sour turn. Most of them now responded that their governor was "out partying with another woman while we pay the bills." But when even more of the missing context was supplied, their responses changed a third time. Students learned that the "unidentified friend" in the caption was actually the governor's wife (Fox, in press). By understanding the larger context through additional facts, the students' perceptions became more accurate and unbiased.

Examine Media for Internal and External Stories

Help students to understand the two stories that are inherent in every media text. The first story is the *internal* one—what we see or hear on the page or screen before us. Viewers must understand the basic narrative elements: the who, what, where, when, how, and why of the commercial.

The second story is the *external* one—which is determined by the same elements. However, here, they are applied to the *actual situation of creating and producing the ad*, not the story *within* the ad.

Let's consider the internal and external story of one example—a logo for an organization, a simple line drawing that appears on its stationery, envelopes, business cards, and brochures. The illustration depicts a duck, wings outstretched, flying upward. Behind the duck is a large sun, with leafy marsh grass and cattails sprouting from below. The bird's beak points to the printed words: "The National Wetlands Coalition."

First, consider the internal story. The "who" is a duck; the "where" is a marsh with cattails, which appears against the setting or rising sun (the "when"). Viewers could also say that the "what" of this entire logo is nature. And what about the "how" of the logo? How do the bird and nature appear? The answer is peaceful, pure, sublime. The scene definitely communicates a quiet, calm habitat, utterly undisturbed by any encroachments of civilization. The color version reveals the duck drawn in fluid, blue lines as it glides upward. The marsh grass and cattails seem to toss gently in the breeze. Behind everything, the huge orange sun encircles them, unifying marsh with bird, earth with life. So far, these elements help determine the "why" of this logo—deep respect and reverence for nature.

However, the external story of this logo is quite different. The external story of this message—the who, what, where (etc.) of its *creation*—is not the story depicted by the picture just described. The "what" is a logo for the National Wetlands Coalition—its trademark or symbol, which embodies what the organization does, what it believes in and values. The external "where" is Washington, D.C., the organization's headquarters. However, a closer inspection of the logo's "who" reveals the following members: Exxon Company, U.S.A.; Berry Brothers General Contractors, Inc.; Badger Mining Corporation; International Council of Shopping Centers; Louisiana Land and Exploration Company; and Phillips Petroleum Company. According to the *New York Times* (1991, A1), the organization represented by this logo urged then-President Bush to redefine the term "wetland"—a change that would have reduced protected wetlands by one-third.

The logo's internal story seems at odds with its external story. Knowing both the internal and external stories of media messages helps kids match one against the other, providing a more complete context, revealing how the *representation* may or may not be compatible with its creators' actual deeds and intentions.

KNOW HOW MEANINGS RUB OFF OF ONE THING
AND ONTO ANOTHER

A key principle of media literacy is that *one sign or symbol can stand for something else*. In fact, just about everything can be thought of as a sign that also represents something other than what it actually is: a bank check stands for money—and money stands for work, and work stands for education and training, and so on. In media, signs include pictures, words, and music. Any person, place, or thing can function as a sign. These signs multiply into intricate networks, because *one sign can suggest or remind us of others*.

Here's an example of this "stands-for" relationship from a Channel One commercial. One ad for acne medication depicted a group of kids sitting at a restaurant table. When a boy approached them, one of the kids said, "Uh oh, here comes Paul, the Pimple King." Some students I talked to told me that this commercial took place in a *pizza* restaurant. When I asked them what they thought about this location, they responded with, "Pizza Face"—an unflattering term for acne sufferers. The point is that signs bear meaning. Here, the images and meanings of pizza, the food, transfers or "rubs off" onto the boy with acne. One sign calls forth others: the circular pizza becomes Paul's face; pepperoni on the pizza becomes his blemishes—each one red, hot, and greasy. Worse, the unsavory images and meanings rub off even further onto Paul's personality or worth as a human being.

Although associating is a natural type of thinking, the problem occurs when we accept these links and comparisons without question, when we accept them as truth, without evaluating their logic or appropriateness. In this ad, noncritical viewers will accept the simplistic notion that acne means ugly pizza faces and that people with acne are less worthy than others. On the other hand, more critical viewers should see how meanings rub off of one thing to another, with little or no logic, reason, or empathy. Following are strategies for helping people to understand how the meanings of signs and symbols stand for other things—how meanings rub off of one thing and onto another.

Ask, "What Is the *Invisible* Thing Being Sold Here?"

After students read or view a *complete* media text, such as the transcript of a Head and Shoulders Shampoo commercial, assign a different part to each person (including the voice-over narrator) and read the transcript aloud.

Head & Shoulders Television Script

Video	**Audio**
1. Living room setting. Teenage boy walks in, bouncing basketball, and sits down on couch.	Brother: So, what's a little dandruff?
2. Older teenage girl walks into room behind brother. Stands over him and speaks to him. Gestures as if to brush flakes from her shoulder.	Sister: OK, imagine you're at the social event of the year and your dream girl says "Hello" just as you do this . . .
3. Brother shrugs shoulders . . . while sister impersonates dream girl . . .	Sister: Her first impression "What a hunk, but only a few flakes."
4. Brother snickers.	Brother: Give me a break.
5. Close up of sister.	Sister: The breaks are you never get a second chance to make a first impression.
6. Brother tosses ball into air.	Brother: So??
7. Sister picks up shampoo and passes it to her brother.	Sister: The regular shampoos won't fix your problem. Try this.
8. Brother examines bottle.	Brother: Head and Shoulders . . . But you don't have dandruff . . .
9. Sister grabs ball.	Sister: Bingo!
10. Close up of product.	Announcer: Head & Shoulders. Because you never get a second chance to make a first impression.

(Mueller and Wulfemeyer 1991, 151)

Begin with *readers'* responses, by inviting them to say whatever they wish about this commercial. Then ask them what they think is being sold. (Most of the kids I asked replied, "shampoo.") Next, tell them that shampoo is indeed being sold here—but that shampoo is the *visible* sale. Next, ask them what "invisible" thing the commercial might be selling. Some students might respond with "popularity" or "sex appeal." If so, ask them to explain—as explicitly as they can—why and how they arrived at their conclusions. It is important for people to verbalize (or concretize) such connections in order to gain greater fluency in critical thinking. Try the same strategy with the "Cavorting on the Farm" description in Chapter 1.

EXPLORE HOW EMOTION IS USED IN ADVERTISING

Most media texts cannot help but communicate emotionally. Why? Because images evoke whole, emotional responses. Edward Hopper's painting, "Nighthawks," might make us feel quiet and alone, whereas the "Mona Lisa" may create feelings of wistfulness. Generally, images induce undiluted, emotional responses, unfettered by numbers or verbal thinking. That is the nature of pictures. Advertising relies on emotion for its main ingredient—not logic, proof, argument, words, or numbers. Instead, what dominates are values, attitudes, feelings, sentiments, sensations, passions. Edell (1990) even states that emotions are "the basis for most decisions"; that they are the reasons we make decisions in the first place. She further explains how emotions may distract us from being logical, which of course limits the number of rational options we might normally weigh when making decisions (xiv).

Advertising employs two potent ingredients: (1) imagery and (2) knowledge about how people think via emotions to create "internal experiences" within viewers: emotion-driven feelings that they have *moved*—internally—from one point to another, from one place in our interior landscape to another place. It's very important for students to explore the frequency and types of emotional changes (or "transformations") that they experience within a media text. In "Where We Live" (Fox 1994), I describe how these internal ups and downs, created by purely visual ads, constitute a kind of visual syntax that viewers can use to better evaluate these transformations.

EVALUATE MEDIA FOR AUDIENCE VALUES AND ATTITUDES

In addition to traditional demographic information (e.g., age, gender, income level), marketing strategists focus on consumers' personal values and use a system similar to that developed by Arnold Mitchell (1983), which identifies and groups consumers according to their values, attitudes, and lifestyles (or VALS). "More than anything else," Mitchell states, "we are what we believe, what we dream, what we value" (3). Mitchell articulates the subtle differences among nine interlocked lifestyles. For example, the Need-Driven groups, typified by illiterate, older, and poor Americans, live on the fringes of society. The Outer-Directed groups are *externally motivated*, people who look *outward* to others for authority and standards: to the church, school, family, co-workers, government, and other institutions. Consider the following summarized descriptions of Belongers and Achievers—two very different lifestyles that nonetheless share an *outward* orientation.

Belongers primarily value family, togetherness, and traditional organized religion, seeking approval and sense of belonging through family, church, and community groups. They have a low tolerance for subtlety and ambiguity; but they are financially stable, valuing tangible objects such as houses, cars, and real estate. Finally, Belongers are politically conservative and patriotic.

On the other hand, Achievers mainly value professional achievements and contributions. Most Achievers are doctors, lawyers, and executives, who seek approval of professional and community peers. They support technological advances and are affluent and successful. Achievers set goals and achieve them, while projecting self-reliance and self-confidence. Like Belongers, Achievers value tangible objects and are conservative and patriotic.

Contrast the outer-directed groups with the inner-directed people, who are *internally motivated*—who look inward to themselves for authority and standards, not outside to other people and institutions. Overall, Channel One commercials are aimed at what Mitchell calls I-Am-Me's—young people who are in the process of change, of shifting from

The comfortable, established, well-defined, deeply outer-directed lifestyle of Achiever parents to the evanescent, fanciful, mercurial, flighty styles of I-Am-Me peers and contemporaries. The change is powered by both love and hate, admiration and disgust, envy and resentment of outer-directeds' way of life. The stage thus is not only I-Am-Me but also I-Am-Not-You. Clearly it is a time full of confusions, contradictions, uncertainties, excesses, and protean changes. . . .

The picture we have, then, is of youths raised in favored circumstances seeking out—often ungraciously and noisily, to be sure—a new way of life for themselves. Average age is about twenty-one, and almost none are over thirty. The majority are students. (17–18)

This glimpse into marketing research illustrates the considerable resources available for constructing persuasive messages and consumer profiles of the people who watch commercials. Such resources and approaches enable commercial producers to precisely target specific audiences. Channel One founder Christopher Whittle's chief ingredient for success has been his development of "target-specific media" and the "single-sponsor concept" (Rudinow 1990, 71).

For instance, the Groovy Fruitopian kids described in Chapter 7 were strongly attracted to values of peace and love, nature and harmony—even a positive, unfocused spirituality that values holistic approaches to life. This subgroup, targeted by advertisers within Channel One's already well-defined audience, bought the products in question and were loyal to them over time. Viewers, then, need to examine how commercials and other media texts are tailored to appeal to audience values, attitudes, and lifestyles. Following are suggestions for helping viewers understand how advertisers link media texts to viewers' values, attitudes, and lifestyles.

Identify and Describe Specific Audience Values in Media

Ask students to explore how specific media texts (e.g., a magazine ad or a popular TV sitcom) are aimed at specific audiences. For a TV program, students should begin with the commercials and ask, Who are the people in the ad? To what socio-economic class might they belong, and how can you tell? What are they doing? What is the ad emphasizing—the people or their actions? The place or the time period? What colors dominate? What do these colors suggest to viewers (e.g., red might signal action; blue might indicate peacefulness or sadness)? Do sharp and angular shapes dominate—or soft, rounded ones? And what do they suggest? Do the figures in the foreground and background, when viewed as a continuous line, point to something in particular? Why?

Another option for focusing on audience values is to ask students to collect three to five magazine advertisements or TV commercials, each for a different product. For each ad, have students write a one-page summary that (1) identifies the audience they think it is aimed at, and (2) explains how and why the ad matches the label they have assigned it.

Simulate What Focus Groups and Advertisers Do

Using real or imaginary products, ask students to role-play what real focus groups do. For example, provide them with two or three brands of root beer, chocolate, or some other product. Place the food or drink into plain containers or wrappers to ensure that they cannot be identified. Number each one. Divide the class into small groups and ask them to complete each of the following steps.

First, working independently, each student should taste each product and describe in writing what it tastes, looks, and smells like. Students should employ similes and metaphors. Next, students should share their choices with their group and reach consensus on which sample their company will promote. Each group should then construct an advertising campaign to sell its product. This campaign could include a written press release, radio ad, TV commercial, newspaper or magazine ad, and billboard. Each ad should be aimed at a different audience. Before students present their entire ad campaign to the rest of the class, each group should describe why it chose to present its product in a certain way. After presenters answer questions, class members should evaluate each campaign's strengths and weaknesses.

Use the Preferred Reading Approach

Stuart Hall's preferred reading approach asks viewers to determine who will prefer a message—and who will *not* (Fiske 1987). In other words, which audience does the text favor or privilege—and which group is downplayed or left out? Is any middle ground possible? Hall's approach helps viewers to identify the primary or dominant audience of a text by linking the text's stated and implied values to this audience. Viewers are asked to read media texts in three ways: dominant, oppositional, and negotiated.

The first way involves readers in determining the text's *dominant* ideology. Readers ask themselves, What are the dominant values communicated by the text—and which group is most likely to hold these values? This group would constitute the dominant or main audience. Second, students reread the text from the *opposite* point of view of the dominant ideology, trying to see it from the minority's position. In the third reading, students try to accommodate the two earlier extremes with their own responses (Hall refers to this as the *negotiated* reading). The three strategies reflect how much (or how little) an audience may agree with the text's meaning.

EXPLORE STEREOTYPING OF GENDER, RACE, CLASS, AND AGE

Most characters in TV-land—from Jed Clampett to *Dynasty*'s Alexis to the "Fresh Prince of Belair"—are very wealthy, even though we never see them working. And all elderly people—from Archie Bunker to Maude to Grandma Walton—are cranky. And all young women—from Gilligan's Mary Ann to Charlie's Angels—are mindless sex kittens. Although this list doesn't account for every character on television, only a few powerful icons are needed to communicate stereotypes—of gender, race, socioeconomic class, and age. Following are ways to help kids understand how media characters, events, and places cannot be universally representative.

Analyze How Media Frames Social Issues

Ask students to examine how one text introduces or frames a social issue such as gender, race, or class. Introductory segments influence kids' interpretations of everything else that follows. Effective openings provide a thematic container into which viewers "pour" the rest of their perceptions of the text. Use a film that students have seen in its entirety, but focus on the opening, including the title screen and credits.

For example, Fehlman (1994) uses the opening title scene of *The Silence of the Lambs*, a film about a serial killer, to focus his college freshmen on issues of gender and power—mainly, "Starling's role in a man's world" (49). Students discussed and wrote informally about the film's beginning scene, which shows Clarice running an obstacle course at FBI headquarters. Fehlman describes how even students' initial responses elicited complex gender issues. Some students seemed to grasp the stalking and paranoid quality of the entire film—discovered on their own, but with the help of a teacher who encouraged students to openly respond to a few minutes of a title scene. This informal analysis and reflection slowed down students who might have otherwise rushed far into the text before consciously beginning their analysis. Consequently, students' thinking became more focused and detailed.

Examine Media for Stereotypes

A popular Newport cigarette ad from magazines and billboards shows two men, wearing jeans and out in the country, carrying a long pole. Each end rests on each man's shoulders. Suspended from the center of the pole by her hands and feet is a young woman. Although everyone in this ad is laughing, the bound woman appears to be the men's prey—a prized deer being hauled out by hunters (Moog 1994).

Ask students to conduct full-blown research projects that investigate how one media genre (e.g., situation comedies, detective shows) portrays one of the following categories: gender, race, socioeconomic class, and age. Let students choose their own genre. If one student wants to research how women are portrayed in "movies starring Jim Carrey," allow her to do so. Ask students to gather all types of evidence, including video clips, and then present their findings to the entire class for discussion and revision.

Compare Media Treatments of the Same Issue

Select three media texts—self-contained clips from programs and films, commercials, print ads, and the like—that illustrate different treatments of one social issue (e.g., age, gender). For example, if your class is viewing three videos for their depiction of women (e.g., *Roseanne, Home Improvement,* and a Cheer detergent commercial), provide students with charts divided into three columns: (1) Details You See and Hear, (2) *How* These Details Are Communicated, and (3) How They Connect to Your Own Life. The simple charts can help students focus their viewing. Allow students time to gather their thoughts and take notes after each viewing. After students have completed the charts, discuss their observations and conclusions. Finally, on the basis of all their viewing, notes, and discussions, students should write an analysis of the three texts.

Match Media Characters with Real-Life Counterparts

Ask students (working alone or in pairs) to describe all the characteristics of one popular media character, striving for as many details as possible. For example, Zack, a character on the TV program *Saved by the Bell,* is tall, has blond hair and blue eyes, wears jeans and plaid flannel shirts, earns good grades, and dates attractive girls. Next, ask students to research ten people they know who share some of the same characteristics as the media character, such as gender and age. Finally, have them compare their conclusions in a chart, as well as in writing, before they report to the entire class.

EXPLORE MEDIA VIOLENCE

Veteran media researcher George Gerbner makes the following observations about media mayhem:

- *The Godfather* produced twelve corpses, *Godfather II* put away eighteen, and *Godfather III* killed no less than fifty-three.

- In 1988, the daredevil cop in the original *Die Hard* saved the day with a modest eighteen dead. Two years later, *Die Hard 2* achieved a body count of 264.

- The decade's record goes to the 1990 children's movie, tie-in marketing sensation, and glorification of martial arts *Teenage Mutant Ninja Turtles*. . . . It is the most violent film that has ever been marketed to children, with 133 acts of mayhem per hour.

- The October 14, 1991, international edition of *Variety* featured 123 pages of ads for new movies, with pictures of shooting, killing, or corpses on every other page and a verbal appeal to violence, on the average, on every page. Leading the verbal procession were *kill, murder, death, deadly,* and *dead* (thirty-three times) and *terror, fatal, lethal,* and *dangerous* (twelve times). Bringing up the rear were *rage, frenzy, revenge, guncrazy, kickboxer, maniac, warrior, invader, hawk, battle, war, shoot, fight, slaughter,* and *blood.* (Gerbner 1994, 134–135)

Media violence tends to breed more media violence, fostering an atmosphere and attitudes that make violence acceptable—and too often, the only choice that viewers perceive. Media provides the language, pictures, sounds, and role models that make it easier for us to think and act violently in real life. Of course, media violence is not confined to movies and television; it's also common in cable TV, music, computer games, and other forms of popular culture. Gerbner, reflecting on a culture whose first generations have now grown up without having escaped television violence, places it within the larger context of daily American life:

Growing up in a violence-laden culture breeds aggressiveness in some and desensitization, insecurity, mistrust, and anger in most (Gerbner 1988). These are highly exploitable sentiments. They set up a scenario of violence and victimization in which some take on the role of violent perpetrators. Most, however, assume the role and psychology of victims. And as victims, they demand protection, condoning, if not welcoming, violent solutions to domestic and world problems . . . where punitive and vindictive action against dark forces in a mean world is made to look appealing, especially when presented as quick, decisive, and enhancing our sense of control and security.

The cult of violence is the ritual demonstration and celebration of brute power—and its projection into sex, family, job, politics, and war. (Gerbner 1994, 135)

The following approaches will help kids evaluate and understand issues in media violence.

Examine How *Other* Factors Affect Violence

Because violence is part of a much larger, intricate web, students should explore other factors that contribute to a culture of violence. These include poverty, inner-city decay, the breakdown of family life, drug addiction, the availability of weapons, a lack of jobs and education, and a high cultural value placed on winning at all costs (Department of Justice 1993). Students should evaluate how these categories are represented in popular films, TV programs, and music. How, for example, do films and TV portray the work ethic? Are media characters shown working or valuing work? How do media represent the multiple consequences of *not* working? How do media portray a lack of education—is violence fairly or unfairly portrayed as a consequence? Students need to explore how such issues affect violence, in media as well as in real life.

Evaluate the Jolts-per-Minute (JPMs) in Media

Assign students to view two media texts—one they judge to be exciting and another they consider to be painfully dull. Then ask them to tabulate the number of jolts in each text. A jolt can be an act of physical violence or psychological violence, as well as any sudden change in equilibrium: a loud bang, a funny line, an explosion, a scream, name-calling, loud music, and the like. Finally, ask students to write an analysis that compares the two texts for JPMs and how they affect each text's level of perceived excitement. Finally, students should examine how each text's level of excitement contributed to (or detracted from) its overall quality or effectiveness.

Describe How Enemies Are Represented in Media

Ask students to construct a profile of the typical enemy in several similar media texts. Are foes usually male or female? Why? What are the effects? Do the types of enemies shift, depending on the genre? To what extent are the main enemies believable characters? What are the effects of media using such "faceless" enemies? How often do the starring characters in media inflict physical violence? Psychological violence? What are the racial, gender, age, and socioeconomic status of enemies in media? How do the enemies behave after they inflict any type of violence? What do they do and say?

Describe How Victims Are Represented in Media

Focus not on the instigators of violence in media, but on the victims. Ask students to explore the following questions: How often (and how realistically) are victims developed and fleshed out? What are the effects of media portraying "faceless" victims, or those who are undeveloped? Do the types or qualities of victims shift, depending on the genre? How often do the starring characters in media suffer from violence? When victims (and stars) survive physical violence, do viewers see any evidence or scars—physical or psychological? What are the effects of violence on the stars versus the secondary characters? What are the racial, gender, age, and socioeconomic status of victims of media violence? How do they respond to violence?

Evaluate Images of Violence in Proximity to Images of Sex

Evaluate media in which sex and violence occur simultaneously or very near to each other in space or time. Media violence expert Park Dietz, a forensic psychiatrist, believes that "A vulnerable youngster may watch a sexy slasher movie and become conditioned to sexual arousal through such images. When that boy becomes a man in his 20s or 30s, society runs the risk that he will seek sexual gratification through actual, not fantasized, brutality" (Kieger 1994, 19).

An ancient maxim (and a verified principle of Gestalt psychology and semiotics) holds that two items placed close to each other are perceived by people to be the same thing. Nowhere is this more true than in film and television, where rapidly cutting between two different things makes viewers lump them together, regardless of logic. Hence, viewers come to believe that violence and sex are compatible: that one is needed for the other to occur; that if one element is absent, the experience is neither whole nor authentic.

To counter this artificial and destructive linkage, Dietz has proposed that media-makers adhere to a "detumescence period" in movies—a five- or ten-minute interval between violent scenes and sexy scenes. The point is that sexual imagery and violent imagery should not occur at the same time or nearly the same time. Dietz is convinced such a rule is needed because of "the number of cases he's worked on in which sexual murder, murder with torture, product tampering, carjacking, or workplace violence was inspired, instructed, or otherwise influenced by mass media" (Kieger 1994, 19).

Ask students to examine film and television episodes for the proximity of sexual imagery to violent imagery. Orally or in writing, they should report the length of the sex segments and violence segments, describing their structure, editing techniques, and transitions. Students should also describe how the episode affects them (and others) as viewers. Also, ask students to describe any other types of transitions or links they observe between violence and sex—or between violence and other topics that occur with or near violent images.

Specify Nonviolent Alternatives within Media

Media texts have long portrayed overly simplistic events wherein characters could exercise few or no options. Indeed, this black-and-white world is especially true of TV commercials, which often elicit boxed-in judgments from kids in which they think they have only two choices, such as Nike or Reebok shoes. It is crucial that kids understand and be aware of options to violent behavior.

One direct approach to helping kids see the larger picture is to have them examine the same program or film for its points of clash or conflicts. Students should record all the nonviolent options that are stated directly by characters or are implied or suggested. Ask students to hypothesize why, in reality, normal people would not have chosen these less violent courses of action. Also have students consider the list of nonviolent options from the director's point of view, by asking, Which nonviolent options could have been used instead of the violent ones—all the while retaining dramatic interest? Finally, students should create their own lists of nonviolent options for each situation and compare their conclusions. For one conflict, teachers should combine all the nonviolent options, so that everyone can concretely see the myriad of possibilities left out.

CONSTRUCT MEDIA TEXTS

Deeper understanding of media occurs when kids actually write, film, edit, revise, and produce their own media. It's one thing for viewers to understand how Orson Welles communicated the power of Citizen Kane by positioning the camera down low, so that viewers must gaze upward at his commanding presence. But they better internalize this concept when they hold the camera and do it themselves. Next, kids should view and critique their work with others, before doing it again.

Kids best learn media conventions, codes, and genres through analyzing other media texts while simultaneously creating their own. Throughout these parallel activities, students should examine values questions such as, When is it okay to make something appear larger in film than it really is—and when is this distortion not okay?

Of course, media production skills also involve considerable reading and writing, as students create scripts, narratives, technical instructions, summaries, proposals, and marketing plans. Media production should encompass all purposes, technologies, formats, and genres—from student-made video documentaries and soap operas, to personal home videos and video mail, to computer graphics and multimedia presentations, to magazines and newspapers, to alternative points of view to mainstream media.

VIEW MEDIA WITH NO AGENDA

All the strategies presented here ask viewers to use language to become more critical of media. This is what's most needed. For media education to be effective, students should engage in it every day. However, once in a while it's also important—especially within school settings—to view media with no agenda; with no introductions, analysis, writing, or discussion.

Even when students view a no-strings-attached film or video, some will comment anyway. Such voluntary talk is excellent (even ideal), but sometimes—especially for emotionally powerful texts (e.g., as Alain Renais's *Night and Fog*)—teachers might impose a rule of no comments allowed, both during and immediately after viewing. The moratorium will allow responses to surface and sort out. There are several reasons for this suggestion. First, analysis will take root better if teachers refrain from overanalyzing everything. Second, allowing class time for viewing a media text with no strings attached demonstrates for students that media, for most people, most of the time, is an aesthetic experience. Third, the no-agenda approach is perfect for showing students a type of film or video that's new or strange to them. For example, some students have never seen a Buster Keaton silent film or an "avant garde" film by Jean Cocteau. Finally, such unfettered media sessions can come in handy later in the year as a context or frame of reference for discussing *other* media texts.

FINAL THOUGHTS

The recommendations made in this chapter have a few common characteristics. First, media has a wonderful way of placing all kids on the same level playing field, because they all have media knowledge and background. The more that kids are on an equal footing, the more they will participate in their learning. Second, these approaches ask kids to discover the meanings in media texts, messages conveyed visually, aurally, and verbally. They ask kids to examine explicit meanings as well as to sift out implicit ones. Third, these approaches ask kids to engage in reflective, critical thinking—to relate media to their own values, lives, and communities; to relate media to larger issues of politics, economics, gender, age, race, and class.

Fourth, these approaches ask students to consistently and vigorously use their skills in reading, writing, viewing, filming, speaking, listening, and collaborating—applying them to specific contexts such as film, video, and magazine ads. Finally, these strategies ask kids to exercise responsible citizenship in an electronic culture—to write letters, to establish ad-free zones, to search for values and prejudice, and to express themselves effectively.

It is clear, in this age of appearances, that images themselves constitute our culture's first and universal language. It is equally clear that the language of images must become our second tongue.

Works Cited

Adams, Scott. "Whittle Communications and Channel One: Rhetorical Strategies of Innovation." Paper presented at the Annual Meeting of the Speech Communication Association in Atlanta, GA. ERIC Document No. ED 339 054, 1991.

Adler, R., and R. Faber. "Background: Children's Television Viewing Patterns." In *The Effects of Television Advertising on Children*, 13–28. Lexington, MA: D. C. Heath, 1980.

Arnheim, Rudolf. *New Essays on the Psychology of Art*. Berkeley: University of California Press, 1986.

"Atlanta Quick City Guide." Guest Informant, a subsidiary of LIN Broadcasting Corp., New York, 1990.

Aufderheide, Patricia. "A Report of the National Leadership Conference on Media Literacy." Washington, DC: Aspen Institute, Communications and Society Program, 1992.

Baker, C. Edwin. *Advertising and a Democratic Press*. Princeton, NJ: Princeton University Press, 1994.

Barber, Benjamin. "America Skips School." *Harper's Magazine* (November 1993).

Barry, Ann Marie. "Advertising and Channel One: Controversial Partnership of Business and Education." In *Watching Channel One: The Convergence of Students, Technology, and Business*, ed. Ann De Vaney, 132–136. Albany: State University of New York Press, 1994.

Bazalgette, C., B. Bevort, and J. Savino, eds. *New Directions: Media Education Worldwide*. London: British Film Institute, 1992.

Beach, Richard. *A Teacher's Introduction to Reader-Response Theories*. Urbana, IL: National Council of Teachers of English, 1993.

Belland, John C. "Is This the News?" In *Watching Channel One: The Convergence of Students, Technology, and Private Business*, ed. Ann De Vaney, 87–102. Albany: State University of New York Press, 1994.

Bennett, William. *What Works: Research about Teaching and Learning*. Washington, DC: U.S. Department of Education, 1986.

Bloom, Alan. *The Closing of the American Mind: How Higher Education Has Failed Democracy and Impoverished the Souls of Today's Students*. New York: Simon and Schuster, 1987.

Bowen, Wally. "Ads, Ads Everywhere! Are There Any Limits?" *New Citizen* 2, No. 2 (Summer 1995): 1.

Carlin, T., et al. "The Perception of the Educational Value of Channel One among Secondary Level Teachers and Students." Proceedings of Selected Research and Development Presentations at the Convention of the Association for Educational Communications and Technology. ERIC Document No. ED 347 980, 1992.

Carmody, Dierdre. "News Shows with Ads Are Tested in Six Schools." *New York Times*, February 1, 1989, p. A28.

Celano, Donna, and Susan Neuman. "Channel One: Time for a TV Break." *Phi Delta Kappan* (February 1995): 444–446.

Christensen, P., and D. Roberts. "The Role of Television in the Formation of Children's Social Attitudes." In *Learning from Television: Psychological and Educational Research*. London: Academic Press, 1982.

Columbia Daily Tribune. "Flashy Beer Commercials Draw Children, Study Finds." *Columbia Daily Tribune*, February 12, 1994, p. A12.

Consodine, David M., and Gail E. Haley. *Visual Messages: Integrating Imagery into Instruction*. Eaglewood, CO: Teacher Ideas Press, 1992.

Consumer's Union. *Captive Kids: A Report on Commercial Pressures on Kids at School*. Yonkers: Consumer's Union Education Services, 1995.

Costanzo, Bill. "Conference on Children and the Media." *Media Matters* 4, No. 2 (Spring 1992): 2.

Cramer, Rebecca. "Channel One as a Current Events Medium for Secondary Students." Unpublished master's thesis. Department of Library Science and Information Service, Central Missouri State University, July 1993.

Department of Justice. "Safeguarding Our Youth: Violence Prevention for Our Nation's Children." Recommendations from the Working Group on Media at the National Consultation, Washington, DC, convened July 20–21, 1993.

De Vaney, Ann. "Reading the Ads: The Bacchanalian Adolescence." In *Watching Channel One: The Convergence of Students, Technology, and Private Business*, ed. Ann De Vaney, 102–137. Albany: State University of New York Press, 1994.

Eco, Umberto. *A Theory of Semiotics*. Bloomington: Indiana University Press, 1976.

Edell, Julie A. "Emotion and Advertising: A Timely Union." In *Emotions and Advertising: Theoretical and Practical Applications*, eds. Stuart Agress, Tony Dubitsky, and Julie A. Edell, xiii–xviii. New York: Quorum Books, 1990.

Educational Technology. "Video News Program Said to Have Little Impact." *Educational Technology* 31, No. 6 (1991): 61.

Elbow, Peter. *Writing Without Teachers*. New York: Oxford University Press, 1973.

Ellul, Jacques. *Propaganda*. New York: Vintage, 1965.

Fehlman, Richard H. "Making Meanings Visible: Critically Reading TV." *English Journal* (November 1992): 19–24.

————. "Responding to Popular Media: Focusing on Gender." *Iowa English Bulletin* 42 (1994): 47–53.

Fiske, John. *Television Culture*. New York: Methuen, 1987.

Fleming, Charles. "Understanding Propaganda from a General Semantics Perspective." *ETC.—A Review of General Semantics* 52, No. 1 (Spring 1995): 3–13.

Fox, Roy F. "Knowing the Dancer from the Dance: Analyzing (and Intuiting) Persuasive Media." In *Media Literacy: Classroom Practices in the Teaching of English*, ed. Carole Cox. Urbana, IL: National Council of Teachers of English (in press).

————. "Manipulated Kids: Teens Tell How Ads Influence Them." *Educational Leadership* 53, No. 1 (September 1995): 77–80.

————. "Where We Live." In *Images in Language, Media, and Mind*, ed. Roy F. Fox, 69–91. Urbana, IL: National Council of Teachers of English, 1994.

Gerbner, George. "Instant History, Image History: Lessons from the Persian Gulf War." In *Images in Language, Media, and Mind*, ed. Roy F. Fox, 123–140. Urbana, IL: National Council of Teachers of English, 1994.

Gombrich, E. H. *The Sense of Order: A Study in the Psychology of Decorative Art*, 2d ed. Ithaca: Cornell University Press, 1982.

Goodman, Ellen. "Turn On 'Channel One,' Turn Off Values." *Los Angeles Times*, March 8, 1989, p. II-7.

Greenberg, Bradley S. "Television and Role Socialization: An Overview." In *Television and Behavior: Ten Years of Scientific Progress and Implications for the Eighties*, eds. D. Perl, L. Bouthilet, and J. Lazar. Rockville, MD: National Institute of Mental Health, 1982.

Greenberg, Bradley S., and J. E. Brand. "Television News and Advertising in Schools: The 'Channel One' Controversy." *Journal of Communication* 43, No. 1 (Winter 1993): 143–151.

Greenfield, Patricia M. *Mind and Media: The Effects of Television, Video Games, and Computers*. Cambridge, MA: Harvard University Press, 1984.

Halleck, DeeDee. "Whittling away at the Public Sphere." *Lies of Our Times* (September 1992).

Harper's Magazine. "Rock-a-Buy Baby." *Harper's Magazine* (April 1994): 22.

Hayakawa, S. I. "Sexual Fantasy and the 1957 Car." In *The Use and Misuse of Language*, ed. S. I. Hayakawa. Greenwich, CT: Fawcett Publications, 1962.

Hirsch, E. D. *Cultural Literacy: What Every American Needs to Know.* Boston: Houghton Mifflin, 1987.

Hite, R., and R. Eck. "Advertising to Children: Attitudes of Business vs. Consumers." *Journal of Advertising* (October/November 1987): 40–53.

Honig, Bill. "And Now This: TV Commercials as 'Educational' Fare." *Los Angeles Times*, June 3, 1993, p. M5.

Hovanec, Carol, and David Freund. "Photographs, Writing, and Critical Thinking." In *Images in Language, Media, and Mind*, ed. Roy F. Fox, 42–57. Urbana, IL: National Council of Teachers of English, 1994.

Johnston, Jerome. "Channel One: The Dilemma of Teaching and Selling." *Phi Delta Kappan* (February 1995): 437–442.

Johnston, Jerome, and E. Brzezinski. "Taking the Measure of Channel One: The First Year." Ann Arbor: University of Michigan Institute for Social Research, April 1992.

Karpatkin, Rhoda H., and A. Holmes. "Making Schools Ad-Free Zones." *Educational Leadership* 53, No. 1 (September 1995): 72–76.

Kieger, Dale. "The Dark World of Park Dietz." *Johns Hopkins Magazine* (November 1994): 18–19.

Knupfer, Nancy, and P. Hayes. "The Effects of the Channel One Broadcast on Students' Knowledge of Current Events." In *Watching Channel One: The Convergence of Students, Technology, and Private Business*, ed. Ann De Vaney, 42–61. Albany: State University of New York Press, 1994.

Kozol, Jonathan. "Corporate Raid on Education: Whittle and the Privateers." *Nation* (September 21, 1992): 273–278.

Lichter, S. R., and L. Lichter. "Does Television Shape Ethnic Images?" *Media & Values* 43 (Spring 1988): 5–8.

Lurzer's Int'l ARCHIVE of Ads, TV, and Posters Worldwide. 1994.

McCarthy, Colman. "Channel One Whittles away Education in U.S." *Columbia Daily Tribune*, November 6, 1993, p. 4A.

Medrich, E., et al. *The Serious Business of Growing Up: A Study of Children's Lives outside of School.* Berkeley: University of California Press, 1982.

Mitchell, Arnold. *The Nine American Lifestyles.* New York: Macmillan, 1983.

Moog, Carol. "Ad Images and the Stunting of Sexuality." In *Images in Language, Media, and Mind*, ed. Roy F. Fox. Urbana, IL: National Council of Teachers of English, 1994.

———. *"Are They Selling Her Lips?" Advertising and Identity.* New York: William Morrow, 1990.

Mueller, Barbara, and K. Tim Wulfemeyer. "A Framework for the Analysis of Commercials in the Classroom: The Decoding of Channel One." *The High School Journal* (February/March 1991): 138–159.

Naparstek, Aaron. "I'm OK, You're OK." *SPIN* (March 1995): 20–21.

Nemerov, Howard. "Gnomes." In *Collected Poems of Howard Nemerov*. Chicago: University of Chicago Press, 1977.

Newsweek. *Newsweek* (March 7, 1994a).

Newsweek. *Newsweek* (October 17, 1994b).

New York Times. *New York Times*, August 3, 1991, p. A1.

Paivio, Allan. *Mental Representations: A Dual Coding Approach*. New York: Oxford University Press, 1990.

Peterson, R. C., and L. L. Thurstone. *Motion Pictures and the Social Attitudes of Children*. New York: Macmillan, 1933.

Plummer, Joseph T. *The Futurist* (January/February 1989).

Postman, Neil, and Steve Powers. *How to Watch TV News*. New York: Penguin, 1992.

Rank, Hugh. "Teaching about Public Persuasion: Rationale and a Schema." In *Teaching about Doublespeak*, ed. Daniel Dietrich, 3–19. Urbana, IL: National Council of Teachers of English, 1976.

Ritchin, Fred. *In Our Own Image: The Coming Revolution in Photography*. New York: Aperture Foundation, 1990.

Rosenblatt, Louise. *The Reader, the Text, the Poem: The Transactional Theory of the Literary Work*. Carbondale: Southern Illinois Press, 1978.

Ross, R. P., and T. Campbell, et al. "When Celebrities Talk, Children Listen: An Experimental Analysis of Children's Responses to TV Ads with Celebrity Endorsements." Unpublished paper, Center for Research on the Influences of Television on Children, University of Kansas, n.d.

Rossiter, J. "Source Effects and Self-Concept Appeals in Children's Television Advertising." In *The Effects of Television Advertising on Children*, 61–94. Lexington, MA: D. C. Heath and Co., 1980.

Rudinow, Joel. "Channel One Whittles away at Education." *Educational Leadership* (January 1990): 70–73.

Schwed, Mark. "TV Commercials & Your Kids." *TV Guide* (February 18, 1995): 19.

Simons, Elizabeth. Personal journal. 1993.

Sless, David. *In Search of Semiotics*. Totowa, NJ: Barnes and Noble Books, 1986.

Solomon, Jolie. "Mr. Vision, Meet Mr. Reality." *Newsweek* (August 16, 1993): 62–64.

Sproule, J. Michael. *Channels of Propaganda*. Bloomington, IN: EDINFO Press, 1994.

Tate, C. "Opinion: Chris Whittles' School-News Scheme." *Columbia Journalism Review* (May–June 1989): 52.

Tiene, Drew. "Exploring the Effectiveness of the Channel One Telecasts." *Educational Technology* (May 1993): 36–42.

————. "How Viewers View Channel One." *Education Digest* (October 1994): 57–59.

Toch, Thomas. "Homeroom Sweepstakes." *U.S. News and World Report* (November 9, 1992): 86–89.

Verhovek, Sam Howe. "New York Bans Sponsored TV from Its Schools." *New York Times*, June 17, 1989, p. A28.

Washington Office of the State Superintendent of Public Instruction. *Report to the Legislature on Commercialism in Schools*. Olympia: Washington Office of the State Superintendent of Public Instruction. Eric Document #EA 332301, January 1991.

Whittle Educational Network. "Scheduling Channel One in Your School." 1989.

————. "Teachers' Guide: Whittle Educational Network News & Programming." October 1993: 5.

————. "Whittle Communications' Educational Network School Agreement." n.d.

Index

About the Author

ROY F. FOX teaches at the University of Missouri-Columbia, where he also directs the Missouri Writing Project. He is the author of *Technical Communication: Problems and Solutions* (1994) and editor of *Images in Language, Media, and Mind* (1994). He has published numerous articles and chapters on thinking, visual/media literacy and culture.